THIS IS A GOOD GUIDE

Also by Marieke Eyskoot
Talking Dress – Alles over eerlijke kleding en lifestyle (in Dutch)

First edition 2018

BIS Publishers, Amsterdam, the Netherlands
Editing: Edmé Koorstra
Translation: Natasha Barton, Marieke Eyskoot
Design: The Green House
DTP: Esther Scheide
Image editing: Naomi Rachèl Timan
Text contributions: Laura de Jong
Author's photo: Melody Lieftink
printed on wood-free FSC paper (Galerie Art Natural),
with Novavit BIO ink from plant-based, renewable raw materials

ISBN 978 90 6369 492 0
ISBN 978 90 6369 516 3 (e-book)

mariekeeyskoot.nl
bispublishers.com

MIX
Paper from
responsible sources
FSC® C016890

THIS IS A GOOD GUIDE
for a sustainable lifestyle

Marieke Eyskoot

fashion · beauty · food · home · work · leisure · tips · stores · brands · destinations

CONTENTS

In good we
trust

INTRODUCTION

This is a good guide. Well... We'll see about that, right? In any case, it's certainly full of good things. And wonderful people and initiatives, sure to bring a smile to your face. Most of the time, that is: some facts included may well make you grumpy. Because there's a good reason for this book: the world could be a better place. But more fun too! Impulse buys end up in the back of our ever-bulging wardrobe, price tag and all still attached, while at the same time we've got nothing to wear. We're all buying more clothes, yet spending less money on them (and they're not necessarily making us any happier either – just like all those gadgets, cut-price chicken or the promise-to-make-you-younger creams). Recognise any of this? Let's start doing things differently.

And we can. One of the most important things I've learned is that we determine the world. We can choose how we want to live, who we want to be, what we like and don't like. Every time you buy something, you're actually saying to the brand or the store: 'I like what you're doing, here, take my money to continue.' You support a particular development, and so can steer it too. Especially when we do it together. Collectively, we have tremendous power and strength, if we choose to use it. Which we sometimes forget to, it seems. But after this book, hopefully no longer.

You probably already knew this. Just as you probably know how necessary it is. People are suffering to facilitate our lifestyle. Not cool, but true. And the earth is too. We need to make changes. Now. Also true, but this time actually cool: this doesn't mean your life should suffer, become sparse or boring. On the contrary, I'm convinced that it can be better, more interesting, and more varied once you stop automatically choosing the easiest and most familiar path. This is what I want to show you.

This is a good guide about sustainable fashion, personal care, food, home, work, leisure and much, much more. So pretty much our whole life, really. I've been working in sustainable fashion and lifestyle for over fifteen years, and at every birthday party, event or meeting I attend, I receive lots of questions: 'Where can I buy ethical fashion?', 'But what about my facial products?', 'How do you feel about flying?', or 'How can I make my workplace greener?'. In this book, I'll try and answer all these questions. Thank you for all the requests via e-mail and social media, as well as up close and personal. This handbook is because of you, for you.

It's impossible to make a good guide alone. Certainly about so many subjects. I started out as a sustainable fashion expert, and in the

4

times more than for regular ones, demand for sustainable products has grown in 2015

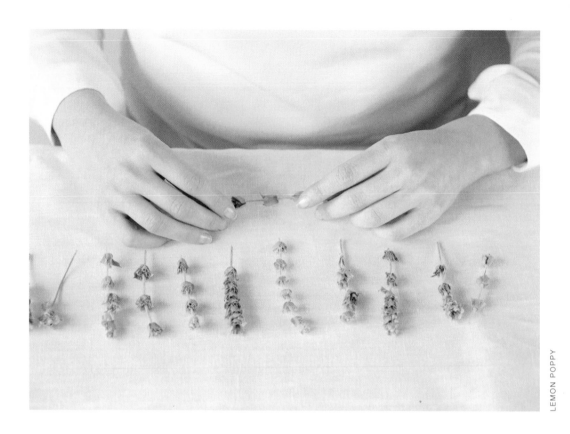

time I've been working in this field have learned a great deal about green and ethical beauty products, restaurants, interior choices, travel options and the like. I've gathered a wealth of information and tips, and met a lot of people. Many of whom have become friends. They do amazing work and I'm incredibly grateful that they're willing to share their wisdom and tips in this book.

This is a good guide, but not a perfect one. I've selected wonderful brands, fab stores, useful tips and inspiring people. And although lots has been included, lots hasn't: it's far from being complete. Developments happen so quickly that they can catch-up and overtake a book. And there are so many great labels and shops, far too many to mention. Even more so, when it comes to an international edition – impossible! I try to provide you with what you need to get yourself started. I've made my own selection, based on what I like and admire, and would recommend to my friends. I'm Dutch; this guide was first published in the Netherlands, but for this edition, I have 'internationalised' it. I've worked for the Clean Clothes Campaign for many years, travelled the world, visited factories and collaborated with workers for better conditions. I also met numerous brands that already have this in their DNA, who want to make great products with respect for people and our environment. It became my mission to put them on the map, to bring them into contact with all those consumers looking for them, and to show everyone that a sustainable lifestyle is not only fabulous, but feasible too. And so, I started as an independent, sustainable fashion and lifestyle expert, giving lectures and workshops, and consulting for stores and businesses. I co-founded the international, sustainable trade show MINT, to make sure that as many good brands as possible get into stores. And continued to receive more questions, about all kinds of topics. Time, then, for an comprehensive guide…

A good guide is one thing, totally living by it is something else. So, that perfection isn't the goal also goes for you. I'm certainly no saint, and you don't have to be one either. Striving for perfection only discourages, because it's simply not feasible. I've written this book to help you make different, better choices that will hopefully improve your life. Sustainability doesn't mean that you can't or shouldn't do things, quite the opposite in fact. It gives you more: quality, options, enjoyment.

For now, there will still be ridiculous choices to make. Between people and the environment, animals and style; impossible. You can ask yourself all sorts of questions. Vegan clothes are probably better, because no animals are used to make them. But aren't alternatives to leather often made of plastic, which in turn comes from oil? And isn't this harmful? Should I buy local to reduce emissions, or fair trade from a developing country to support the people there? And what is this zip made of, how much did the person earn who made it, how long did he or she have to work for it? And how sustainable is this laptop and how long was I under the shower this morning? All very important things to ask yourself. But don't let them drive you crazy.

And most of all, don't let them stand in your way. There's not yet an answer to everything. That's fine. Choose what you feel is best and what's within your capabilities. That's all you can do. Every step you do take, is one you wouldn't have taken before. Of course, the more, the better – but trust me, this will happen naturally. Sustainable living is a little bit like chocolate in that respect. However much I want to devour an entire bar in one go, I always seem to enjoy it more when I choose to eat it more slowly and with a little bit more attention. It's really hard for me to do this with chocolate (perfection wasn't obligatory, right?), but fortunately I seem to manage it with most other things. A sustainable lifestyle also means consuming less and putting quality above quantity.

A good guide about a sustainable lifestyle for me definitely is about top brands, great stores and smart tips, but also about the way in which we interact with the world and each other. About equality, diversity, wanting to understand and help each other. Freedom for everyone, regardless of background, preferences or appearance. It's about truth. Authenticity. About what you do, not what you say. And about trying, sometimes stumbling/failing, but always doing your utmost with the best of intentions.

For me, sustainable living is modern living: in amazing style, with respect for people and our environment. It's modern, because it both looks to the future and is very much in the here and now. Life is to be celebrated, not to be tossed away or wasted with stuff that's actually not good enough for us anyway.

Enjoy this guide, and a huge thank you for using it. This is a good time.

Marieke

79%

of young Americans would engage with a brand that could help them make a difference

WHAT KIND OF GUIDE IS THIS?

I've written this guide as a magazine, so you can read, browse, skip, fold, underline; up to you. Every chapter consists of a collection of tips and tricks, alternated with interviews and facts & figures. The figures have been collected by journalist (and my husband), Edmé Koorstra. They give a good impression of the current state of affairs and developments, but are not the holy grail – sometimes, for example, there are various results relating to one particular aspect. And although we've collected them with as much integrity as possible, their main purpose is to give you an idea of the issues. This is why I mostly avoid source references in the text, this is not a scientific book and readability is paramount. Every chapter concludes with a guide, filled with online and offline addresses. I've selected very stringently, to end up with some of the best. Not easy, but definitely necessary. This book is published in countries including America, Australia, Canada, Denmark, Germany, Finland, New Zealand, Norway, Sweden, the United Kingdom – and unfortunately, I can't include all addresses from everywhere. You'd now have a much thicker, and more quickly outdated 'telephone book' in your hands. But I try to get you started with some well-chosen examples – just take it from there, you'll discover the rest once you get going. I curate the brands, stores, restaurants and initiatives based on my experience. I've developed my own method to distinguish between what is real and what isn't. For MINT, for example, I've been selecting brands for years, based on where and how it is made; from what, by whom, who verifies this, how transparent that is, the approach to women's rights, to transport and packaging, and the company culture. I particularly look for credibility, not perfection. Of course, you need to very much be on the right path, and have a clear idea of what's optimal, and where improvements still need to be made. But being 100% sustainable is often still a challenge.

Every little bit helps and well begun is half done. Don't ever think that you don't matter, or that you can't achieve much on your own. One droplet is enough to change the colour of an entire jug of water, I wrote in a previous book. Something I still believe. Just think about the impact one mosquito can have in your bedroom…

WHAT IS SUSTAINABLE?

For me, it means: with respect for people and our surroundings. So, made under good working conditions, from environmentally and animal-friendly materials. Exploiting nothing and nobody, and causing as little damage as possible.

As far as I'm concerned, we on our own cannot fully define what sustainable is. The people making our products, in India, Bangladesh or the Ivory Coast, know best what a good salary is, how many working hours are reasonable, and how they want to champion their rights. So, taking their voices into account is essential. It's about human rights, fair trade, local skills, the position of women, transparency, organic, non-toxic, safe and animal-friendly, recycling, energy, waste, emissions, transport etc. It's also about authenticity, credibility and a real story. That's the story I'm trying to tell, without 'greenwashing', which makes something look much better than it is (so old-fashioned). Buy green and ethical products, choose quality above quantity, buy less where possible, reuse if you can, and recycle what is left. That's it.

FRAENCK

SUSTAINABLE IS NOT EXPENSIVE

That something is cheap, doesn't mean it costs little, but that someone other than you is paying the price. Fair fashion is not too expensive, regular brands are too cheap. Such prices are simply not possible, without people, animals and the environment having to suffer. They're being exploited to clothe us. The real costs are passed on to them: low wages and environmental damage are subsidising our standard of living. Sustainable labels source differently, they don't force prices down and are often considerably smaller, meaning they have less products to distribute their costs over. Despite this, there are plenty that have the same price level as 'normal' brands. And their products often last longer, so there's your profit right there. Choosing quality that's durable, means we're better off than buying something new that's short-lived.

Using less also really makes a difference, is more enjoyable than you might think and of course, saves money. Do you really need it all? Does it make you happy? Or does it only add to the mountain of stress-inducing things in your life? We can't just improve the world by buying more. For everything we consume, resources are needed. Does everything have to be new? Or can it also be second-hand? With new items, go for quality and timelessness, so that they last, and can have a second life once you're finished with them. But I'm getting ahead of myself. First this: of course, you can buy things. But we can do it differently – more fun, a little less and with more value for our money.

THIS IS AN INDEPENDENT GUIDE

No brand, store or initiative has – in any way, shape or form – paid to feature in this guide. I have chosen them because I rate them in terms of style and story. In addition, I've considered availability and diversity as much as possible. Some are so special that I just have to include them, even though they come from afar, or require a larger investment. Hopefully, in this way, I can bring them a little closer. I am independent and have no affiliations (apart from 'the society of the good life'). There are many more labels, shops and people working on this subject, unfortunately I couldn't include everyone in his book. But a major shout-out to everyone doing good things.

NO ANIMALS WERE HARMED

This book is printed on FSC-certified paper, with inks from plant-based, renewable raw materials. There is also an e-book available. Nevertheless, I can hear you thinking: 'Hmm, talking about buying less, using less resources and then making a book. How sustainable is that?!' You're right, of course. I'd have probably burdened the environment less if I hadn't made it (although, all those hours sitting stock-still at my desk, I wasn't doing other more polluting things). But by inspiring as many people as possible to take some good steps, I hope that the positive outweighs the negative, and the net effect is favourable.

HELLO

Please don't hesitate to get in touch via **mariekeeyskoot.nl**; for a key-note/lecture, workshop or consultancy, or if you want to book me as (English language) presenter or moderator. On social media you can find me here:

Instagram: mariekeeyskoot
Facebook: talkingdress
Twitter: mariekeeyskoot

I look forward to seeing you there!

IMPRINT MAC / PHOTO: LAILA COHEN / DESIGN: NELLY ROSE X ODETTE STEELE X DIAN BELANGI

01

FASHION & ACCESSORIES

INTRODUCTION

10,000

litres of water go into
the making of one outfit
(jeans, T-shirt)

11.8

billion kilos of
clothes and textiles
end up in American
landfills every year

80

billion: the amount of
clothes we produce
annually worldwide
(11 pairs of jeans, jackets
or dresses per person,
4 times more than in 2000)

Where would we be without clothes, right? Or bags or shoes? Nowhere. Many people ask me: so, how do you *do* it? Isn't sustainable fashion a lot more expensive/more difficult to find/uglier than regular clothes? Not per se, sometimes and no. In this chapter I'll show you why. I actually like buying clothes now a lot more than I used to. Because I no longer do it indifferently. Where's the joy in being indifferent? Indifference towards your food is no fun, nor towards living or learning. It's much more interesting and satisfying to buy (or eat or learn) something you really want. The same goes for clothes – I enjoy my purchases much more, because I don't just buy the first thing that looks okay and is cheap. Compare it with the (mindless) eating of an entire bag of crisps, in contrast to an exquisite piece of cake. You'll probably feel guilty, nauseous and big after finishing the crisps, and while the cake might be a bit more expensive, you'll have enjoyed it more. And once you've finished it, you still do. That's what I mean.

So overall, I buy a little less, but spend a little more. Yes, you've guessed it: quality over quantity. I've had to learn this, I sometimes find spending money quite difficult. And my partner too. We were pleased to realise that we've started spending more money recently. On life in general, but certainly also on clothes, shoes and bags. Because if there's one thing I've learned over the years, it's this: cheap doesn't mean that it doesn't cost much, but that someone else is paying the price. Sustainable products are not expensive, regular ones are too cheap.

Fortunately, sustainable, good-quality products generally last longer, making the 'price per use' lower, so that we're actually better off in the long-term. Because the cliché is true: you get what you pay for. If you choose something that doesn't cost a lot and you subsequently can only wear a few times because there are holes in it, or looks like a piece of rag after three washes, you need to keep buying, ultimately spending more. Not smart, but definitely how we've become programmed. We should really shake off that short-term way of thinking. Buy better quality items that cost more, use them for years and you'll spend less. More may seem better, but a growing number of people are questioning this.

Including me, so I try to only buy what I need. If I have to replace something, or because it would be good to have so that I can combine and actually wear more of my clothes. I don't just randomly grab something that I 'like'. It's easier now than it used to be, because I better understand my own body and style. Bad buys are not only a waste in terms of money, but also in terms of the environment

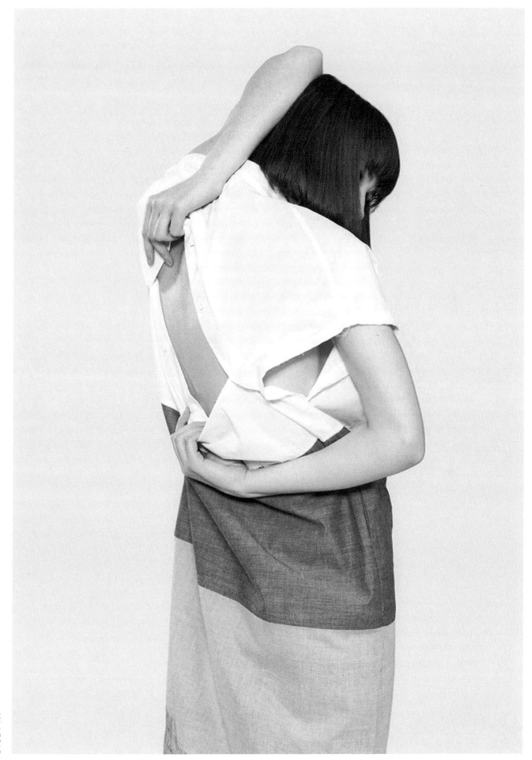

and the effort of the people that have made that skirt. So, I know my own taste, and that actually, I never wear skirts. Many people have said clever things about this. Pioneering fashion designer Vivienne Westwood says it best: 'Buy less, choose well and make it last. In fact, don't buy this collection at all.'

85

million trees on average are cut down each year to make fabric (30% of which are from primary forests and threatened areas)

At nearly every workshop or lecture I give, it turns out that everyone wears about 20% of their wardrobe 80% of the time. We need to bring this more into balance. Being sustainable with your clothes, bags, shoes and jewellery is also about much more than buying new things. It's about second-hand, swapping and sharing, repairing, washing and recycling. People sometimes think that most doors close if you want to be sustainable, that you aren't allowed anything anymore. But actually, all kinds of doors open: you discover new stores and brands, as well as possibilities. You have a lot more freedom, you no longer have to buy and wear everything the regular fashion chains want. Great! But what *can* you wear? And how do you find it? That's what this chapter is about.

10%

the percentage of the total CO_2 emissions caused by the fashion industry (in comparison: the aviation industry is responsible for 2.5%)

60

euros is the minimum wage in the garment industry in Bangladesh, what they need to live from is around 294 euros – so this is 20%

ELSIEN GRINGHUIS

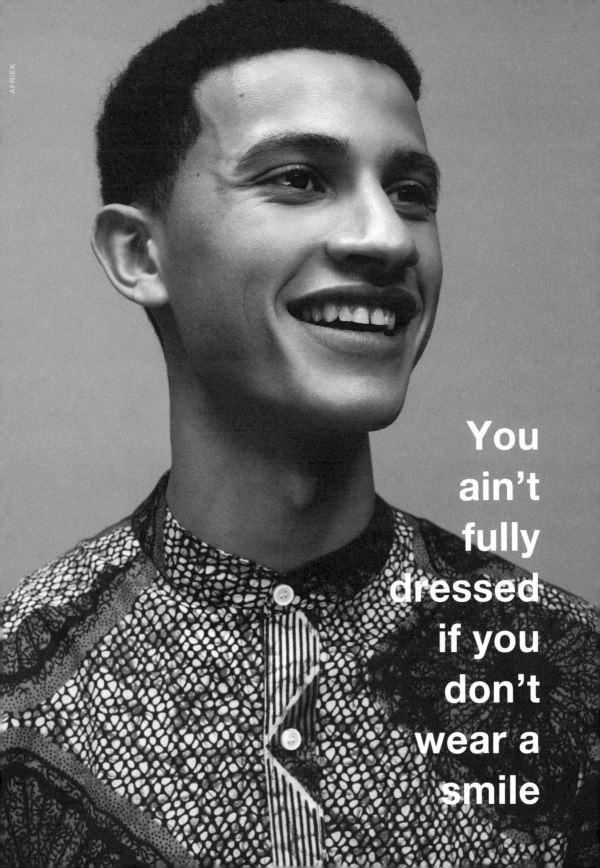

AFRIEK

You ain't fully dressed if you don't wear a smile

FASHION

AURÉLIE CHADAINE / LAURA BONNEFOUS

The average British woman buys about 3,100 items of clothing in her life, including 270 pairs of shoes, 185 dresses and 145 bags. In total, she spends approximately 105,000 euros on clothes. At the same time, 60% say often not to know what to wear.

Preparation

Know your Wardrobe

One of the first stops for sustainable fashion, is your own wardrobe. The longer you make do with what's in it, the better. It may sound corny, but it's not. Because the contents can often be quite surprising. We don't always know exactly what we have. But that knowledge is quite useful, as it tells you all kinds of things: what you like to buy, what you like to wear (which isn't always the same thing), what you have lots of, and what's missing from your collection that you could combine some of your other items with. Having a thorough rummage through your wardrobe is one of the best ways to make it more sustainable (and it clears up nicely!).

> Your clothes are made of all kinds of different materials, from cotton to polyester and from lycra to modal. But what is what? Have a look when you're going through your wardrobe, also at what you prefer. This will help make your next purchase something you will actually wear and suits you.

> You have the whole world in your wardrobe: it's quite amazing how many countries your clothes come from, and from how far away. Read the labels, it gives you an idea of how global the fashion industry is – and maybe, a wish list of places your clothes have been, but you haven't (yet!).

Clearing Out is Great (or It Can Be)

I actually don't do this often enough, even though I know it works. Clearing out your wardrobe really helps: with less clothes, you better know what to wear and what you still need. In short, go for it! Like this, for example:

01. Make three piles: 1) Definite keepers, 2) To go, and 3) Unsure.

02. Looking at the 'Unsure' pile, consider this:
> Does it still look good? Is it still in one piece? No? Get rid of it. Has it lost its shape, are the colours faded or is the wool bobbling? Out with it.

> Does it still fit? If not, it can go (it's not going to fit any better).
> Have I worn it in recent years? No? Ditch it. Unless you easily can come up with something else in your wardrobe to combine it with.

03. Divide the pile that can stay into two: basic items (jeans, black trousers, white shirt, blazer, jumper, cardigan, sneakers, flats, those kinds of things) and items that allow you to vary and combine (the more colourful, unique items). The ideal ratio is said to be 70/30, but don't hold me to that and see what suits you.

04. Take a good look at the piles. What items are you missing, to combine so that you can wear as much of your wardrobe as possible? Go in search of them.

05. Of course, don't throw away the clothes and accessories you're getting rid of. Sell, swap, donate or give as a gift. More about this later (see p. 059).

06. Be strict with yourself. Difficult now, great later.

Well, that's better. This is your basic collection.
And Now Stick with It:

» One in, one out. So, if you buy a new dress or coat, another one goes. If you're given a new bag, another one goes. You get the gist. This will keep your wardrobe nice and tidy and you'll really be able to use everything.

» Invest in your signature item (or items, of course). The thing you always turn to if you want to feel fantastic, powerful, beautiful. For me it's a jumpsuit, yours maybe a jacket or good shirt. Something you wear your entire life, your go-to item (guys, this sounds familiar too, doesn't it?).

» Always choose quality over quantity. Always. So often, that I'll talk about this a lot more later.

» Go for timeless. Again, as often as you can. Trends pass, and everyone looks the same. And suddenly that print is a real no-go in a few months' time (which in itself is bizarre, so never mind that if this trend happens to be your perfect style). Your clothes will go together much better and be easier to combine if you choose classic items – and you'll be able to wear them a lot longer.

» Is there an item you don't have that would make it easier to get dressed every morning? Buy it (not something else).

The average British woman doesn't use 60% of her wardrobe. An American study showed that women consider 21% of their clothes unwearable, 33% too tight and 24% too loose. 12% are new, unworn clothes – which leaves just 10%...

Style is Everything

You can buy, swap, sew, borrow and steal clothes, but not style (okay, you *can* steal that). Style is how we put our look together, our personal fashion language, our je-ne-sais-quoi. It's not about expensive things, big names or following the crowd. Often quite the opposite. The choices you make about your top, jeans, coat and bag, and how you combine them, say a lot about you. About how you want to be seen, your taste and what's important to you. Knowing your style matters, because it can prevent bad buys. You of course look better if you know what suits you and what makes you feel invincible. Invest in getting to know your style, then you won't get carried away by hypes and you'll buy the right things.

> What colours work best for you? Depending on your eyes, hair and skin tone, you probably fit into a colour type. This can help you find your style and enhance your appearance.

> What's your body shape? What clothes, styles and prints suit this well? Good to know – and be honest with yourself. It'll ultimately be for the best. Also if you think you're perfect and can wear absolutely anything. That's your prerogative.

> Tastes differ, but in general, these things won't benefit your style:
» Try not to buy counterfeits. Fake is for wannabes, it plays into the hands of dubious industries, unregulated in terms of working conditions or the

environment. The quality also often leaves a lot to be desired too.

» Sandblasted jeans (it gives workers lung disease and cancer) or sequins (fiddly work, so more often done by children).

» Fabrics that make you sweat, in a colour that shows it. Believe me, you won't wear it again once it's happened to you.

Germans buy approximately 31 items of clothing and pairs of shoes a year, the Danish 35 (15 years ago: 27).

Clothes are Cool

We don't always realise how important clothes are for us. But they actually matter quite a bit, and have all kinds of functions. They protect us against cold, rain or sun. They give us attitude for an interview, class at a wedding and the right look for an evening on the sofa. Clothes hugely determine how you feel – sharp, chic or relaxed – but also how people see you. Ideal if you're a fireman or chef: the uniform immediately clarifies your goal. Your outfit communicates (I'm tough), inspires (I love that bag!) and implies (I like to stand in the foreground). Your clothes say who you are. But clothes also make your entire life possible. We can't actually function in this society without them. The chance that you're reading this guide completely naked is pretty small. Clothes are of vital importance – so why then do we take them for granted? We barely stop to notice how unique it is that we wear clothes (the only ones on this planet), or where they've come from. We attach little value to the manual labour they have taken, buy them by the dozen and throw them away just as easily. My grandmother was surprised at how this has changed so rapidly in the last fifty, sixty years. She only bought clothes if she needed them, chose quality and often made them herself. She'd dress up, for an evening out, for example. Special outfit, hair curled, husband in a suit. Clothes can mean a lot, and sustainable ones even more. You definitely feel better about yourself putting on something that's exploited nothing or nobody. What we wear doesn't only determine our style – it's also a statement. When you wear sustainable fashion, you can give a good answer to the question where you got that amazing coat, not only to other people, but yourself too.

Men are on their way up. They spend increasingly more money on clothes (and their appearance). In recent years, global sales of men's fashion have been growing faster than women's, and this will probably continue for a while yet.

LIVIA FIRTH

Livia Firth (1969) is creative director of Eco-Age, a brand consultancy specialised in sustainability. She likes to question things constantly, and describes herself as curious and an 'agitator'. If something doesn't add up, she wants to act on it. Livia is the wife of actor Colin Firth, and even cooler than he is.

Why do you do what you're doing?
'Because we're on a train heading for a big crash, and we need to make sure we divert the tracks towards a future which is possible. Businesses, governments and citizens all have huge responsibilities and today, I think the most powerful change can come from businesses – which are driven by citizens and often dictate to governments.'

What is your '30 wears challenge'?
'Ethical-living expert Lucy Siegle and I were talking about how to convince people to move away from "Which brand is good and which is bad?", as this creates confusion and impasse. How do you take a step back and actually look at the big question of "Should I buy it?" as most purchases today are made impulsively. So, we came up with the idea that when we want to buy a garment, we ask ourselves, "I like it, but would I wear it a minimum of 30 times?". Probably most people would answer "Not really, no" – and that's the solution. Put it back and walk away, as you're about to contribute to disposable fashion.'

Why did you start the Green Carpet Challenge?
'It was born on the red carpets and is a way to showcase, on the most powerful communication platforms ever, the stories behind what we wear. So not purely saying, "This is what I am wearing", but more, "This is who I am wearing, and these are the stories behind it". Today we do all sorts of events and collections, it's become our communication arm of Eco-Age.'

Where would you like you and your work to be in 10 years?
'At home in pyjamas – smiling at the revolution that we all managed to achieve and how fast fashion has been destroyed for ever.'

Do you have a life motto?
'Stop bitching and start a revolution. It was on a sticker that someone gave to me in Venice Beach years ago.'

Who is your hero?
'Any person who says, "Let's change this".'

Buying

Here We Go

How do I buy ethical fashion, what should I pay attention to and where can I find it? These are the questions people have asked me most frequently. I don't have one comprehensive answer for you, but I do have all kinds of possibilities (and the request to not strive for perfection).

This is How You Buy Sustainable Fashion

01. Choose ethical brands

This one's rather obvious of course, but hey, who said it was going to be difficult? Buy from brands that make beautiful products and treat people, animals and our surroundings as well as they can. The number's growing, in all types and price ranges – from basic to high-end and from affordable to expensive. Just as in regular fashion. By buying these brands you support them, show there's a need and a business case for ethical fashion. At the end of this chapter you'll find brands and stores to help you on your way.

02. Buy smart

This is one of the best tips I can give you. It saves money. It's better for the environment and better for your morning ritual (and your relationship). Before you go shopping or decide to purchase something, ask yourself these questions:

» Do I really need this? Or is it more of the same?
» Will this enable me to wear other clothes I have more often?
» Does it fit well?
» Does it look amazing? Do I feel a million dollars in it?
» Am I really going to wear it? Or do I enjoy buying it more than wearing it?
» Can I easily combine it? Can I think of at least a few outfits that I can wear it with?
» Will it last?
» Can I see myself wearing this in a few years?
» Is this investment worth the money? Is this bargain worth my money?
» Does it suit my style? Or is it something I'd have bought a few years ago?
» And: does it have to be dry cleaned or can I wash it? Does it crease easily? Will that annoy me?
» Does the idea of wearing it make me really happy?

03. Take quality over quantity

Invest in good items, and make sure that you don't end up with a pile of 'not-quites' as I used to. It may feel expensive, but this is generally not true. You can wear it so much more often that it's actually cheaper than continually buying new tops that may cost less, but you only wear three times. Save for something special, you're worth it.

04. Go for timeless and take your time

Choose the piece that you can still wear in ten years, but then combined with something else. Buy what you want instead of what you see. Spotted a must-have? Sleep on it for a night. Or two. Still even thinking about it?

05. Appreciate second-hand

This is one of the best and most fun things you can do for a more sustainable wardrobe. The landfills shrink, no new resources are used, the item has a second life and you have something unique. And: it's much cheaper than new. You may need to search for a while, be patient and keep your eyes open, but the chase is part of the thrill. Is there a brand you love, but that isn't sustainable? Look for it in second-hand shops or on eBay, and you might be able to wear it anyway. More about this strategy for a better wardrobe on page 063.

06. Shop local

Nearly all our coats and bags come from far away and have already made a huge journey before they land in your wardrobe. If the environment's important to you, then you can choose to shop as locally as possible. It's wonderful to support regional craftsmen, small stores and designers. Meanwhile, many brands choose to have their products made in developing countries, to stimulate employment and trade and improve conditions. Do I buy clothes that people abroad make for us and try to help them, or do I shop locally to cause less environmental pollution? There's a case for both, of course – but it can be pretty challenging to find an affordable outfit made close to home.

Most ethical brands try to keep the transport impact to a minimum by finding as many factories as possible for weaving, dyeing and sewing in the same region, and by shipping their collections in one go.

07. Buy less

It may sound like the least appealing tip, but secretly it's the most fun. Reducing feels great. And there are savings to be made everywhere. Firstly, logically, money. Time, also for sure. Think about the hours you spend browsing, hunting down the lowest price, the best deal, the most exciting find. On trying on, doubting, deciding and returning. On shopping, choosing, talking about it. On not knowing what to wear every morning. On stress, because of this and because of all the stuff. The more stuff, the more stress, it turns out. And so, this tip's a life saver. It has really helped me in recent years. Less is more.

Fast Fashion
(A Race to the Bottom)

Every year we consume about one and a half times what our earth can make in raw materials in that time – at a gigantic speed. The fashion industry plays a huge role in this, partly because it produces at a lightning rate, and the throwaway culture is part of the system. The objective of fast fashion is to get everyone buying as much as possible in as little time as possible. Nothing else. Do you need new clothes twelve times a year, or even six? Most major chains want us to believe we do. The consumer culture that emerged in the sixties has gained momentum in the last twenty years. Thanks to internet, everybody knows everything, and wants everything, immediately. The newest it-bags, the latest trends, that celebrity's outfit. Quickly assembled copies come straight off the catwalk.

Computer drawing makes handcrafted design redundant, materials are getting cheaper. Making it easier and easier to offer multiple collections a

Worldwide, we spend nearly 775 billion euros annually on clothes and shoes. In the Netherlands, we spend about 1,700 euros per household per year on clothes: approximately 5% of our budget. My mother and grandmother estimate that they used to spend a quarter of their income on clothes, while they bought much less than we did.

KOWTOW

ELSIEN GRINGHUIS   EKN FOOTWEAR   BY MÖLLE / STUDIO OINK

year. By outsourcing to low-wage countries, this can all be done at a bargain price. And we lose out: similar, cheap, bad-quality clothes. The emergence of fast-fashion chains is the result. They push us into a vicious circle: cheap clothes mean disposable clothes, which means you need to keep buying. It also puts enormous pressure on the people who have to make these clothes at breakneck speed for as low a price as possible. Storage is expensive, so there's no stock: if an item's a hit, it has to be put together in no-time. Feel your clothes are badly sewn? They're made by professionals, but even for them, this pace is too high. And that's not to mention the impact on the environment from the dyeing and transportation. Some brands design 40,000 items per year, of which 10,000 reach the stores. Every few weeks there's a new supply. Supposedly because *we* want that, but I may have missed that memo. You? Do you even realise it's happening? And does this all really make us happy – these clothes and this way of doing things?

Desire/Pressure and Self-Image

Where does that need to keep buying new clothes actually come from? We've got more than enough, and we don't go shopping because our only pair of trousers is split, and we literally don't have anything to wear. So why do we? Because we want to belong. Because we get bored quickly. Because we can. Because we've seen it in a magazine, or it seems to be the solution to our problems. Because we want to reward, comfort or cheer ourselves up. Retail therapy should make us feel better, but I don't believe it does. Keep

buying more, so that we need to keep working harder to earn the money? Wouldn't we be better off investing the time we spend shopping and working in experiencing life, in friends, making love, volunteering? The fashion industry (just like the beauty industry) has been criticised for years because of its contribution to the low self-image of women in our society, and problems such as depression and anorexia. The link between fashion and self-respect is a strong one. The fashion world thrives on bringing its customers down. The message that you're not thin, successful or beautiful enough resonates all around us. That pair of shoes, bag or dress will fix everything. Which is never the case, of course. Yet still, you keep trying. Have you ever been so obsessed with a bag that you can't get it out of your head? Shopping addiction is perhaps an exaggeration for most people. But make sure you claim back your freedom and resist the temptation. These initiatives can help you:

> #30wears – Livia Firth (see p. 021) is committed in various ways to sustainable fashion, including the promotion of the #30wears concept. She asks you to only buy clothes that you will wear at least thirty times. Doesn't sound like much, but if you think about it, bizarrely it's actually quite a lot.
> Project 333 – Every three months you choose 33 items from your wardrobe which are the only things you'll wear. Including shoes, coats and jewellery, excluding underwear and sport clothes. Save (or get rid of) the rest, but do not use them. You'll see that you don't miss some clothes at all. Because you select exactly what you want to wear, you get to know your own style and wear your favourite items the most.

JANINE ABBRING

Janine Abbring (1976) is a Dutch television maker and presenter. She's editor-in-chief of the prize-winning current affairs show *Zondag met Lubach* and hosts a major interview programme.

How do you use your profession for a better world?

'Before I take on an assignment, I always look at whether it actually fits with who I am. My agent has been known to roll her eyes when I refuse a well-paid job because the client isn't to my liking. Companies that pollute the world, have no respect for human rights or are involved in the bio-industry, I won't work with them. This does thin out what's on offer, but that's just how it is. I still remember stopping at Kentucky Fried Chicken, when recording in South Africa. I refused to go in, even turned down the coffee. So, there I was, sulking like a child on the steps outside, ha ha!'

Do you approach clothes differently now to a few years ago?

'Yes, completely. Up to few years ago I was buying an absurd amount of clothes, my wardrobes (yes, plural) filled to bursting. I'd unscrupulously spend hundreds of euros online, ordering a certain style of skirt or sneakers in several colours. Now it's very different. I have fewer clothes, I'm more selective. And the cliché is absolutely true: having less stuff really is liberating.'

How do you buy or choose clothes?

'I pay attention to animal, human and environmental friendliness. This means: stay as far away as possible from the major mass-production fashion chains, preferably shoes without leather, second-hand shopping. Fur, down and angora are no-goes. I have several Etsy webshops selling vintage clothes I like to browse. But then of course you sometimes face the fact that whatever you order

has to be flown from the other side of the world. It's damned difficult to be 100% sustainable.'

What do you worry about?

'Animal abuse really gets to me. This sounds rather nonsensical – after all, who's *for* animal abuse – but I do notice that I'm more sensitive to it than those around me. Most of my friends have no problem separating the steak on their plate from the cow it once was. They choose not to think about the suffering or the environmental impact. I can't. That rabbits are plucked alive, screaming, for their angora wool, is for me an appalling idea. I'm the irritating Facebook friend that keeps circulating all those petitions.'

What are you most proud of?

'In my television work, I try to make my "green voice" heard. As editor-in-chief of a satirical talk show, I'm very aware of this. Although it's a comedy programme, we do tackle important themes. We have the opportunity to get people thinking, an unbelievably valuable position. I'm most proud of the item we made about why we should be eating less meat. Many meat eaters have told me that because of this programme, they have altered their eating pattern. Isn't that fantastic? I'm really conscious however of trying not to preach. A wagging, green finger will achieve very little, in my experience. Hold on to your principles, but don't become bitter!'

Janine's tips

Clothes 'My shopping behaviour changed considerably after I got professional colour advice. It's a misconception that this is only done by middle-aged ladies who tell you what isn't allowed. I don't really have any shopping mishaps now, and all my clothes match.'

Skincare 'Don't let magazines or beauticians talk you into the feeling you need creams, lotions and masks for daytime, nighttime, winter, summer, wrinkles, a greasy or combination skin, the T-zone and, not to forget, around your eyes and cleavage, because "the skin is thinner there". All marketing bullshit. Since I've been cleansing my face with coconut oil and a warm washcloth, I've led a silky-smooth and spot-free existence. If you want to delve deeper into simple skincare (and making, for example, scrubs and masks yourself), then the book *Skin Cleanse* by Adina Grigore is a must. I also swear by Living Libations products, based on natural oils and herbs.'

MATT & NAT

BEWARE OF GREENWASHING

Sustainable fashion is big business. More and more people are looking for it, so an increasing number of companies are seeing an opportunity to make money. Which means you can't take what everyone claims at face value. Of course, you're a critical consumer who pays attention and thinks, but just to be sure, a few questions to help you recognise greenwashing:

— Are vague words such as natural, fair, green or environmentally friendly, being used?
— Is the brand itself claiming all kinds of things, or is there independent verification, such as certification?
— Does the brand window-dress, meaning it sells one good product (a shirt made of organic cotton, for example) to distract attention from the rest?
— Is there something about sustainable policy on the website – and are these concrete actions or just woolly ideas?
— Does the brand consistently behave sustainably, so also addressing, for instance, packaging or transport?
— Does the website mention a sustainable policy – and are these concrete actions or just woolly ideas? Do they talk about the people who make their products, and their environmental impact, in a meaningful way?
— Do they provide (credible) answers to your questions, are they easy to get in touch with, or do the store assistants know their stuff?
— Do others (online) say anything about their sustainable achievements?
— What does your gut feeling tell you? Is this real? (Actually, this should be at the top).

Slow Fashion: Easy Does It

We've had enough. Who still wants to come home with seven large bags of tops, skirts and sequins, to not even wear half because they're too tight, don't suit or don't go with anything? It may partly be wishful thinking, but I really feel more and more people are becoming fed up with all that buying, buying, buying. We need to break the circle, and I think it's happening. Slow fashion is the sister of slow food: prepared and consumed with attention. We view and use clothes differently (and more easily) than food, because we have less experience with preparing them. Everybody cooks, but few make their own clothes, so we don't appreciate how much effort and manual labour goes into them. Slow fashion shifts the focus from quantity to quality, long term, craftsmanship, fair distribution and conscious choices. Just as with food, we need to learn to value a variety of tastes, styles and colours. Good design can be a weapon for change. Modern designers make beautiful clothes that fit well and can be cherished for years.

Seasonless is the Future

I'm convinced that we need to shift the focus from seasons and rapid changes, to the promotion of timeless collections in which designs retain their value. The industry of the future is about quality over quantity, collections that grow or don't change, and styles that aren't suddenly 'out' once summer turns into autumn. The strict fashion calendar puts extreme pressure on producers and consumers and creates waste. But modern fashion no longer allows itself to be restricted by seasons. And do these actually still exist? Stores are left with mountains of surplus stock if the weather is slightly different than expected. How often have you not been able to buy a winter coat anywhere when you needed it? For some reason, clothes often don't seem to be in the shop at the right moment. And who has a special summer or autumn wardrobe anyway? We mix and match, opt for layers and pay increasingly less attention to the 'rules'. The entire industry is configured to design for a short life-cycle – and this doesn't just apply to clothes. It's not innovative, not inspirational and definitely not sustainable.

— Luxury brand Burberry is turning things around: from now on you can immediately buy what you see on the catwalk. Normally, there would have been a period of waiting (and longing), once they'd displayed their newest creations. The pieces were only available months later, now instantly. What impact this acceleration has on the people who actually have to make the clothes remains to be seen, but it's certainly a different perspective on seasons.

— More and more brands work seasonless, such as Study NY and AYR ('All Year Round').

— Many ethical fashion brands create timeless classics and variations on styles that are popular, keep best-sellers in the collection or work with a basic staple collection, adding something new, or an on-trend item, every now and again.

INTERVIEW

STUDY NY

Tara St James (1976) is owner of modern and ethical fashion brand Study NY: designed and responsibly made in New York, from environmentally-friendly materials.

You want to change the fashion world and work with an anti-calendar model. What does this mean?
'I have a love-hate relationship with the fashion world. I love creating and solving problems – finding the right materials and a way of designing that creates no, or very little, waste. But I hate how many clothes have already been made, how many resources wasted. If I was to make a truly sustainable collection, it would mean making nothing: no

new clothes and products, because we simply don't need them. But that's not my reality, so I now make timeless collections that don't adhere to the fashion calendar and don't have to be worn in a particular season.'

Why did you start working like this?

'I'm embarrassed to admit that I used to view fashion as something disposable. I was a slave to trends and loved finding cheap items. I had the advantage of travelling to Hong Kong four times a year for work, where I saw huge quantities of easily accessible counterfeits and on-trend items. When organic cotton came onto the market, I started to delve into the effects of pesticides, chemicals, water wastage and cheap labour. Once I'd learned about this, I couldn't "unlearn" it. I put myself into rehab, started buying less and implementing these values into my work.'

Do you have a hero?

'My mother is a successful entrepreneur and a single mum, who was always there for her family. She encouraged me to follow my dreams, however challenging or crazy they seemed. She's my muse, incredibly stylish and wears everything I make. If she likes it, I know I'm on the right track.'

Tara's guide for Brooklyn, NY

Package Free Shop – 'All things necessary to live a package-free life, including bamboo straws!'
Zero Waste Daniel – 'Fashion brand upcycled from production-waste salvaged from local NYC manufacturers.'
Kaight – 'Retail pioneer in the sustainable fashion movement, carries exclusively ethical brands.'
Bhoomki – 'Multi-brand shop that also make their own collection using artisanal fabrics from India.'
Adaptations – 'Beautifully-curated vintage furniture.'
10 ft Single by Stella Dallas – 'My favourite vintage clothes shop in Brooklyn, give yourself lots of time to explore!'

STUDY NY

The quality of our clothes is deteriorating, and they can be reused less and less. Now, only 35% of the items collected in the Netherlands are good enough to be worn again straight away, a figure that used to be much higher.

Once we need less,
we will have more

QNOOP / PEGGY KUIPER

There's No Such Thing as Cheap

» Really, there isn't. That something is cheap, doesn't mean it doesn't cost much, but that someone other than you is paying the price. Sustainable fashion isn't expensive, regular fashion is too cheap.

» We've lost sight a little of the relationship between price and quality. If we see a low price in a mainstream store or major chain, we believe this to be the real price of a product. But this is only the price if the person that grows the resources gets paid the lowest market value, if it's made in a low-wage country for too small a salary, if it's produced in such enormous quantities that the costs can be spread across a multitude of items, if the shop staff aren't paid well, if the costs of environmental damage are not included, and so on. Our low prices are being subsidised on all sides by people much worse off than we are, and by the planet on which we live.

» The consequences of the race to the bottom, when everything has to be done faster and cheaper, are passed on to the weakest. I so often hear that 'they should be happy to have work'. But I believe that nobody should have to live this way and having a job doesn't mean that you can be exploited.

» Something that costs little, but you can only wear a few times, is actually expensive. Something that costs 50 euros and you wear 50 times, costs 1 euro per wear. A 10 euro item worn 3 times, costs over 3 euros per wear. Simple.

» We all suffer as a result: environmental pollution, uniformity, loss of ethics and less and less value for our money.

» If we buy less for a higher price, the wages can go up and the working hours down. Of course, this is too simplified, but broadly speaking, it's true.

» From what you pay in the store, approximately 42% goes to the store, 21% to the brand, 19% to the factory (material is about 13%), 16% to the government, and 2 to 5% to the worker. This is an average of course and differs per item. But still, if you were to double the wage, something that would have cost 40 euros will cost 41 euros. Doable?

This distribution may not be very fair, but it can be much worse. Worldwide, Kanye West is opening pop-up stores with his own label. He boasts that in New York, in just two days, he earned more than a million dollars. This is how:

A KANYE WEST HOODY

Sale price (108 dollars)	**96,78 euros**
Factory and manufacturing costs	**13,44 euros**
Sea transport and insurance	**0,90 euros**
Import tax	**2,24 euros**
Store costs	**2,70 euros**
Tax	**1,80 euros**
Profit	**75,70 euros**

A lesson in getting rich.

Major Chains: Yes or No?

I'm often asked if you should buy from a major chain such as H&M or Zara or not, from their more sustainable line, for example. This is what I think:

» If you really want to shop at a chain, then choose something from their more sustainable line, such as H&M's Conscious or Zara's Join Life collections. This is at least an improvement on their normal range, as they're made of more sustainable materials. This way, the people in charge see there is a demand, and will then hopefully improve the whole brand.

» At the same time, don't be fooled: such lines are often not completely sustainable, and form only a very small percentage of the total on offer. Certainly, in terms of working conditions, it frequently leaves a lot to be desired. C&A and H&M are both major users of organic cotton, but not pioneers in the field of workers' rights. The Swedish giant has started a living wage-related project (not many big chains work on this), but this doesn't seem to have much to do with the Conscious collection. H&M is relatively rather transparent and discloses where their clothes are made, which is a good step.

» At some chains, you can hand in old clothes in exchange for a credit voucher. But if you use this voucher to buy yet more cheap clothes, we're not really getting anywhere.

» Chains have huge budgets for marketing, making projects quickly appear bigger than they actually are. If we take the previous example: chains take in clothes to reuse, and to make collections with the material; but we're talking relatively small numbers. Of course, something is always better than nothing, but it can easily appear to the outside world as if they are, for the most part, doing good work.

The value of the global fashion industry is estimated at 2,700 billion euros. These are, according to FashionUnited, the richest people in the fashion world:

62.8 billion	28.6 billion	24.6 billion
Amancio Ortega of Inditex (richest man in the world, of, amongst others, Zara)	Bernard Arnault of LVMH (including Louis Vuitton, Dior, Céline)	Axel Dumas and family of Hermès

22.4 billion	21.0 billion	17.5 billion
The Brenninkmeijer family of C&A	Phil Knight of Nike	Stefan Persson of Hennes & Mauritz

Minimum wage per month of garment workers in:

54 euros	58 euros	60 euros	87 euros	91 euros
Sri Lanka	India	Bangladesh	Cambodia	Indonesia

» With size comes power. A small step made by a large brand has an immediate, real effect, but this size also increases responsibility, and entitles us to expect more. Giants can change the entire industry, if they were to take the lead. Now this is being driven by the smaller players.

» Ultimately, major chains must produce less, and of a better quality. As long as they don't, and continue to make such massive amounts of clothes at such a speed, becoming truly sustainable is not going to happen.

» I would never call for a boycott. The people making our clothes then have less work, as they're not in a position to choose whose collection they sew. You're also no longer a customer, which means you lose some of your power. You do though have the choice every day of how you spend your money, and which brands you want to support.

Is Luxury Still Luxury?

Luxury brands used to sort of resemble today's sustainable brands. Handmade, high quality, with attention and appreciation for the product. But then extremely expensive. You bought a lifestyle, an image, a fairy-tale almost. This is no longer always the case. Luxury brands aren't only made in Paris or London anymore, but outsourced to low-wage countries. Because they also have to watch costs, the quality of the material is becoming less. Material that definitely can't be called sustainable – they frequently use leather, fur or exotic animal skins. The social aspect remains somewhat more underexposed, as so often, but there are certainly reports of people made to work hard for little. The sector is closed like an oyster, because the spell must not be broken... Today's luxury is about transparency, craftsmanship and innovation. About timeless, seasonless, quality and authenticity. And about daring to do things differently. To put 'good' on par with 'beautiful'. Luxury is special, and costs time to make. Fortunately, there are luxury brands that show there's hope. Stella McCartney is the first vegetarian, luxury label in the world (also see p. 256), and doesn't use leather, fur, skin and feathers. She proves you can have a luxury brand with popular it-bags, without leather. Plenty of people were sceptical when she started, especially because accessories make up such a large part of the turnover of luxury brands. Former parent company Kering (that also owns Saint Laurent and Gucci) is one of the first major fashion conglomerates to report on issues including water use, CO_2 emissions, use of harmful materials, and to formulate objectives around these themes. They're not there by a long way, but it's definitely a step in the right direction.

LOVIA

Anna Lehtola (1995) is a sustainable fashion entrepreneur from Helsinki. After running an online second-hand company, she's now the CEO of ethical luxury brand Lovia, which creates bags and accessories from high-quality leftover materials, rescued from different industries. Each bag is numbered, carrying detailed information about the makers, materials and price. She's lived in Scandinavia and San Francisco – these are some of her favourite recommendations.

Arela – 'A Finnish brand creating long-lasting designs in quality materials. They work hard to increase people's awareness of consumption choices and clothing waste.'

Carcel – 'This Danish label's clothes are made of local materials by women in prison in countries with high rates of poverty-related crime.'

Cosa Buena – 'Makes clothes and homeware in collaboration with indigenous artisans from remote Mexican villages.'

Pure Waste – 'Finnish brand which creates new fabric from cotton waste. They sell comfy, everyday basics and make fabric for other companies too.'

tonlé – 'American/Cambodian zero-waste brand that ethically produces clothes from mass-manufacturers' scrap waste.'

And a bonus: 'Get a real sauna experience at **Löyly**, a sustainably-built design sauna in Helsinki, right by the sea.'

(Online) Shopping and Shipping

It's impossible to imagine life without online shopping anymore. It's fast, easy and the offer is huge. Also in terms of sustainable fashion, more and more is available online.

Yet filling your wardrobe online does have its disadvantages. The working conditions in large distribution centres often leave a lot to be desired: it's hard work for little, the same applies to the package deliverers. Margins are low, and competition is brutal. Parcel transport causes considerable pollution and CO_2 emissions. Particularly if you buy several sizes to try and for sure will need to return items. Or shop abroad, meaning that your clothes have to come from even further away. Are you ever surprised by the huge box delivered to your doorstep containing a tiny necklace? And plastic, filling, you name it (although I do love receiving a fun, personal card). Try not to get things sent backwards and forwards, recycle packaging as much as possible and if you can, get your purchases to come from as close to home as possible.

In Australia in 2016, online clothes shopping rose three times faster than in physical stores. It's estimated that fashion makes up 26% of the online market.

STUDIO JUX

Carlien Helmink (1983), is co-founder of Dutch brand studio JUX, available in eighty stores worldwide.

What is studio JUX?
'Studio JUX is a sustainable fashion and design label from Amsterdam. "Jux" is the German word for "having fun". Fashion should also be enjoyable for the tailor and the cotton farmer, not just for us. This is why JUX has had its own factory in Nepal since 2010, with 35 employees that work according to fair trade standards. To put minimal burden on the environment, we are committed to as small a footprint as possible, by using for example organic cotton, linen and hemp.'

How does studio JUX fit into current times?
'Daily, we can be in contact with people from all over the world, meaning that a colleague in China can sometimes be closer than your neighbour. Social control and support are no longer limited to your family or village. Additionally, the younger generations see that the mass consumption of their parents, and the associated hard work, does not necessarily make them happy. Rather, stressed and over-stimulated. Because what do you do with all these things if you haven't got the time to enjoy them? With studio JUX, we take care of a large group of vulnerable people and we make timeless, high-quality collections you can enjoy for a long time.'

What are your favourite sustainable tips?
'Decide that your next purchase will be a sustainable one: second-hand, organic or fair trade. And not all at once, as this is an unrealistic expectation. See it as a process. What you do, is good enough. Choose sustainable alternatives that are easy for you. Willpower is like a muscle, you can't continually strain it. This is why people can stick to a healthy lifestyle, but not a diet. The same is true of sustainable choices. If you ask too much of yourself, one day it becomes undoable. So, my tip is: don't be too hard on yourself, it's all about what you do right, not about what needs to be better. For example, I replace minced meat with soya mince. You hardly taste the difference in a well-seasoned Bolognese, but you do *make* a difference.'

Carlien's favourites
Cus 'Refined women's fashion made from European fabrics in social workplaces in Barcelona.'

Quazi design 'Amazing jewellery produced in Swaziland from old advertising brochures.'

Werner 'German family business making beautiful shoes from organic and naturally-tanned leather.'

Jan 'n June 'Edgy, young and affordable German brand that works with recycled materials.'

Beaumont Organic 'English, high-quality ladies brand, also great for larger sizes.'

Kaliber 'Young, vegan bag brand from Berlin.'

Sales: Hurray or Nay?

Who doesn't love the sales? Most people do, and I also sometimes find them hard to ignore. But as you can imagine, they're not very sustainable. The clothes aren't sold for the original price, so there's less money for everyone who worked on them. For brands that try and make their clothes sustainably in particular, this money is needed to be able to do business ethically. Sales put even more pressure on the supply chain, driving prices down. Nowadays, we know how much everything costs, but not what anything's worth. If we want things to be different, we're going to have to be prepared to pay a realistic price. There are an increasing number of brands that don't do sales anymore, such as Kuyichi and Joline Jolink. This also means that their collections don't change as frequently and that there's less often room for new items. A risk, but the future.

Reduce Bad Buys

In 1930, the average American woman owned nine outfits. Now, women in the US buy on average more than 60 new items per year. And make about 1,100 euros' worth of bad buys. Buying may give instant satisfaction, but afterwards it can be less fun.

Another study showed that 78% of American women regret certain purchases, and that nearly a quarter return clothes at least once a month.

» Never go shopping if you are feeling lonely, angry, hungry or bored. This often leads directly to impulse buying.

» Pay attention to the washing instructions. Dry-clean only? Not very sustainable (more later). Don't buy it, or be happy to hang it in the bathroom or an open window.

» Hand-wash only? Consider whether you'll really do this or want to risk putting it through the delicates programme in the washing machine. This is usually okay, but there's no guarantee of course. Don't buy it if you're not feeling these options, as once dirty it'll probably remain unworn.

» Do creased clothes annoy you? Test it in the shop, by crushing a piece of the fabric in your hand. Don't take it if it indeed looks crumpled, you'll probably not wear it.

The Perfect Fit (and Size)

» Only buy it if it fits well now. It's not going to fit any better later.

» Gosh, those sizes! Standard sizes are strange anyway – nobody is average. But don't get thrown by all the numbers. They say very little. They're there to facilitate mass-production.

» Sizes vary per country, brand and even per item within a brand. Don't feel bad if you need a larger size. It's arbitrary and based on a very limited target group. Wear the size you think is right.

» One size fits all, that one's funny too! Unfortunately only for those who aren't very tall or short.

» Some brands do vanity sizing: giving the clothes a smaller size than they actually are. This may make you feel better, but it's only to make you buy it.

» Have doubts while trying it on? Ask other shoppers. They don't know you and will be more likely to give you an honest answer than some store assistants, as they have no invested interest.

» No time to try? The circumference of your neck is often about half that of your waist. Hold trousers by the corners of the waist and wrap around your neck. Fits? Then the trousers probably will too.

» Shopping online? Measure yourself well, and aim to mostly buy from stores that show the measurements of the clothes. With shoes, I sometimes e-mail to ask for the length and width. Why not?

» One of the most frustrating things about online shopping, is that everything is shown on supermodel-sized, perfectly (in the eyes of the industry) proportioned people. So it'll never look the same on you, and you can only guess if it might fit or suit. Resulting in disappointment, frequent returning/environmental pressure (also because of buying in multiple sizes, as you just don't know!) as well as insecurity about our bodies. What would really help, and what I'd love, is if webshops would show models with different body types and sizes alongside each item, so you can see it in size 36 or 44. Asos has announced plans for this, I can't wait.

» In any case, more diversity in sizes, colours and types of people would be a huge improvement. The fashion industry is by no means inclusive enough. I'll get back to this later.

» 3D-printing is also going to help: it'll make bespoke clothes a real possibility.

» Digital changing rooms are coming, where you can scan yourself or submit a picture, and 'try on' the clothes. Hopefully this is the new normal soon.

THIS IS TRUE

> Many clothes (by non-sustainable brands) are designed to fall apart.
> Items by major brands that you buy hugely reduced or in outlets, are often made for that particular purpose, from a poorer quality.
> The fashion industry deliberately tries to make you feel 'out' after the first few times you've worn something, by hanging new things in the stores 52 times a year.
> Sequins and beading can be a sign of child labour: this often takes place at home, where children work alongside their parents.

FILIPPA K

Elin Larsson (1975) is Sustainability Director of modern Swedish brand Filippa K.

What are you proud of, and what more needs to happen?

'I'm proud of how sustainability is integrated throughout the entire company. It's quite rare for everyone to be involved, and it takes a lot of time to get them onboard. But once you've done it, you're incredibly powerful. We still have a lot to do though. We want to undergo a complete transformation: change the materials, production process, everything. And it's pretty urgent! What I want to change most, is how we deal with seasons. We have four collections per year, while other brands have 52. But we're still stuck. There must be a better way to do it. Both from a business perspective and a quality one – I'd like to have more time to develop the products. We haven't found the solution yet, but we're working on it.'

Filippa K makes sustainability promises – which?

'By 2030, we'll be working solely with sustainable materials. So, the fabric, the lining, the thread, everything. And all our designs must be recyclable or biodegradable. We also want to produce our goods in a sustainable and responsible way. To do this, our chain must be completely transparent. We don't want to produce more than is needed and want to be a resource-efficient business with a minimal footprint. So we're looking critically at our energy use, transport, stores, etc. Everyone who works on and with our products must be respected and treated well. From the person working with the raw materials to the person selling it in the stores. And lastly, we want to run a successfully sustainable company, based on long-term relationships with factories, shops, warehouses and of course, our customers. We also want to make a profit, to grow naturally, and not be dependent on investors.'

How are you making this happen?

'We believe the circular economy is one of the answers. We focus on reducing, repairing, reusing and recycling. How can we make our products as sustainable as possible, use as few resources as possible and ensure they can be reused? You can already bring our clothes to all our stores to get them repaired, and we provide tips on how to take good care of them. We have a second-hand store in Stockholm, and are looking into whether we can also offer second-hand clothes in our regular stores. Rental will be a major part of our future. Do we have to own everything we wear? If you rent, you can keep your wardrobe up-to-date without contributing to over-consumption. This is already possible in a few shops worldwide, and in Amsterdam we are collaborating with LENA, the fashion library. Many people own clothes they no longer use, but that are still in good condition. We take these in. Currently, we sell them in the second-hand store, but in the future, we also want to recycle them into new fabrics for our collections. Additionally, we send our material residues to our Italian factories, who make new fabrics from them, and we try to design patterns that create less waste.'

Will Filippa K produce and sell less?

'We make 1.7 million pieces per year. Our objective is to have economic growth but produce less clothes. This is a shift in values, we're going to adjust and vary our business model and combine multiple channels.'

What is your favourite sustainability tip?

'For me, the most important thing is to slow down. We seem to be running so fast that we're missing the purpose of life and have no time to make conscious decisions. Practically, I've decided to only have 40 items in my wardrobe. If I buy a new piece, or even better something old, I must sell or give away something else, and for special occasions or temporary updates I rent or borrow.'

Elin's Stockholm-tips
AfroArt 'Stores with artisan and fair-trade products from all over the world, founded in 1967.'
Nudie Jeans 'Great stores from this Swedish, sustainable jeans brand.'
Houdini 'Shop from the Swedish, sustainable outdoor label.'
Paradiset 'Wonderful sustainable supermarket, with a good restaurant and beauty department.'

How your Clothes are Made

They Don't Grow on Trees

Before an item ends up in your wardrobe, it's made quite a journey. If it's made of cotton, there's first been sown, land cultivated, harvested, thread spun, fabric weaved or knitted, dyed, there's been after-treatment, patterns drawn, cut, parts sewn together, zips, pockets, buttons, holes, hems, belt loops inserted, finished, ironed, packed per piece, packaged, transported, distributed, unpacked, hung and sold/bought. A great number of these steps happen in different countries. Of course, mood boards have also been made, designs created, orders placed, marketing done, advertisements produced, etc. All in all, there were on average 170 people involved in making sure you can wear those jeans, half of whom have touched them with their hands (including your underwear).

The Facts about Fabrics

Daily, you wear all kinds of material on your skin. Some more sustainable than others, although it often remains a choice between for instance natural origins and long-lasting. Below, a short overview of the pros and cons, per type of fabric.

Cotton
» Has already been used to wear for 5,000 years; it's in about two-thirds of our clothes.
» It's cheap, comfortable to wear and reasonably strong.
» Each year, we grow enough cotton to give each person on the planet 18 T-shirts.

» More than 100 million households worldwide are involved in cotton production (according to the film *The True Cost*, the fashion industry is so big that approximately 1 in 6 people in the world work in it).
» Not much is natural or vegetable about cotton. 16% of all pesticides globally are used to grow cotton. 2.5% of farmland is used for cotton (an area 10 times the size of the Netherlands), which also involves the use of lots of insecticides and artificial fertiliser.
» About half of what it costs to make cotton is spent on toxins. The jerry cans are kept at home because the poison is so valuable, and once they're empty, reused to store water or food.
» Cotton's also a very thirsty plant: 10,000 litres of water are needed to grow one kilo – so a shirt and a pair of jeans.
» Colouring and anti-shrinkage treatments make it even worse, requiring even more chemicals (and water), that are extremely dangerous for the cotton farmers.
» The World Health Organisation calculates that every year, one million cotton workers end up in hospital due to pesticide poisoning. Annually, 20,000 to 40,000 people die as a result – including many cotton farmers. The market is worth billions and in the hands of just a few major players, which is why pesticides have not (yet) been outlawed.
» The people that grow cotton earn far too little, work excruciatingly long hours and do very gruelling work. Suicide is relatively common. Since 1995, around 270,000 Indian cotton farmers have committed suicide, among other things due to debts because they had to buy extremely expensive, modified cotton seeds.

The market for sustainable fabrics will grow in the future by 12% per year, to 79 billion euros.

Organic cotton

» Certified organic cotton is better than regular cotton. No toxins, fertilisers, pesticides and insecticides are used. Genetic manipulation is banned.

» Lots of water is still needed, but less.

» Many farmers choose to go organic themselves, because they want to keep their soil healthy and fertile. It's still hard work, but they do often get paid more for it.

» There is also Fairtrade certified cotton, for which farmers receive a guaranteed price and extra compensation for the community. Within fair trade there are also rules for pesticides and toxins.

» H&M and C&A compete each year for who's used the most organic cotton.

» There are also brands that only use organic cotton, such as Patagonia and Vaude.

» There's also Better Cotton – sounds better, but is a little less so than organic. Less use of pesticides, less water and genetic modification is permitted.

» You'll find more about certification on page 054.

Recycled or residual cotton

» These are the most sustainable forms of cotton: new fabric from old.

» Recycling cotton is not yet very easy, because the quality suffers as a result. It's happening more and more though, and there's lots of innovation, so we can expect something in the years to come. Making new clothes from our cast-offs: great.

» Pattern cutting leaves lots of excess material. This is mostly discarded, but of course it's a valuable resource that can be processed into new fabric.

Viscose, modal and rayon

Fabrics made from soft wood, but heavily processed with chemicals.

Lyocell (and Tencel)

Lyocell comes from wood from sustainable forests (often eucalyptus), is processed in a closed system without loss of resources, with non-chemical substances, and is biodegradable. Tencel is the brand name, the material looks like silk, absorbs liquid easily and is soft and strong.

(Organic) hemp

Grows quickly and easily, does not need fertilisers or pesticides, can be produced in many climates, is extremely strong and long-lasting. It's quite stiff though, so often needs to be mixed with other materials to make it wearable.　　⟶

YOUR CLOTHES ARE THIRSTY

It takes an enormous amount of water to make clothes, particularly cotton ones. The Aral Lake in Uzbekistan is a good example. Formerly the fourth largest lake in the world, only 15% now remains. Pumped away to cotton plantations. All 24 species of fish are gone, and it has ruined the people who lived from them and the fertile land. And all of this, while the pipes leaked so heavily that much of the water didn't even ever reach the cotton fields. Nowadays, more and more's happening to reduce water consumption. Major brands such as Levi's are developing new ways to recycle water, and organisations such as the Better Cotton Initiative and the World Wildlife Fund support water-saving projects.

(Organic) linen

Is strong, doesn't need a lot of toxins (but does get them quite often, so choose organic), and is often high quality. Can grow in moderate environments, so doesn't always have to come from far. Does crease terribly, so must receive after-treatment or you need to iron lots (or accept the creases).

(Organic) bamboo (Monocel)

Is soft and quick-growing and is therefore seen as quite sustainable. But bamboo's a stiff plant that needs lots of chemicals to turn it into fabric. Organically certified or produced in a closed system (Monocel), it can be sustainable.

Polyester

» Synthetic fibres such as polyester are, besides cotton, the most important materials for clothes, used to make at least half of them.
» Polyester is the most-used artificial material – like PET, of the bottles.
» It's cheap, colourfast, long-lasting and doesn't crease.

» Made of oil (that's running out), and the production uses lots of energy, water and toxins.
» Polyester is often mixed with other fabrics, making it difficult to recycle.
» It takes up to 200 years before polyester starts to decompose in landfills.

Recycled polyester

» Recycled polyester is strong, long-lasting and old plastic is used to make it.
» The technique to recycle PET bottles can also be used to make fabric.
» Up to 25 bottles go into one fleece jumper.
» The bottle fibres also contain harmful substances that were never intended for the skin.
» Plastic fabrics discharge microfibres, which if you wash them in our water, cause environmental pollution and are eaten by animals.
» Big names such as Pharrell Williams see a future in the plastic floating in the sea. His company, Bionic Yarn, fishes for plastic and turns it into yarns and fabrics, including for certain G-Star collections (a company he co-owns).

PLASTIC IN YOUR JUMPER

Over 60% of our clothes are made from plastic or a mix of cotton and polyester (such as nylon, fleece from PET bottles or acrylic). Millions of plastic fibres are released every time it's washed. About half a jam-jar full of particles smaller than half a millimetre. Via our waste water, they go straight through the filters into the sewer, and out to sea. In the ocean they end up along the coastline, and they become part of the so-called 'plastic soup'. The salty water makes them disintegrate even more. They're a threat to small animals such as fish, birds and seals, because they ingest them. Eventually, the particles end up, through drinking water and eating fish, in us.

ANNE GORKE / SCHMOTT

There are also experiments with clothes made of soya, milk, seaweed, corn, cow manure, bananas, pineapples, coconut, coffee and tea. If they succeed in processing these into fabrics with environmentally-friendly processes, exciting things could be on the horizon (if they don't compete with food-growing).

If I ever let
my head
down,
it will
only be
to admire
my shoes

Animal Materials
(and Vegan Alternatives)

Why should animals suffer for our outfit? A rhetorical question, of course. There's an increasing number of good alternatives for leather, wool and silk. Stella McCartney is the most well-known vegetarian designer, but attention for a cruelty-free lifestyle is growing rapidly. Here, some of the ins and outs of animal materials and alternatives.

Leather

Leather is a difficult one. It's often a bi-product of the meat industry, we're told, but does that make it any better? The animal is still killed for our 'needs'. The industrial livestock industry is terrible for animals and the planet (more about this in the chapter about food). Leather is also bred especially for the fashion industry, such as snake or crocodile leather: a real no-go. The environmental impact of leather is quite significant, it often comes from far away, is tanned with chrome so it doesn't rot, and washed and dyed, processes that involve lots of toxins, water and environmental pollution. Working in a leather factory is incredibly hard, dirty and dangerous. Leather may last a long time but doesn't decompose very well due to the heavy metals, and causes (toxic) waste. You can consider this:.
— Naturally tanned eco-leather comes from animals that are kept organically, and the skin is processed using plants. Not perfect, but better.
— There are also vegan fake-leathers, for example from recycled television screens or cork (natural, strong, grows fast). Be careful that it isn't just plastic, as this is made from petroleum and isn't much better for the planet.
— Brands also use industry leather residues (there are lots of cut-offs as animal skin is irregular), which saves on waste, or leather is reused (as by for example Reformation or Naomi Rachèl Timan).
— The Leather Working Group is a group of brands and manufacturers that started collaborating in 2005 to improve the industry. Big names are members, including adidas, Dr. Martens, Burberry, Timberland and Nike.
— I try to go for second-hand as much as possible, for example with shoes.

Wool

Many people wear wool, it warms you when you're cold, and vice-versa, and is moisture and dirt repellent. But just like leather, it travels huge distances before it gets here, which costs lots of energy and CO_2 emissions. The hide is processed with chemicals to keep away insects and stop it rotting or going mouldy. Then of course, the dyeing, pollution, water etc. Animals are often treated horribly: angora rabbits are plucked alive, sheep

are mutilated (their tail and parts of their rear are removed to prevent parasites). Reason for some brands to say they no longer want to sell angora wool from rabbits. There are other possibilities:
— No chemicals are used for organic wool; the animals are treated better and the wool dyed using natural methods. British brand Izzy Lane saves sheep from slaughter, keeps them in as animal-friendly conditions as possible and makes collections with their wool.
— Local wool from your region saves on transport and thus environmental pollution.
— Wool is ideal for recycling, so choose that if you can, or of course go for second-hand.

Silk

Silk represents luxury. But for the silk-worm, life isn't such a party. It hangs on the mulberry tree, eats as many leaves as possible and then wraps itself up by spinning a thread around itself up to 100,000 times. One single cocoon sometimes produces more than one kilometre of silk thread. After two weeks, the worm has transformed into a butterfly and emerges. Breaking the silk thread. Which is not what the fashion industry wants, as long threads make for a glossy fabric without ruptures. Therefore, the worms are killed in hot steam or boiling water. The dyeing process also uses lots of toxics. This is a difficult and labour-intensive process, which is often still done by hand, by families in low-wage countries. These could be options:
— Wild silk comes from cocoons collected after the butterfly's flown away. The threads are broken, so have small knots in them. Organic silk exists too, but in general this only means that the worms feed on organic mulberry leaves before they die, and are still boiled to death. See it as an eco-Last Supper.
— Materials such as lyocell/Tencel (from eucalyptus trees) have a comparable look and feel to silk, but are considerably less damaging.

Fur

Fur equals animal cruelty. No doubt possible, in my opinion. Worldwide, millions of animals are being bred in distressing conditions, often killed brutally for their fur. Think small cages, stress, boredom, clamping, hunting, electrocuting. To keep us warm, but more often just to show off. You may believe that most fur collars on coats are fake. Think again. The Netherlands is one of the largest fur producers in the world. Every year, breeding farms gas nearly five million minks (that's an international third place). But not for much longer, because in 2013 the mink breeding ban came into force, and by 2024 the entire industry must be gone. And rightly so. Fur is also incredibly environmentally unfriendly: tanning, dyeing, sick workers, everything. The impact of a kilo of mink fur is five times bigger than one kilo of textiles. There are a few alternatives:
— Fake is better than real. But even then: you maintain fur's visibility on the street, so that's something to think about. It's often synthetic, so harmful. It can also be done well: the brand Hood-Lamb, for example, makes fake fur from hemp.
— Fur Free Alliance has a list of brands on their website that have proclaimed themselves fur free, and tips to distinguish fake from real.

Down

Down is made from the feathers of ducks and geese, and is therefore viewed as a bi-product, and even a waste product. Sounds very sustainable, but isn't, because the animals are often plucked alive. Horrific. This is why there's the Responsible Down Standard, that brands such as H&M, The North Face and Fjällräven support. Patagonia has introduced its own Traceable Down Standard, as they want to go even further.

Your Clothes are Dirty

The fashion industry is the second biggest polluter in the world, you often hear. Only the oil industry is worse. Not just the cultivation, but in particular the dyeing and finishing (making your clothes water repellent or crease-free) are nasty. Every year, tonnes of chemical pigments are used for our clothes. 40,000 to 50,000 tonnes of dye are dumped into rivers, and heavy metals are needed to fix your favourite colour. Cheap pigments are quick to rub off onto your skin or while being washed, and then get into the water. The darker the colour, the more dye you need. Hello, navy handbag or little black dress...
— Greenpeace took successful action to ensure that brands stop using toxins. Many major brands have joined the Detox campaign, including H&M, adidas, Nike, C&A and Puma. They promise to stop using any carcinogenic, polluting and harmful substances by 2020. ⟶

O MY BAG

Paulien Wesselink (1984) is owner of eco-leather bag brand O My Bag. They work closely with the factories and tanneries (and tell you all about them online) and have a second-hand bag programme.

How did O My Bag come about?

'As a student, I wanted to work for the United Nations. A first step was a placement at the Ministry of Foreign Affairs, but I couldn't use my creativity there. So I left to New York for six months. In America, entrepreneurship was much more encouraged than in the Netherlands. Back home, I was bursting with ambition and worked on a business plan. There had to be a sustainable bag brand, that promoted fair trade. It wasn't easy, but I persevered and in India, together with a Dutch leather tanner, I developed our eco-leather. This leather even won us the Sustainable Leather Award. When travelling, I discovered that it's possible, as an individual, to make a difference for someone else. A simple fact that worked as an accelerator for me to make it happen.'

What do you worry about?

'60 million girls don't go to school. Because they have to work, due to traditions, or because there's simply no school nearby. Education is essential in ending child marriage and providing the confidence and knowledge to participate in society. Because poverty causes this problem, I try to do something about it.'

What makes you happy?

'It was Gay Pride yesterday, that gives me so much joy! I love that we can all live together in peace and equality. Especially nowadays, with attacks and growing intolerance, I am extra thankful for these accomplishments. We should never take that for granted. When everyone is equal, we are all more free.'

Do you have a hero?

'I'm an Oprah Winfrey fan. She's a television guru, actress, new-media magnate and philanthropist. She keeps exceeding expectations and makes her own rules. I love that. As a small girl, she was told she didn't have to go to school because she'd only become a cleaner for a white family anyway. Later she was told that she was too ugly for television. Then, many people doubted whether her own network would be a success. Meanwhile, it's clear: Oprah truly is boss.'

Paulien's sustainable tips

Everlane 'Wonderful brand that addresses the lack of transparency in the fashion industry by communicating clearly about how prices are established.'
Apolis 'The slogan of this inspiring label is "Advocacy through Industry", they also use the power of trade to bring about social change.'
Reformation 'Really cool, sustainable brand with great marketing: all the hip super models are wearing it.'

— Hormone disrupting 'phthalates' were even found in underwear brands, and in bedding, formaldehyde, which is associated with cancer. Not a bad idea to give some tender loving care to our intimate parts and our sleep, and to for example choose organic cotton.

— Kering, the parent company of amongst others Gucci and Alexander McQueen, annually analyses the environmental damage it causes, expressing it in euros. In 2016, the impact was 858 million euros.

Jeans are your Best Friend

Jeans are the Netherlands' most popular item of clothing (and maybe even the world's). Just 17 million people live there, yet they seem to buy 45 million pairs per year. 95% wear them and own an average of 5.4 pairs. But what do we know about them? Researcher Babette Porcelijn found out:

— The biggest climate impact of a pair of jeans is caused by washing and drying: about 12.5 kilos of CO_2 equivalent. This compares to two trees. It does depend on how often you wash and how you dry them: on the line or in a machine.

— From the water used to make one pair of trousers (up to 10,000 litres), you could shower 200 days for 6 minutes.

— 32 kilos of CO_2 are released when making a pair of jeans: the same as driving a car 150 kilometres.

— 10 m² of farmland is needed to grow the cotton for one pair.

Old is New

Shop, shop, shop, use quickly and discard is old, circular thinking is now. Within this system, all resources retain their value, so nothing is waste. All materials must be put to good use in another product, after their life in the original product. Ideally, no quality is lost, residues are used, and it's entirely climate neutral. Such a closed cycle has been put on the map by cradle-to-cradle pioneers William McDonough and Michael Braungart, and is being used increasingly by brands. Fabrics made from worn and scrap cotton, biodegradable threads, jeans from jeans, wool jumpers from wool jumpers, and so on. Many of our clothes are made from a mix, for example cotton and polyester. This makes it more difficult to recycle into new material, because they first need to be separated – which is hard. The new thread is subsequently a little weaker, which is why, currently, our clothes usually don't contain more than 40% reused material. But there is a lot happening.

— The ReTuna Återbruksgalleria shopping centre in Sweden is dedicated entirely to circularity. The fourteen stores only sell recycled and upcycled products, you can hand in furniture, electrical equipment and clothes (which are then refurbished and resold on the spot) and you can even study recycling.

— Ecoalf makes stylish clothes and shoes from used fishing nets, ground coffee and car tyres, adidas trainers from plastic from the ocean, MUD Jeans jumpers from old denim, etc.

If all the textiles thrown away in America every year would be recycled, the environmental impact would be the same as taking 7.3 million cars off the road.

PEOPLE TREE

Safia Minney (1964) is founder of the British/Japanese fair-trade fashion brand People Tree, director of sustainable shoe brand Po-Zu, consultant and activist. She wrote the books *Naked Fashion* and *Slow Fashion*, and worked on the film *The True Cost*. Recently she's launched the Slave to Fashion project, to put modern slavery in the fashion industry on the map, together with best practices in the fashion world to eliminate it.

What for you is the most important thing about People Tree?
'I founded People Tree 25 years ago, when only a few people were concerned about the true price of fashion, and the ethics behind it. People would laugh and ask: why an organic dress if you can't eat it? They didn't realise how destructive cotton can be for the ecosystem and the lives of farmers, and the big difference that organic makes. Nowadays, more of us want to be part of the solution, not the problem. It's time for a major transition to transparency and responsibility. We have slavery in our supply chains, which we are responsible for if we buy things the regular way. People Tree puts people and our environment at the heart of the design. We challenge the way the industry works and lead the way to improvement and empowerment.'

Why do you do what you do?
'Because I know that another way is possible, and that it's usually arrogance, greed and laziness that stop change. I'm an optimist. The ethical fashion world is growing rapidly. I would love to see the pioneering work of People Tree develop and become accepted and made mainstream by the industry. Hopefully, one day, this will be the norm.'

Safia's favourite sustainable tips
» Don't buy anything new unless it is ethical.

» Watch a short video or read something interesting every day – keep learning!

» Worry more about the health of your body and mind, more than about what you are wearing.

» Make an effort to dress as part of the celebration of life!

» Go walking instead of shopping, read a book rather than shop online – but if you do these things, then at least do them sustainably.

» Concept stores:
The Netherlands Charlie + Mary in Amsterdam, BrandMission in Haarlem and Eigen in Apeldoorn
Germany Friedrich in Heidelberg, DearGoods in Munich and Greenality in Stuttgart
Japan Kagure in Tokyo, Ethical Penelope in Nagoya and Kikuya Zakkaten in Kyoto

Workers Deserve Much Better

When it comes to sustainable fashion, it's often all about the material. Because you can see it, feel it and make relatively easy choices about it. But everything you wear has been made by hand. By thirty to forty million people, the majority of whom are female. And life is extremely tough for them. I've seen it during my travels, for example, to Bangladesh. The workers I spoke to there, their shacks I visited, their suffering and courage. It's made an everlasting impression on me. How's it possible that people have to live like this for our prosperity? How can this be allowed; how can it be legal? I've visited many production countries, such as Thailand and Turkey, been to the homes of workers and worked with them. But I still can't imagine what it must be like to be one of them. At the factory, day-in day-out, stressful, boring, from early morning to late at night. Dirt, danger, intimidation. Hours and hours, repetitively inserting

the same zip: mind-numbing assembly-line work making you fast, effective and cheap. You learn nothing and aren't allowed to open your mouth, so any chance of advancement is miniscule. And on top of all this, the conditions are degrading. I'd want to say a lot more about this, because the heroes that make our clothes deserve all our attention. But I think you know. They must get a better life as soon as possible; the urgency is real. People are getting poisoned during cotton harvesting, going hungry and living without prospects. The newest kid on the block: terminator seeds, which produce plants that don't make seeds themselves. Poor farmers have to *buy* new seeds after every harvest, from a multinational like Monsanto.

» Factory workers don't have it much better. Working hours are too long: up to 14-16 a day.
» There's often no question of a contract, meaning that if orders are low, they lose their job.
» There's a lot of inequality and intimidation on the

work floor: supervisors are often male, workers female.

» Child labour still exists in the industry, although a lot less than it used to. The cotton harvest and finishing phase of embellishing clothes are the most vulnerable areas.

» Trade union freedom is not a given, meaning there's little opportunity for workers to stand up for themselves.

» Wages are too low. Really too low. Everybody has the right to a living wage, meaning a salary from which you can actually live, so they do too (see the figures on p. 032).

» It's deadly. On April 24th, 2013, the Rana Plaza factory in Bangladesh collapsed. The building wasn't built as a factory and had three illegal extra floors. 1,138 people died. 2,500 were injured. Brands such as Benetton, Gap and Mango had

HONEST BY

According to Oxfam, the CEO of one of the top 5 fashion brands only has to work for four days to earn what a Bangladeshi garment worker does in his or her entire life.

their clothes made there. This disaster caused shock waves, and hopefully improvements too. But it wasn't the first time something like this happened. In 2010, fire broke out in two factories, causing 28 and 21 deaths. In 2012, the Tazreen factory went up in flames, killing 112 people. This is just the tip of the iceberg. And it has to stop.

What *do* we want? Workers that are proud of their work and what they make. Who can use their skills, develop and have a voice. Who are involved in the entire production process, feel empowered, and earn enough to lead a good life. Who can be happy, healthy and free. Just like us.

Show It All

The fashion industry is pretty shady. You'd probably already realised. It's rather difficult to find out how and where your clothes are made. Which is of course what manufacturers want, if they've something to hide. Transparency is hugely important to create improvement: only once we know what's happening, do we know what needs to change. Fortunately, progress is being made. Big brands are making their production-sites public, pioneers such as Everlane and Lovia communicate on their website and labels about price mark-ups and factories, reporting has improved and innovations such as QR codes make the story behind your clothes more visible. Fashion Revolution's Transparency Index reviews and ranks hundreds of brands and stores worldwide, based on what they make public about their chain, policy and impact. The major forerunner in the area of transparency in the fashion sector is the Belgian Bruno Pieters. He's worked for Martin Margiela, Christian Lacroix and Hugo Boss, and had his own label. In 2010 he took a step back and embarked on a two-year sabbatical. Everybody feared losing a major talent, but he returned – and how. During his travels he realised that things had to be done differently, better and more respectfully. In 2012 he launched Honest By, a revolutionary, radical and completely transparent brand, made ethically from sustainable materials. On his website, he shows exact calculations of costs for each piece – including the material, zip, thread, safety pin and price tag. Which factory made them, how long that took and what the CO_2 emissions are. It's an honour that he shares his vision in my book.

INTERVIEW

BRUNO PIETERS

Belgian designer and pioneer Bruno Pieters (1975) is the founder of Honest By.

Why did you start Honest By?
'I was looking for a brand that could tell me everything I wanted to know about my purchase. From the raw materials right up to the packaging. No 100% transparent brand existed. And so I decided to do it myself. Honest By is a tool for change. I love fashion and now's the time for the story behind the clothes to become as beautiful as the piece itself. In the best-case scenario, you can describe today's industry as "just legal". I'd like to turn it into something we can all be proud of.' $\longrightarrow$

What's your most important message to everyone that buys clothes?

'If you buy from major fashion chains, you've got the guarantee of child labour, animal cruelty and environmental pollution. This is the certainty these brands give you. I don't have to name names – use your computer, do some research. There are hundreds of alternatives. Online, you can find ethically-made clothes in all kinds of styles and price ranges. Why would you not do it?'

What does your wardrobe look like?

'I'm always trying to simplify it. I am looking for a "uniform" that I can wear daily. My favourite item is a T-shirt. It's so simple, unpretentious and efficient.'

Do you have a life motto?

'"Be the change you want to see in the world", by Gandhi: so powerful and so essential. If you really want to see change, you need to start with yourself. I'm not a magician, and no longer have expectations. If people change, become more aware, then it's because they're ready. You can only remind people what it means to be a human being, and to care about their own and other people's wellbeing. This is why my heroes are people such as Buddha, Gandhi, Dr. Martin Luther King, Jane Goodall, Kip Anderson... People that bring out the best in others and help them advance.'

Bruno Pieters' tips

'Every purchase is a vote. Do your research. Find out what you're voting for and stay true to your own values and opinion.'
Shoes Rombaut, Good Guys
Beauty ISUN alive & ageless skincare
Food Antwerp Eten vol Leven, Carotterie 2000

Tech is Leading the Way

Technological progress can make a huge difference in the fashion industry. These space-age innovations are hugely exciting and interesting.

» 3D visualisation makes it possible to design clothes without making them. By showing the new piece virtually and having a (also virtual) model wear it, no fabric or other materials are needed to develop new collections. Result!

» The number of virtual showrooms is increasing, meaning that brands don't have to fly samples around the world and can make fewer clothes.

» Holograms are even being worked on, replacing clothes and models, for instance on the catwalk.

» Energy-generating clothes are coming. Designers integrate solar cells and motion sensors into the fabric, so that you generate energy and can, for example, charge your phone.

» There's experimentation with clothes that can keep you warm or cool you down. Handy post-exercise (wearables that measure our physical performance are also getting better and smaller)!

» More and more brands provide 'bespoke' shopping. If we can choose our own colours, fabrics and designs, it fits better, and we get exactly what we want.

» 3D printing creates clothes to order, before your very eyes: tailor-made, no travel, no emissions or waste material.

» Online fitting rooms and virtual fitting ensures that what you order online fits and suits you, so you don't have to return it.

» Self-cleaning and self-repairing fabrics will do exactly that.

Men are Sustainable

There is less choice for men. Both in the regular and the sustainable world of fashion and lifestyle. This is ridiculous, of course. But also, slightly their own fault. They buy much less, so less is made for them. Because of this, they are at the forefront of the sustainable movement. Well done!

Zalando conducted research among men. Quite surprising results!

71	the percentage that enjoys shopping
47%	of men talk about fashion
57%	don't care about trends, 54% aren't interested in brands
92	the percentage that finds quality important
101	euro what men spend on clothes, on average, per month

What the Certifications Say

There are different certifications and organisations that try and identify how well a brand produces. In the fashion industry, this isn't easy. Because so incredibly many different steps are needed to make something, it's impossible to find one stamp that fits all. This is why there's not one sole certification for sustainable clothes. Verification also differs per certification and is often quite problematic, precisely for that reason. There are also 'labels' that companies put on their brand themselves, or that have little significance. So, above all keep thinking for yourself, and don't be tricked by a label. Here's an overview of certifications:

Global Organic Textile Standard (GOTS)
Founded to certify the entire process from resource to organic clothing. Seen as one of the most trusted in the area of environmentally-friendly materials. A minimum of 95% of resources must be organic, and the production process environmentally aware and socially responsible: there are also clear guidelines for working conditions. Before a fabric receives GOTS certification, all steps are verified by an official body such as Soil Association.

Oeko-Tex
Clothing that meets this standard *no longer* contains substances damaging to the health. So this

doesn't mean they never went into it. Both natural and synthetic fabrics can get this label.

MADE-BY
Non-profit organisation, and not an actual certification – but is used as such. Above all specialised in environment and material, affiliated brands score well in these areas, but also with guidelines for working conditions. Their achievements are transparent and featured on their website, and MADE-BY develops tools for companies to produce more sustainably.

EU Ecolabel
Foremost an environmental label: reduced water usage, a list of toxic substances that are not permitted, and the use of harmful substances must be limited. Products with this certification are less taxing on the planet. There are also guidelines for organic and working conditions, but these aspects count for less in the assessment.
>> *Sometimes you see Ecocert or Soil Association: these are mainly used for personal-care products, so you can read more about them in chapter 2 (p. 090).*

Fair Wear Foundation (FWF)
Internationally seen as one of the most progressive organisations in the field of improving working conditions. Affiliated organisations must make a plan for the entire chain and implement the strict norms as adequately as possible. FWF trains country teams with local experts, who independently monitor conditions in the factories. Workers can also report complaints to this organisation, that isn't an actual certification, but is seen as such. Brands that decide to join, show they take good working conditions seriously.

Fairtrade International
Independent certification for Fairtrade cotton (and of course, coffee, bananas, etc.). If you see this label on clothes, it only stretches to the cultivation of the cotton under fair conditions, not the complete production process of the item. This means good working conditions for the farmers and workers in terms of areas like wages, safety and strict environmental rules. Work's being done to tackle the entire production chain, to also impose better demands at, for example, weaving and sewing factories. This new approach has just been

'I worry about the carefree society in which we live, I don't understand the irresponsibility and lack of interest in how our environment is changing. I once raised a deer. He now lives independently in the forest, but still pops by sometimes. This is how I was brought up, with appreciation for the world. Appreciate real design and creative talent. Don't buy a copy from a chain. Understand the look and create it yourself with second-hand or sustainable clothes.'

Sustainable designer Anne Gorke

launched and is awaiting major commitment from the fashion sector.

World Fair Trade Organisation (WFTO)

Membership is only allowed if you comply 100% with fair trade rules. This encompasses the ten principles of fair trade, from fair prices to transparency. The companies are verified both internally and by an external organisation.

>> You may run into the Higg Index. This comes from the Sustainable Apparel Coalition, a collaboration of major brands such as adidas, Asics, Gap, Patagonia etc. They represent around 40% of the global market and have made their own index to measure their sustainable activities. There are also B Corps: companies that uphold standards in the areas of people, planet and profit, and focus equally on profit and doing good. Possible shareholders must also agree. Dopper, EILEEN FISHER, Patagonia and Tony's Chocolonely are examples of B Corps.

>> Better Cotton Initiative works with big brands such as Benetton and Esprit to improve the cotton industry, and, for example, reduce water and pesticide use. If 5% of their cotton is Better Cotton and they have a plan to make that 50% within five years, brands can use the logo.

>> Rank a Brand ranks brands, based on the policy they publish on their website or their answers to a questionnaire. This is therefore primarily a judgment about their transparency (which of course is also very important), not about their performance or actual implementation of that policy.

>> Ethical Clothing Australia works with fashion companies in Australia and accredits them, to make sure their Australian supply chains are transparent and legally compliant.

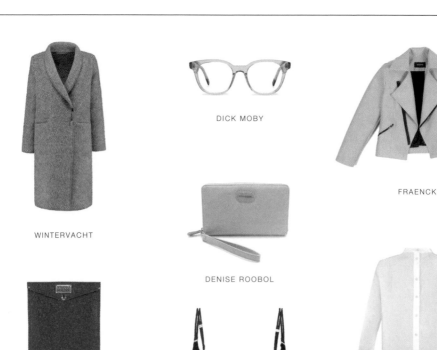

WINTERVACHT

DICK MOBY

DENISE ROOBOL

FRAENCK

FRAENCK

WORON

JAN 'N JUNE

Maintenance

Keep your Clothes Happy

Treating your clothes well and looking after them means they'll last much longer. I wouldn't go as far as calling myself lazy, but it's not something I do automatically. So, this section is as much for me as it is for you.

Storing
Are your clothes neatly folded and piled in your wardrobe? Do you air them regularly? Do you sew a button back on the minute it falls off? Well, right, um, it would be better. Here are a few tips to keep your clothes in good condition for as long as possible:
» Store knitted items flat or folded, as they'll lose their shape if they're hung up. Are they starting to pill or fluff? Try removing it with sticky tape. You can also use a razor blade, but please be careful with your clothes and your fingers.
» Don't let your clothes lie around too much or pile up in the back of your wardrobe. Also, don't try to cram too much in your wardrobe at once. It'll crease and smell, and creepy crawlies love it.
» Now and again, air items that you don't wear that often. And the ones you do wear too.
» I struggle with leather items, because you should really treat them with that special stuff to prevent drying out and spray them against moisture. But these products are always so horrible and not really environmentally friendly. And so the leather dries out, which is even worse. So do do it, I guess, and remove stains with a damp cloth while you're at it.
» Put tea bags in your sneakers if they smell, or stick them in the freezer for a while in a plastic bag. Apparently, you can whiten them with toothpaste; fabric-made sneakers can also be washed.

Washing
The majority of a regular item's CO_2 emissions and energy use comes from washing. This is more than material, production and distribution together. It's true. So you can make a big difference here.

Less
Isn't it great, that doing little is best? The less you wash, the better. Jeans look much better if they rarely see the washing machine. 'Never wash' is an actual jeans movement, and how dirty are we really? Nothing a damp cloth and a good deodorant can't sort out – few of us still work on the land. So hang it outside or in front of an open window, sun also helps banish bacteria.

Colder
90% of the energy a washing machine uses is for heating the water. Make some easy money and wash colder. 30°C is ample for most things, and you can go even lower.

Environmentally friendly
Use detergent that contains no toxic or damaging substances – filtering it all out of our water costs energy (and some may escape). And you can probably also use a little less (another saving!). Washing powder has a slight preference to liquid, it uses less water to produce.

Full
Fill your washing machine to the (advised) limit, this saves time, money and energy (don't forget to turn your clothes inside-out first).

Energy efficient
Choose an efficient as possible washing machine. Buy a new one if yours is very old. Washing machines use 20% of your water and 7% of your energy, so this makes a real difference.

Hang
Don't use a dryer, hang your washing on the line. A dryer uses on average 90 euros worth of energy each year.

Dry-cleaning free
Don't take your clothes to the dry cleaner. The chemicals they use are severe, and bad for your clothes too. Many items that claim they need to be dry cleaned, actually don't have to be. You can also hang them in the bathroom when taking a shower, wash by hand or use a hand steamer. There are also an increasing number of green dry-cleaners, you can find them online. ⟶

Iron free

Try not to buy clothes that crease easily, or make peace with the crease. Ironing uses lots of energy, including yours. Only iron clothes if you can't wear them otherwise. And don't sit down for the rest of the day, or you can start all over again.

Repairing

Repairing your clothes if they're broken is of course extremely sustainable.

» Sew on that button, it's not difficult and there are heaps of shops that sell the buttons that you've of course lost (and from now on, save all those extra buttons attached to your clothes in a handy box – I'm talking to myself, of course).

» Or bring your clothes to your local tailor, your friends surely know of a good one.

» Find a good friend who enjoys sewing and give him/her lots of presents.

» Find a local Repair Café, where they have tools, expertise and advice.

» The internet is full of films showing you how to do things and handy tips, such as on Love Your Clothes, Instructables and iFixit.

» Zip stuck? Rub both sides of the zip with chalk to get it running again.

» More and more brands offer a repair service. Nudie Jeans, Filippa K and Kings of Indigo for example, and Patagonia even promises a lifetime guarantee.

» Of course, you can also make your own clothes. I wish I had such skill and talent. There are a number of webshops selling sustainable fabrics, such as Offset Warehouse or Sew Natural.

---

01. Are your clothes not dirty, but do they smell a little 'off'? Put them in the freezer, this kills the bacteria that cause the scent. Works well for jeans, for example. Do put them in a proper freezer bag, as normal plastic bags can break, and you'll end up with frozen pizza stuck to your outfit. Leaving it overnight is usually best.

02. Sweat patches in your (white) clothes? Try ox-gall soap before washing or rub in half a lemon. Spray with a bit of water, allow to dry and fingers crossed.

03. Chewing gum comes off your bum by putting your jeans in the freezer and then scraping it off.

04. Talcum powder is meant to be good for oil stains, shaving cream for make-up on your collar, salt for nearly everything and hairspray (or first salt and then milk) for ink. Why not give it a go?

ELSIEN GRINGHUIS / TSE KAO

Discarding

At a certain point, it's over. You've tried everything and it's time to part ways. Then you can discard your clothes. But not throw them away. Ever. Instead, this.

Donate (and Feel Great)

You can donate your clothes to charity shops. Or put them in a collection bin if there's one in your area. They'll then be sold in second-hand shops; the rest is sold-on on the second-hand market or donated to developing countries to sell on the local market. The latter does raise some questions, because it can suppress local brands and workers in those countries. Most organisations put proceeds of the discarded clothes into projects to help the country.

You can also put damaged clothes in most collection containers. They are used as filling for car seats, or to make dusters. Really, it's allowed!

» Americans throw away an average of 13.6 billion kilos of textiles a year. In less than 20 years, the amount of clothes tossed has doubled, according to *Newsweek,* to 36.3 kilos per person.

» 90% of clothes handed-in in Canada go to textile recyclers, 10% are sold in thrift stores.
» About half of the textiles handed-in in the UK are reused, the other half recycled. Over 60% of wearable clothes are sent abroad.
» Taking textiles to the collection bin saves ten times more CO_2 as putting glass in the glass container.

Major brands such as H&M, C&A, Marks & Spencer and Zara are also take up recycling. You can hand in clothes in the store and receive a voucher for new clothes. Great of course, especially if they then use these clothes as raw material for new collections. This is only happening on a limited level, also because the technology isn't yet advanced enough (or they're not yet investing enough in it). They sell the rest of the clothes on the second-hand market (Marks & Spencer donates them to development organisation Oxfam), which generates lots of money. And so our clothes sponsor the brands; the money no longer goes to the projects of development organisations. And: you can use that voucher to buy yet more non-sustainable clothes, in a quality not always suitable for reuse. In short: it's great that brands are taking steps to reduce waste, but it comes with a catch.

The British are getting better with their clothes. In the last five years they've thrown away 51 million kilos of clothes less, they're ironing and using the dryer less, and wash using colder temperatures. Annually, this saved over 711 million kilos of CO_2 emissions.

Swap or Give Away

How fun is it to make someone else happy with clothes you're fed up with? I've got a bag ready next to my wardrobe, for all the things I don't wear anymore. When friends visit, they can always have a quick look, who knows – they might go home with a find. Giving away is wonderful, although I do recognise that knot in your stomach when someone puts something on you've discarded, and it looks great... But there was a reason you never wore it: it's too big for you, it itches, or she's blonde, tall or has no waist, which is why it suits her so well. You can of course also donate your cast-offs to a charity shop or put them in a container. Or plan a swap evening with a few friends (second-hand and swapping is also handy for men!), everyone brings some good items, a few snacks – ready to go! Do agree on a few ground rules in advance about what you'll do if multiple people fall in love with the same top, to keep it sociable. Also, more and more dedicated swap parties are being organised – maybe also in your neighbourhood?

Get Rich from your Wardrobe

Well, rich... But you can of course sell those coats and shoes you've had enough of. On eBay, at second-hand markets, Etsy, via special websites such as Designer-Vintage, The Next Closet and Vestiaire Collective, car-boot sales, Instagram etc. I've earned quite a bit of money from too-tight shoes (I've got wide feet) and red clothes (which really don't suit me).

INTERVIEW

THE NEXT CLOSET

Thalita van Ogtrop is co-founder, together with Lieke Pijpers, of The Next Closet, an online marketplace for second-hand designer fashion.

Why The Next Closet?
'We make it easy for women to sell their second-hand clothes online and to earn decent money from them. At the same time, we curate all items on style and authenticity, meaning we've the best designer outfits on offer. We want to change the fashion chain and inspire women to invest in quality and reusing.'

What are your favourite sustainable tips?
'If you're in a fortunate position and want to improve the world, then you really have to start with yourself. Personally, I benefit from yoga and meditation. I notice that I'm more connected to myself, kinder and gentler towards those around me, and make more conscious choices. Also, certain documentaries have given me a push in the right direction. Thanks to *Cowspiracy,* I'm now largely vegetarian and because of *The True Cost* I love my work even more.'

The Next Closet recommends

Initiatives
Nowness – 'Video channel featuring inspiring films, photos and stories.'
TED – 'Cool videos in which scientists, entrepreneurs and creatives share, in a few minutes, their fascinating story.'

Berlin
The Store by Soho House – 'Concept store with special brands; also great for lunch.'
Concierge Coffee – 'The best coffee in Berlin.'
VooStore – 'Wonderful store with original brands.'

Recycling costs energy. Nevertheless, collecting and processing second-hand clothes is much more economical than making new ones. Replacing one kilo of new cotton clothes with second-hand saves 65 kWh of energy, in the case of polyester even 90.

LISA KONNO / TOMEK DERSU AARON

SECOND-HAND

Second-Hand is the Best

Few things are more fun for a more sustainable wardrobe than buying second-hand. And few things better: using clothes and thus resources that are already there is always greener than new ones. You can give yourself a unique edge with them, find hidden gems, and are often better off too. In short: there are no disadvantages. It may take a bit of time to dig up something good. But it'll be well worth the effort. This can help:

» Check in the store whether there are any holes in it, buttons missing or other things wrong that you don't want to, or can't, mend. Moths could've also found it first, particularly in knitted items, so pass your hand under the entire piece to check if you can see your skin through. A loose seam is easy to sort out, but other faults maybe not.

» Look out for stains, particularly in the armpits or collar. They're often impossible to remove.

» Try the zip, and other fastenings. Everything still work?

» Don't be fooled by sizes. They used to be very different, and even now vary enormously per brand. So, try on. Online? Ask if the item can be measured if you're not sure.

» Pay attention to quality. Older fabrics may have become brittle or fragile.

» Do you feel overwhelmed by the quantities in a charity or vintage shop? Keep the items you're missing in your wardrobe in mind and look specifically for these.

» Be honest with yourself. Are you going to get it repaired if something (small) needs to be done? Are you going to get it altered if it doesn't fit properly? Even if it's a good deal, it's a waste if you won't wear it.

» Look for timeless pieces such as trench coats and jackets.

» Trust your instinct. If you shop second-hand more often, you'll start recognising the good from the bad.

» Only buy online from shops with a good reputation that you trust. Make sure you can return, and if you buy at auctions, that you have proof of authenticity. Don't exceed the price you've planned to spend.

Borrow, Rent, Share

The sharing economy is here to stay. Fortunately, because there's more than enough clothes to go around, and what's more fun than enjoying things together? Moreover, it's a very good idea to try before you buy, to prevent bad buys. These are your options:

Join a fashion library
A few years ago nobody could imagine it, but this movement is now growing. What could be better than an endless walk-in closet where you can

---

In 2017, 44 million American women shopped second-hand: that is 1 out of 3 (in 2016, this was 35 million, so an increase of over 25%).

---

choose what you want, return it once you're done with it, and still do good for the environment? That's a fashion library. It works the same as with books, but then with clothes and accessories. At most you can not only borrow, but also buy – which means you can try an item first, and see if you really wear that bomber jacket, tailored suit or woollen jumper before you purchase it. That can save quite a few bad buys. Ideal. Also great for a special occasion such as a wedding (how often will you re-wear that 'special' outfit?), but for variety in your day-to-day wardrobe too. There are already libraries in, for example, Amsterdam (LENA), Paris (L'Habibliotheque), Gothenburg (Klädoteket), Stockholm (Sabina & Friends), Copenhagen (KALO) and Cologne (Kleiderei), and hopefully more will come soon (or start one yourself if there are none near you?). I can highly recommend it.

Borrow from a brand

Brands are slowly beginning to realise that it's a good idea to give clothes a second life. Sustainable, but also a way for them to earn money twice. That's allowed, of course! The Swedish Filippa K has a second-hand store in Stockholm, and in an increasing number of their stores you can borrow a part of the collection. The Dutch MUD Jeans is a pioneer in leasing. As one of the first they not only let you buy, but also borrow jeans from them, recycling them afterwards into new pairs. The Finnish Anniina Nurmi is developing a new model for the fashion industry: 'clothing as a service', based entirely on borrowing (from a brand, store or other consumer).

Rent your outfit online

This is becoming increasingly common. Celebrities are walking the red carpet in second-hand dresses. Special websites, such as Bag, Borrow or Steal for designer bags are growing (this site was even mentioned in *Sex and the City*). Rent the Runway is for designer items (Beyoncé hired-out the contents of her wardrobe on it); and you can turn to Le Tote (where you can select five items at a time to try/return) or The Black Tux (for tuxedos and other suits). The Dutch REWEAR unites designer lovers: via the website you can borrow high-end clothes, shoes and bags from someone else's wardrobe. It goes by day, the items are insured, and the idea is to create a community from Amsterdam to New York.

In the US, fashion resale is growing 24 times faster than regular retail. The second-hand market was worth over 16 billion euros in 2017, estimations for 2022: 34 billion.

MUD JEANS

LENA THE FASHION LIBRARY

Suzanne Smulders (1985) is co-owner of LENA the fashion library.

Why do you do what you do?
'After my studies in fashion I'd had enough of the industry. It's a commercial and fleeting world, and on top of that, very damaging for the planet. It didn't feel right to be working this way, so I went looking for added value to make fashion fun again. I hope that not just LENA, but above all borrowing clothing itself, is a household term in ten years' time. The most normal thing in the world. We want to be driving forces behind a massive change in the chain.'

What bothers you?
'I can get really annoyed by people that hide behind the crowds. I can understand that not everyone makes responsible choices on all fronts, and there's nothing wrong with that. But nothing is more frustrating than someone shouting: "Yes, but it doesn't make a difference anyway!". I'm convinced that every little bit helps.'

Suzanne's motto

'My mum always says: "You're better off regretting the things you have done, than the ones you haven't." This is so true – and you also learn from your mistakes. Don't walk around with ideas for too long, make them happen and pursue your dreams.'

> In the Netherlands, more than a third of all clothes leave stores with reductions of up to 75%.
> This happens because shop owners have wrongly predicted trends or the weather, or the size, fit or colour isn't right.
> 1.23 million new clothes are destroyed annually (the Netherlands has 17 million inhabitants). Approximately half are recycled into felt, the other half is incinerated: fashion brands want to protect their image, and not distort their own market.
> Of course not just in the Netherlands, but worldwide the growing pile of unused clothes is a problem. In 2017 alone, H&M for instance had 3.5 billion euros worth of unsold stock left (7% more than the year before).

DORA

On average, British women have 8 handbags
(3% have more than 100). They contain about 330 euros'
worth of things.

ACCESSORIES

Much of what I have written in this chapter about clothes also applies to accessories. But bags, shoes and jewellery also have their own sustainable challenges.

Bags

Go for timeless: a bag you can wear with everything and will still use in ten years, is the best.

— Leather is a tough one – here, everything from page 044 holds true too. Look for naturally tanned, recycled or waste leather, for example from Aurélie Chadaine, Lovia, MYOMY or O My Bag.

— Do you prefer buying cruelty-free and vegan? Great! Check you're not just buying plastic though, or leather alternatives deriving from oil that are also bad for the environment (such as PVC). Investigate whether the glue's not made from bone remnants (which is often the case). With the PETA or Vegan-approved label on it, you're fine. Denise Roobol, FRAENCK, FREITAG, Kaliber and Matt & Nat are good options, for example.

— Buy second-hand where you can. More sustainable and cheaper. Pay attention to the quality, whether the handles, zips and seams are still strong.

— Got a great bag? Sell it if you want another one – a good bag can raise quite a bit.

— Don't fall for a fake it-bag: there's a huge number of counterfeits out there, so know the features of a luxury brand before you buy. The fake industry is also used to finance groups in countries with civil wars and terrorism, they're linked to child labour and the money doesn't go to the people and brands that you want to support. Don't be part of it.

— A shoemaker or tailor can also repair bags, just like your shoes.

— There are more and more bags featuring solar panels, so that you can charge your laptop and telephone, such as those by Voltaic Systems.

— Bags made of fish leather, cork, canvas, jute, car seatbelts, bottle tops? All possible – take a look at for example 959 and Bottletop.

— An organic/fair-trade cotton tote or bag is al-

DENISE ROOBOL

ways a good option, particularly when you're going shopping (that you of course, no longer use plastic bags for).

— Store and treat your bags well: protect them, spray them, clean them, air them sometimes, those kinds of things.

Shoes

Shoes are perfect to buy second-hand. Especially as they're often discarded because they're uncomfortable, and therefore hardly worn. Frequently you'll see them offered with box and all, as good as new. Ask if they can be measured if you buy online, to avoid having exactly the same problem later.

> Go for quality, choose shoes that will last. It's also handy if you can wear them with lots of different outfits.

> Apparently, it's good to change your shoes frequently – for your feet and for wear and tear, of course.

> Too small after all, but made of leather or another natural material? Put on some normal socks, with a really thick pair on top, and then squeeze into the tight shoes. Grab a hairdryer and blow warm air over the tight areas until they become a bit looser. Keep them on until they've cooled down and try again if they're still tight.

> Do you really want leather? Look for naturally tanned or recycled, like that from Caboclo (also for men), ekn footwear or Werner. Timberland only uses leather from the best Leather Working Group factories, more sustainable cotton and develops new recycled material, such as fake canvas made of PET bottles.

> Rather no leather? There are vegan options, such as Bhava, Beyond Skin, Melissa, Matt & Nat, Good Guys and Brave Gentleman.

> Sneaker fan? Buy them second-hand (via eBay for example) or go for ones by Ethletic or Veja. The latter are made fairly, from environmentally-friendly materials such as organic cotton and their self-developed eco-leather without chrome. Veja

cooperates with small Brazilian farmers, paying them a premium for the natural, wild rubber from the Amazon.

> Sport shoes can also be easy to find second-hand (because of the number of people that start a sport – and then give up again).

> Treat shoes with loving tender care: spraying against dirt and water, immediately removing mud, snow and moisture, and storing them tidily really helps.

With shoes and bags, there's often little attention for working conditions; it's mostly about the material. It is very important though, so if you buy something new, ask the brand or store about it. By doing so we send the message, together, that we want things made by people who are treated well.

> Have your shoes repaired if they (threaten to) break. Really one of the most sustainable things you can do and money-saving. The shoemaker may not use the most environmentally-friendly materials, but wearing your shoes longer is better than buying new ones.

> And then we also have socks, of course. There are socks made of organic cotton (by The Conscious Step or Qnoop, for instance, and department stores offer them now and again), or of bamboo (but make sure they are organic). H&M sometimes sell socks and tights of recycled waste. Some sustainable brands also have socks in their collection. Tights are strange products anyway! They're made of oil and tear almost by just looking at them. Luckily there's now a brand tackling this: Swedish Stockings.

British men nowadays own more shoes than women – partly due to the popularity of sneakers, and because they are less likely to sell unworn pairs. Women have about 400 euros' worth in their wardrobe, primarily stilettos (over a third admit to buying unnecessary shoes because they were in the sale).

INTERVIEW

SWEDISH STOCKINGS

Nadja Forsberg (1988) is co-founder, together with Linn Frisinger, of Swedish Stockings, the world's first environmentally-friendly tights brand. They want to be sustainable, but also bring back luxury and quality to stockings.

What do you do?
'We make beautiful tights from recycled nylon threads. Our factories also use environmentally-friendly dye, purify the water after dyeing and use lots of solar energy. Every year, two billion pairs of tights are produced, a portion of which are only worn once and then thrown away. Nylon thread for tights is made of petroleum, which is incredibly harmful for the environment. The production leads to a lot of damaging CO_2 emissions – and not only are they terrible for the planet, but they also only last for a short while. We do it differently.'

Nadja's top Stockholm tips

Ecoist 'A wonderful lunch spot with delicious food.'
Örtagubben 'A health food store where you can buy herbs, supplements, beauty products etc. It's where I go for everything I need.'
Snickarbacken 7 'One of my favourite lunch spots, they have the best acai bowls in Stockholm.'

Jewellery

Clothes, shoes and bags are utilitarian objects, you really need them. Not so much for jewellery, which primarily exists to decorate us. Extra important, then, that it's made ethically. And that's possible.

Gold and silver

A lot of jewellery is made of gold and silver: a radiant exterior, but a dull flip-side. The working conditions in the large-scale mines (in countries such as South Africa and Colombia) are often unbelievably harsh. People are digging up the most valuable substances on earth at risk of their own lives, getting only a pittance in return. They work with poisonous cyanide to separate gold from the soil, or with mercury in the small-scale mines. These substances also leak into the groundwater and the sea. They don't get a fair price for their work and hardly have rights. Forced labour is abundant, and in places where gold is found, (indigenous) people are driven out. When the gold-seekers depart, they leave the nature dilapidated and poisoned.
— The Fairtrade-Fairmined Standard has been developed in collaboration with Fairtrade International, for small-scale miners, with criteria in the areas of environment and working conditions. Luxury brand Chopard uses it, but also an increasing number of smaller labels. The Initiative for Responsible Mining Assurance is developing a standard and independent verification of environmental and working conditions in the mining industry.
— You can also choose brands that use recycled gold and silver (or get something made from old, family pieces). AUrate and Mumbaistockholm for example uses only recycled gold (and conflict-free diamonds).

Diamonds

The reality behind diamonds is also considerably less sparkling than the stone itself. Most diamonds come from conflict areas in Africa, where they're sold illegally to finance weapons. Resistance groups and gangs sell them to smugglers, and with these 'blood diamonds' keep the war and struggle in existence. The diamonds themselves are also fought over – in countries like Sierra Leone and Angola, many people (millions, allegedly) have already died because of them. Now that this is becoming more well-known, sales are decreasing. Pressure groups such as ActionAid are forcing companies to act. The Kimberly Process has also been established, a partnership between governments, social organisations and the diamond industry. This has improved things, but there's also criticism, because it's voluntary and lacks binding verification. In June 2016, the new EU agreement about conflict minerals was signed, although it's seen as being too weak. The diamond trade is worth more than 50 billion a year.
— Leonardo DiCaprio made the film *Blood Diamond*, about the illegal diamond trade in Sierra Leone and how this finances the bloody civil war. The film created a lot of waves. He now invests in diamonds that are 'cultivated' in a laboratory (the Diamond Foundry). It's technologically possible to create a diamond with the same quality and purity, without all the drawbacks. In the Netherlands, House of Eléonore for example uses these lab-diamonds, in combination with Fairtrade gold.
— For other gemstones too, the circumstances are often not good: emerald mines, for instance, destroy land in Latin America. There are some sustainable pearl nurseries, such as in Fiji and Mexico.
— Second-hand is your friend if you really want to wear diamonds or gemstones.

Wild animals

Ivory, coral, reptile skins, tortoise or mussel shells: never a good idea.

Recycled and second-hand

Many brands use recycled jewellery or materials.
— ARTICLE 22 creates ethical jewellery from bomb fragments.
— EcoBling makes jewellery from recycled wood and glass, the label Made from reclaimed brass, and DORA creates necklaces from residual shipbuilding wood.
— Thea Grant turns old, vintage jewellery into new, contemporary designs.

>> *Avoid cheap (ear)rings and necklaces: they often contain heavy metals and toxic substances.*
>> *Fashion brands such as People Tree and Komodo also sell ethically-made jewellery.*
>> *Jewellery often improves with age, look for second-hand in charity shops, on Etsy and at your parents or grandparents.*
>> *Do you enjoy wearing wood? Opt for used or local wood or FSC certified. And if you like beads, try to find recycled glass.*

The value of the international jewellery market is 264 billion euros. 56% of all gold is in jewellery.

Watches and sunglasses

Something else you can second-hand shop for to your heart's content – there's lots and it's great. Should you still want something new, then try a watch from WeWood: made of wood, and the brand plants one tree per purchase in a project chosen by you. Dick Moby makes cool sunglasses from recycled and biodegradable material. Ballo from South Africa does this too, and Vinylize creates glasses from old LPs in Budapest. You can also get glasses made from your own record collection.

LAURA EN JAMES

Laura de Jong (1984) collects green alternatives on her Dutch blog, Laura en James. Additionally, she runs the online pregnancy calendar poppy to PUMPKIN, where she helps parents make sustainable choices for their (future) child. She's the kid expert of this book, and in every chapter, provides you with the best tips, facts, brands and shops.

What do you blog about?

'I blog about all the fun, sustainable options out there for parents. Not things that should or shouldn't be allowed, but an honest story, so you can make your own choices. Before the birth of my children, I chose sustainable as much as possible, now I find that even more important. When you become a parent, you're much more aware of the choices you make and their consequences for the future. It's not difficult to choose sustainably: more fun even, more tasty and stylish.'

What bothers you?

'People who see price as an argument not to consume sustainably, yet who drive a lease car and make long journeys. I like beautiful things too, but I don't buy just for the sake of buying anymore.'

Laura's favourites

Colour and style advice – 'Invest in good advice. You'll immediately understand why you always get so many compliments about that one sweater and you'll prevent bad buys.'

Peppermint – 'Australian quarterly magazine focusing on style and sustainability.'

Caboclo – 'Stylish shoes developed with local craftsmen in Brazil, from eco-leather and soles of old car tyres.'

By Mölle – 'If I could live in a dream world, I'd choose this one. I've been a fan of this Dutch home label for ages, with plaids of recycled denim and linen bedding.'

GREEN KIDS by Laura de Jong

Pass it On

Do you have friends or family with children? Pass clothes on to each other. This works easiest in boxes per size. Make clear agreements, for example whether you want the clothes back for a possible next child. Don't be scared to ask around if anyone has cast-offs, lots of people are pleased to find them a good home.

Sustainable Pregnancy

Wear your own clothes for as long as possible. Choose for example a maternity shirt with your normal cardigan on top. You can also continue to wear dresses and tops with stretch for a long time. You're better off getting maternity clothes second-hand or via friends. You wear them for a relatively short time, so they often still look fine.

Perhaps unimaginable if you've just become a mum or dad, but did you know that your baby grows on average six sizes in the first year? This is why children's clothes are great for sharing, they usually don't wear them that long.

Don't Buy any New Clothes in the First Months after Giving Birth
Preferably, wear your maternity clothes for a while if you don't yet fit in your old clothes. During those first months you're more likely to make bad buys that you won't wear afterwards. Believe me, there will come a time when 'practical' and 'stain-proof' are no longer top of your list.

Think Big
Buy some of your child's clothes, such as dresses, cardigans and leggings, a size bigger. Fold up the sleeves or legs and you'll be able to use them for a lot longer.

New-born Essentials List
Most lists are far too extensive. Items that parents rarely use include, for example, a bath thermometer, cuddly toys, baby shoes, a complete selection of baby creams and powders, and baby clothes with a hood. Don't buy too much while pregnant, only when the baby arrives will you know what you like and still need.

'Together with many other green brands, we aim to be an opposing force in a time when everything has to be faster, cheaper and easier.'

Maaike Groen, owner Miss Green

GUIDE

This is only a selection of what can be found internationally – I've tried to give an initial starter for every region (and many webshops deliver internationally). Including everything would result in a gigantic phone book, so hopefully this is a good kick-off, and you'll then be able to find more locally.

STORES

AUSTRALIA AND NEW ZEALAND

Ecoture
webshop (Aus)
Fashion, shoes, bags (m/f), beauty products and home accessories.
ecoture.com.au

EKOLUV
webshop (Aus)
Here you can't only buy, but also rent outfits. Offers several labels besides own brands EKOLUV (fashion) and EmilyKate (jewellery from recycled materials): clothes, accessories, beauty (f) and lifestyle.
ekoluv.com

Green Horse
Melbourne + webshop (Aus)
Well-curated selection of sustainable and local brands (and a stylish store): clothes (f), beauty, shoes, home and kids.
greenhorse.com.au

Shift to Nature
webshop (Aus)
Clothes, accessories, (m/f/c), bed linen, active wear and more, inspired by native Australia.
shifttonature.com.au

Thread Harvest
webshop (Aus)
Clothes and accessories (m/f/c); you can choose based on impact, for example living wage, empowering women or upcycled.
threadharvest.com.au

We-Love
webshop (Aus)
Fashionable collection of clothes (primarily female, also own brand), accessories, shoes, swim- and underwear.
we-love.com.au

Well Made Clothes
webshop (Aus/NZ)
Well-curated store (and good blog) with clothes and accessories (f) from a large variety of brands (primarily from Aus/NZ), selected by values such as local, transparent, gender equality, fair, vegan, minimal waste.
wellmadeclothes.com

AND ALSO
brandsforgood.com / ecomono.com.au / orangeoranges.com.au / shopkinobi.com / thesocialstudio.org / velvety.com.au

GERMANY

DearGoods
Augsburg, Berlin, Munich + webshop
Five stores (three in Munich) and a webshop with a broad range of casual and vegan fashion and accessories (m/f).
deargoods.com

Fairfitters
Cologne + webshop
Concept store with fashion, shoes and accessories (m/f).
fairfitters.de

Glore
Augsburg, Hamburg, Munich, Nuremberg, Stuttgart + webshop
Extensive collection of brands (m/f/c), from basic to fashion. Also, yoga wear, personal-care products and home accessories.
glore.de

Greenality
Hannover, Stuttgart + webshop
Large selection of brands (m/f/c): fashion, bags, sunglasses, shoes etc.
greenality.de

Homage
Berlin + webshop
Clothes (m/f), accessories, beauty, interior, gifts etc.
homagestore.com

LOVECO
Berlin + webshop
Two concept stores for vegan and fair trade fashion and accessories (m/f), beauty and lifestyle products, and more.
loveco-shop.de

Moeon
Berlin + webshop
Concept store with modern brands – fashion (m/f), accessories, shoes and more.
moeon.de

Wertvoll
Berlin + webshop
Large selection of clothing, bags and shoes (m/f).
wertvoll-berlin.com

AND ALSO
avocadostore.de / fairaporter.com / @friedrichheidelberg / kaalee.de / standard-saubere-sachen.de / wesen-berlin.com

THE NETHERLANDS AND BELGIUM

Charlie + Mary
Amsterdam + webshop (NL)
Pioneer in sustainable concept stores: 'true fashion' (m/f) and accessories, lifestyle products, books etc.
charliemary.com

Geitenwollenwinkel
Amsterdam + webshop (NL)
Vegan sustainable fashion and lifestyle (f), with clothes and accessories from own brands, Goat Organic Apparel and REAL FAKE, and other contemporary labels.
geitenwollenwinkel.nl

Het Faire Oosten
Amsterdam (NL)
Clothes (m/f), (home) accessories, beauty, books and food from local, artisan and sustainable brands.
hetfaireoosten.nl

Juttu
Antwerp, Bruges, Roeselare + webshop (Bel)
Sustainable and local brands, and labels with a story: clothes (m/f), accessories, food, homeware, beauty and gifts.
juttu.be

MHOOM
Amsterdam + webshop (NL)
Responsible store and sustainable hairdresser. Clothes and accessories (m/f), haircare and make-up.
mhoom.com

Nukuhiva
Amsterdam, Utrecht (NL)
Casual clothes and accessories (m/f), books, candles, detergent etc.
nukuhiva.nl

studio JUX + co.
Amsterdam, Utrecht + webshop (NL)
Concept store with fashion (m/f) and (home) accessories from own brand, and other modern labels.
studiojux.com – see also p. 035

Sukha
Amsterdam + webshop (NL)
Stylish store with, besides regular brands, well-curated ethical labels (f) and own brand Atelier Sukha: knitwear, homeware and accessories.
sukha.nl

Supergoods
Ghent, Mechelen + webshop (Bel)
Clothes and accessories (m/f/c), and furniture, homeware, beauty and toys.
supergoods.be

Verse
Amsterdam + webshop (NL)
Innovative and sustainable fashion brands (m/f), personal-care products, accessories and interior items.
versegoodstore.com

AND ALSO
brandmission.nl / harvestclub.be / inlevel5.be / takeitslowfashion.nl

SCANDINAVIA
AWAKE
Helsinki, Riga + webshop (Fin)
Concept store and gallery with sustainable and designer clothes (m/f), accessories and interior products.
awake-collective.com

Ecosphere
Stockholm + webshop (Swe)
Stylish clothes (m/f), bags and shoes.
ecosphere.se

Grandpa
Gothenburg, Malmö, Stockholm + webshop (Swe)
Mix of regular and sustainable brands, in five stores (three in Stockholm) and an extensive webshop, with fashion, outdoor wear, accessories, shoes (m/f), personal-care, interior and bath products etc.
grandpastore.com

Just Fashion
webshop (Nor)
Selection of slow fashion and designer brands (m/f/u): clothes, personal-care products and jewellery.
justfashion.no

My Fair Shop
webshop (Den)
Many brands for clothes, accessories, personal-care products (m/f/c), lifestyle, yoga etc.
my-fair-shop.com

69B

My Favourite Things
Copenhagen + webshop (Den)
Wide selection of stylish brands: clothes, accessories, personal-care products (m/f), perfume, gifts, etc.
myfavouritethings.dk

Nudge
Helsinki + webshop (Fin)
Large variety of well-curated fashion, accessories, personal-care products (m/f), homeware and gifts; shares the building with a sustainable restaurant.
nudge.fi

Stil & Ansvar
webshop (Swe)
Stylish collection of bags.
stilochansvar.com

The Replik
webshop (Swe)
Scandinavian/minimalist selection of fashion brands (f).
thereplik.com

Weecos
webshop
Market place featuring more than a hundred stores and brands, with Scandinavian, local and sustainable clothes, accessories, personal-care products (m/f/c) and homeware.
weecos.com

UNITED KINGDOM
69b
London
Well-curated boutique by stylist and fashion expert Merryn Leslie, with modern fashion, jewellery, shoes, bags (f), personal-care products and make-up.
69bboutique.com

Asos Eco Edit / Marketplace
webshop
If you enjoy shopping from Asos, then go for their more sustainable range of fashion and beauty brands (m/f). The Marketplace offers vintage and boutiques from young (sometimes sustainable) designers.
asos.com

Ethical Collection
webshop
Boutique for positive change: brands (f) with a good story. Artisan and well-made fashion and accessories.
ethicalcollection.com

FASHION-CONSCIENCE.COM
webshop
Large collection of stylish brands (f): fashion, bags, shoes and accessories (and vegan range).
fashion-conscience.com

Gather & See
webshop
Fashionable web store (and blog) with a well-curated selection of labels for fashion, bags and shoes (f).
gatherandsee.com

Rêve En Vert
webshop
Large variety of fashionable brands: clothes, activewear, accessories, beauty (f) and an inspiring blog.
reve-en-vert.com

The Acey
webshop
Stylish fashion and accessories (f) from well-curated labels.
the-acey.com

The Keep Boutique
London + webshop

'Brands with integrity. Clothes to keep.' Fashion, shoes, accessories (m/f), personal-care products, gifts.
thekeepboutique.com

The Third Estate
London + webshop
Vegan and more sustainable shoes, bags and accessories (m/f).
thethirdestate.co.uk

UNITED STATES AND CANADA
allTRUEist
webshop (Can)
Luxury clothes, bags and jewellery (m/f).
alltrueist.com

Bead & Reel
webshop (US)
Fashion, accessories and skincare (f), chosen according to ethics such as female owner, made to order, gender neutral, zero waste. Also: a good blog, activist's book club, vegan info and a charity of the month.
beadandreel.com

Bhoomki
New York + webshop (US)
Fashion, bags, jewellery (f) from labels with a positive story.
bhoomki.com

Ethica
webshop (US)
Wide selection of fashionable and independent brands, accessories and beauty products (f).
shopethica.com

Fashionkind
webshop (US)
High-end fashion and accessories (f), selected using criteria such as LGBT rights, anti-violence, women's empowerment, anti-slavery, capsule collection, vegan or emerging economies.
fashionkind.com

Faubourg
webshop (US)
Mindful collection of stylish labels; fashion, accessories (f) and blog.
shopfaubourg.com

Hazel & Rose
webshop (US)
Strong selection of feminine brands: fashion (also vintage and plus-size),

accessories, skincare, books, and blog.
shophazelandrose.com

Kaight
New York (2x) + webshop (US)
Fashion, bags, jewellery, shoes, outerwear, personal-care products (f) and interior accessories from independent and sustainable labels.
kaightshop.com

Master & Muse
web portal
Project of model Amber Valetta to put stylish sustainable fashion on the map. Selects smart and innovative brands and refers you to points of sale.
masterandmuse.com

Modavanti
webshop (US)
Wide range of fashionable brands (m/f/c), accessories, homeware and personal-care products.
modavanti.com

MooShoes
Los Angeles, New York + webshop (US)
Extensive and strong selection of vegan shoes, bags, belts (m/f), socks, tights, personal-care products etc.
mooshoes.com

A.BCH

New Classics
webshop (Can)
Timeless designs from artisan, eco, fair trade, handmade, organic, recycled, vegan, zero waste or vintage labels: fashion, accessories, shoes, beauty (f) and more.
newclassics.ca

otherwild
Los Angeles, New York + webshop (US)
Special store, studio and event space; fashion (including The Future is Female shirts), homeware and apothecary – founded to stimulate ethical practices, advocacy and activism.
otherwild.com

Topo Designs
Boulder, Denver, Fort Collins, New York, San Francisco + webshop (US)
Own brand outdoor clothing, bags and accessories (m/f), with a repair service, lifetime guarantee and environmental-protection programme, as well as other, befriended labels (personal-care, hammocks etc.).
topodesigns.com

Zady
webshop (US)
Stylish and timeless brand (m/f), that focuses on quality and collaborates with amongst others Emma Watson. Also fashion, accessories and stationery from other labels.
zady.com

AND ALSO
aligolden.com / intheknowfashion.com / makenewcollections.com / shopgoodcloth.com

VARIOUS
aboynamedsue.co (Hong Kong) / atriumdublin.com (Ireland) / dressingresponsable.com (France) / ecolabo.ch (Switzerland) / kagure.jp (Tokyo) / littlegreendot.com/marketplace/fashion (Singapore) / troo.ch (Switzerland)

BRANDS

Many brands are available in the stores featured in this guide (and lots of other shops) and most have a webshop. Some also have their own stores; if so, it's mentioned.

Fashion

A.BCH
Transparent designer-basics label from Australia (m/f/c), that shows where every item is made (mostly in Melbourne) and from what (mostly

organic cotton) – down to the thread and buttons, how it's packaged (in recycled material) and more. Clean sweaters, tops and shirts.
abch.world

Amour Vert
Extensive range of clothes in classic silhouettes, and jewellery, shoes (f/c), made from more sustainable materials in the US – where they also have several stores.
amourvert.com

Apolis
American timeless brand for global citizens (m/f), that wants to achieve social change via their motto 'Advocacy Through Industry'. Known for their market bags, which just as with their (sweat)shirts, you can customise, but also offers trousers, jackets and swimwear. Stores in LA and NY.
apolisglobal.com

Armedangels
German contemporary, casual brand (m/f) with a large collection of tops, dresses, hoodies and jeans. Sold in many stores, uses Fairtrade cotton, is GOTS certified, largely vegan and member of Fair Wear Foundation.
armedangels.de

bon
Modern label for fashion and activewear (f): timeless wardrobe essentials with a French twist. GOTS certified, recycled or made-to-order material, made in Australia.
bonlabel.com.au

Ecoalf
Innovative Spanish brand with fashion, shoes and accessories (m/f) made of recycled tyres, fishing nets and coffee grounds. Works with big names; own store in Madrid and Berlin.
ecoalf.com

EDUN
High-end, modern fashion brand (f) that wants to stimulate ethical trade with Africa through long-term relationships and the revaluation of craftsmanship. Set up by the wife of Bono; store in NY.
edun.com

EILEEN FISHER
Feminine label with a wide range. Is active in many areas in the field of sustainability (including production in the US, more sustainable materials, certified dyes, clothing deposit programme).
eileenfisher.com

Everlane
One of the pioneers in transparency: shows the cost of materials, labour, tax and transport of every item, and therefore also what they earn. The website features what factory each piece is made in too, as well as supplier profiles. Offers clean, stylish fashion (m/f), accessories, swimwear, shoes and bags, but as of yet not of (many) sustainable fabrics – own store in New York and showroom in San Francisco.
everlane.com

Filippa K
Swedish, fashionable label with an extensive collection (m/f). Member of Fair Wear Foundation, pioneer among the bigger labels, with a growing amount of sustainable materials, a second-hand store and borrow-system.
filippa-k.com – see also p. 038

Honest By
First totally transparent fashion brand in the world (m/f). Sustainable, ethically-made fashionable designs from the Belgian pioneer Bruno Pieters (or in collaboration with other designers). Store in Antwerp.
honestby.com – see also p. 051

HoodLamb
Innovative Dutch brand with coats, knitwear and warm hoodies (m/f) made of hemp, recycled polyester and self-developed fake fur. Also sell summer tops and T-shirts, and support Sea Shepherd.
hoodlamb.com

Industry of All Nations
American fashion brand (m/f) with clean, cool basics, jeans and sweaters – many made of organic cotton, and dyed naturally. Wants to celebrate craftsmanship, and have products made in the regions they originally came from. Views shopping as the equivalent of voting; stores in San Francisco and Venice.
industryofallnations.com

Katharine Hamnett
British sustainability icon in the fashion world, known for her shirts (m/f) with bold, committed statements (for example, for refugees or against Brexit). High-end collection, made in Italy of sustainable materials.
katharinehamnett.com – see also p. 254

Knowledge Cotton Apparel
Fashionable Danish men's brand with good shirts, jackets, trousers, underwear and socks.
knowledgecottonapparel.com

Kowtow
Minimalistic, clean label from New Zealand (f), using Fairtrade and organic cotton and GOTS certified dye. Basic collections and changing shirts, dresses, jeans and accessories.
kowtowclothing.com

CAMILLA ÅKRANS FOR FILIPPA K

Patagonia
American outdoor brand (m/f), pioneer in the field of fabric innovation and recycling. Old clothes are collected to be made into new ones, they give a lifetime guarantee and repair. Many own stores worldwide.
patagonia.com – see also p. 230

People Tree
British frontrunner in ethical fashion and accessories (m/f) made of organic and Fairtrade cotton. Uses fashion to give workers their power and pride back and combines trends with traditional techniques.
peopletree.co.uk – see also p. 048

Reformation
One of the few brands with their own factory: in Los Angeles (you can visit). There, they strive for a living

wage (already half are earning one), and are able to make small batches to test in the stores and adjust according to feedback or replace, to prevent over-production and waste. Also produce elsewhere, both in the US and worldwide – from for instance more sustainable, recycled, vintage or overstock fabrics. Have a second-hand store (in LA) and collect discarded clothes from your home. Women's dresses, jeans, jumpsuits, accessories etc., stores in LA, NY, Dallas and San Francisco.
thereformation.com

Skunkfunk
Basque brand (f) that wants to be as sustainable as possible: zero waste, better materials, certified factories, eco-packaging and economical stores (where they take-in clothes). Feminine tops, dresses, jackets and accessories; own stores in Spain, France, Germany, Ireland, Portugal, Sweden, US and Chile.
skunkfunk.com

Stella McCartney
Major frontrunner within the high-fashion world (m/f), makes eco-fashion modern. First luxury brand that uses no leather (and fur, feathers or PVC) at all and offers innovative alternatives. Various stores worldwide.
stellamccartney.com – see also p. 256

studio JUX
Stylish fashion, accessories (m/f) and interior items, made in their own factory in Nepal. Store in Amsterdam and Utrecht.
studiojux.com – see also p. 035

Study NY
Unique, conceptual label (f), that aims to challenge the fashion system. Works seasonless and transparently, with materials that are as sustainable as possible. The designs are wearable in multiple ways or statement pieces and are made in NY according to the zero-waste principle.
study-ny.com – see also p. 028

Untouched World
Sustainable fashion and accessories made in New Zealand (m/f/c). Part of money raised goes to their own charity for young sustainable leadership, and works with the United Nations. Various own stores – big names

including Barack Obama and Joanna Lumley are enthusiasts.
untouchedworld.com

Vetta Capsule
Clean capsule collections of 5 pieces that together form 30 outfits, made in the US from sustainable or deadstock materials.
vettacapsule.com

Vivienne Westwood
British legend who makes striking designs (f/m). Campaigns against disposable culture and says: buy less, but better. Various own stores worldwide.
viviennewestwood.co.uk – see also p. 256

wunderwerk
Large German brand (m/f), with a complete collection of casual-chic trousers, shirts, sweaters and blouses. Store in Düsseldorf.
wunderwerk.com

afriek.com – Dutch design combined with positive African craftsmanship (m/f).

alasthelabel.com – Fashionable Australian pyjama brand (m/f, also active and daywear) made of organic cotton or recycled polyester.

alchemist-fashion.com – Feminine Dutch brand (f), combining quality, style and ethics.

annegorke.com – High-fashion label (f) with a cheerful twist, produced in Germany from environmentally-friendly fabrics.

arelastudio.com – High quality and timeless basics (m/f), from Finnish brand that mends and takes back clothes, and raises awareness of materials, maintenance and choices.

bassike.com – Clean Australian brand (m/f/c), locally made from partially sustainable materials.

beaumontorganic.com – Complete collection of feminine fashion from British brand (store in Manchester).

behno.com – Special, high-end American-Indian label (f) that works with local NGO to revolutionise labour.

bibico.co.uk – British easy-to-wear women's brand made of natural materials (store in Bath).

bleed-clothing.com – German vegan, extensive casual brand (m/f).

bravegentleman.com – Forward American slow fashion and vegan

men's brand (store in Brooklyn).

bysigne.com – Clean, Danish, timeless women's label.

carcel.co – Danish minimalist brand (f) of local high-quality materials, made by women in prison.

carriercompany.co.uk – Locally made, high quality, classic British outdoor clothing (m/f).

cossac.co.uk – Fresh British brand (f), offering an alternative to the high street with contemporary slow fashion.

dedicatedbrand.com – Cheerful Swedish streetwear label (m/f), with a growing collection and own stores.

ekyog.com – Stylish, feminine French brand, with an extensive collection and many own stores.

elsiengringhuis.com – Minimalist, fashionable and zero-waste Dutch design (f) made of sustainable materials.

goatorganicapparel.com – Affordable basics from vegan, minimalistic Dutch brand.

groceriesapparel.com – Extensive collection of laid-back fashion (m/f), made in the US from natural materials and dyes.

hundhund.com – Modern German brand (m/f), made in Eastern-Europe of more sustainable materials. Wants to be affordable and so not for sale in other stores, a price structure accompanies every item.

isabelldehillerin.com – German designer with French sense of style and elegant designs (f), uses traditional and local skills.

izzylane.bigcartel.com – British, locally made, classic wool brand, from own flock of rescued sheep: wants to save the UK fashion industry and give animals a voice.

jannjune.com – Clean, feminine, German design, made of sustainable materials in a Polish family-run factory.

junglefolk.com – Swiss classic, timeless label (f), also with 'never out of season' line. Sewn by craftsmen in Colombia, from sustainable fabrics.

komodo.co.uk – Extensive collection of easy-to-wear fashion (m/f), from British frontrunner of the sustainable fashion world.

lanius.com – Wide range of feminine fashion; the German brand is member of Fair Wear Foundation and shows factory profiles online.

liminal.org.nz – Fair trade, organic basics and accessories (m/f) from New Zealand.

lovjoi.com – Easy-to-wear design label (m/f), made in Germany from sustainable fabrics.

maggiemarilyn.com – High-end fashion brand from New Zealand (f); distinctive pieces, sustainably made.

marahoffman.com – High-end, stylish American brand (including swimwear), made of sustainable materials and often locally produced.

maska.se – Swedish, stylish label (f), produced in the EU from natural fabrics.

miss-green.nl – Strong basics, supplemented with fashionable pieces, from Dutch GOTS certified label (f).

nmbq.store – Bold, limited edition 'body positive' clothes (m/f), printed and made from sustainable fabrics in Melbourne.

nou-menon.com – Dutch brand with feminine, vegan fashion from eco and recycled fabrics.

okewarainwear.com – Ethically, New Zealand-made stylish raincoats from Bluesign material.

outsiderfashion.com – British, chic womenswear (dresses, jackets), made of natural fabrics.

pelechecoco.com – Cool, reworked vintage biker jackets and denim – flagship in Copenhagen.

purewaste.org – Clean basics (m/v), made of cotton waste. Concept store in Helsinki.

recreatestore.co.nz – New Zealand brand with Fairtrade made fashion (m/f/c) and homeware, from certified organic materials.

rhumaa.com – Special Dutch design brand (m/f), inspired by African artists.

studio-august.com – Contemporary design from Estonia (f), made of natural materials.

sudara.org – American pyjama brand (m/f/c), made by former victims of human trafficking.

thesocialoutfit.org – Colourful fashion (f), made by former refugees (who receive training). Materials are often donated, store in Sydney.

tonle.com – Women-owned US zero-waste brand (f) with items made of mass manufacturers' scrap waste.

tricotage.dk – Contemporary Danish design label (f) made from more sustainable fabrics.

twothirds.com – Two-thirds of the earth is ocean, which is what this Spanish casual label (m/f) is asking attention for.

vautecouture.com – Vegan coats and sweaters, made by American craftsmen out of as much recycled and organic material as possible (m/f/u).

vegethreads.com – Sustainable basics made in Australia (m/f) and yoga, swimwear and underwear for real bodies.

uniformsforthededicated.com – Swedish men's brand with sleek shirts, suits and coats made of recycled or natural materials. Store in Stockholm.

wintervacht.nl – Coats made from old blankets (f) in the Netherlands.

KUYICHI

AND ALSO

bhaloshop.com / bysannejansen.com / citizenwolf.com / cus.cat / cuyana.com / fridaysproject.com / ilovelowie.com / iouproject.com / lisakonno.com / maium.nl / nelly-rose.com / realfakestudios.com / resiste-et-reve.com / sogoodtowear.com / thercollective.com / thinkingmu.com

Jeans

Hiut Denim
The British village Cardigan used to play a major role in the jeans industry. Hiut Denim revives this, and sells locally-made, organic cotton and naturally-dyed jeans (m/f).
hiutdenim.co.uk

Kings of Indigo
Dutch innovative brand (m/f) offering jeans, fashion collections and accessories. Member of Fair Wear Foundation,

motto 'Recycle, Repair, Reuse'.
kingsofindigo.com

Kuyichi
Jeans brand from the Netherlands (m/f), pioneer in organic cotton. Offers a seasonless basic collection, supplemented with casual tops and sweaters.
kuyichi.com

Monkee Genes
Hip and colourful British jeans and chino brand (m/f/c). As they say themselves: no slave labour, no child labour, no blood, no sweat, no tears.
monkeegenes.com

MUD Jeans
Dutch brand (m/f), made of organic cotton and recycled denim. You can buy or lease the jeans, and returned pairs are used to make new fabric.
mudjeans.eu

Nudie Jeans
Smart, Swedish denim and streetwear brand (m/c). Member of Fair Wear Foundation and uses sustainable materials. When you hand in your old jeans for reuse, you receive a discount on a new pair. Store in Stockholm.
nudiejeans.com

AND ALSO
haikure.com / indigoferajeans.com / parcofashion.eu

Underwear and Socks

Anekdot
Stylish German/Swedish lingerie, leisure and swimwear brand, using high-quality waste materials from brands such as Speedo.
anekdotboutique.com

Do You Green
French lingerie, made from local, sustainable pinewood trees and lace from Calais.
doyougreen.com

Lonely
Lingerie, swimwear and fashion, consciously made in China, that celebrates the female body and diversity in a cool, inclusive way.
lonelylabel.com

NICO
Australian ethically-made under-,

swim- and leisurewear, from sustainable or recycled materials.
nicounderwear.com

Qnoop
Dutch brand with colourful socks made from organic cotton (m/f), with a button so they don't get separated in the wash.
qnoop.com

Swedish Stockings
Environmentally-friendly and fashionable tights made from recycled threads.
swedishstockings.com – see also p. 069

Underprotection
Danish lingerie made of organic cotton, bamboo and soya, with colourful, graphic patterns.
underprotection.dk

Woron
Danish minimalist underwear brand (f), with pants, bras, bodies and leggings made of sustainable materials.
woronstore.com

AND ALSO
allvarunderwear.com / consciousstep.com / lafilledo.com / organicbasics.com / thenudelabel. com / saintbasics.com / soxs.co / wearbalzac.com

> See the guide of chapter 5 about leisure for more outdoor, sport and swimwear.

Bags and Jewellery

ARTICLE 22
'From bombs to bracelets'. Special American jewellery brand, made of aluminium scrap metal that the inhabitants of Laos find on their land. Laos is the most heavily bombed country per capita in history – this label works towards providing craftsmen economic livelihood. The name refers to the Universal Declaration of Human Rights.
article22.com

AUrate
Handmade American jewellery, from recycled gold, certified diamonds and better pearls. Stores in NY, Boston and Washington.
auratenewyork.com

Aurélie Chadaine
Minimalist handcrafted label made in Paris, with bags and accessories, inspired by the beauty of natural materials, such as vegetable-tanned and reused leather.
aureliechadaine.com

Denise Roobol
Stylish vegan handbags, sleeves and laptop bags made of fake leather, in the Netherlands.
deniseroobol.com

FREITAG
Smart, Swiss bags made of used truck tarpaulin, both in casual and fashionable styles. Now also offers compostable apparel collections (m/f).
freitag.ch

House of Eléonore
Dutch brand with jewellery and jewels made of Fairtrade gold and laboratory diamonds.
houseofeleonore.com

Lovia
Finnish luxury bag and accessories brand from rescued leather: Nordic elk or excess fabrics from industries that can't utilise these materials. Each bag comes with a product DNA (including price transparency), and is made in Italy.
loviacollection.com – see also p. 033

Made
Handmade jewellery and bags of recycled materials; the British brand supports communities and craftsmanship.
made.uk.com

Matt & Nat
Conquers the fashion world with stylish vegan bags. Instead of animal products, this Canadian brand uses material recycled from plastic bottles, cork, rubber and nylon – big celebrities are among the fans.
mattandnat.com

Mumbaistockholm
Swedish jewellery from recycled gold and silver, and conflict-free diamonds. You can hand in your own jewellery which they reuse (and you receive a discount).
mumbaistockholm.com

MYOMY
Dutch bags and accessories of vegetable-tanned leather, made in ethical conditions in India.
myomydogoods.com

Naomi Rachèl Timan
Handmade Dutch bag collection of reused fabric and leather from old sofas and clothes.
naomiracheltiman.com – see also p. 191

O My Bag
Classic bags with a fashionable twist, ethically made from Indian eco leather. Stores in Amsterdam and The Hague (NL).
omybag.nl – see also p. 046

AND ALSO
959.it / abeautifulstory.nl / baggu. com / dorakloppenburg.com / ecobling.com.au / fraenck.com / joannacave.com / kaliberfashion. berlin / kazmok.com / mokokolabs. com / pucbag.nl / taj.nl / we-wood.com

Shoes

Beyond Skin
British label with a varied collection of vegan shoes, made in Spain (f): from ballerinas to pumps and from boots to wedding shoes.
beyondskin.co.uk

Bhava
American, stylish vegan shoes (from pumps to flats and boots), handmade in Spain and Mumbai.
bhavastudio.com

Caboclo
Spanish brand with shoes and sandals (m/f) of vegetable-tanned leather, made with Brazilian craftsmanship. Two stores in Barcelona.
caboclobrasil.com

ekn footwear
German label with shoes and accessories (m/f), made in Europe from vegetable-dyed leather and natural materials (also a vegan line).
eknfootwear.com

Good Guys
French vegan shoes made of microfibre, canvas and natural rubber. Fashionable sneakers, brogues, boots and heels (m/f) – have won several design prizes.
goodguys.bigcartel.com

Melissa

Vegan and colourful shoes (f), made in Brazil, where waste and water are reused as much as possible. The material isn't always environmentally friendly, but increasingly from recycled PVC and old shoes. Collaborate with designers such as Vivienne Westwood.
melissa.com.br

Po-Zu

British ethical and sustainable footwear (made in Portugal): sneakers, boots, sandals (m/f/c).
po-zu.com

Timberland

American brand, known for the yellow *boot*, but also makes shoes, sneakers and accessories (m/f/c). Only uses leather from the best Leather Working Group factories and develops new recycled materials, such as fake canvas from PET bottles.
timberland.com

TOMS Shoes (and Eyewear)

For every pair of shoes (m/f/c) that this US label sells, it gives a pair to a child in need. They also apply this principle to sunglasses (they provide optometry), coffee (access to water) and bags (birth support). Part of the (not always sustainably-made) collection is vegan.
toms.com

Veja

Stylish French sneakers (m/f/c), Fairtrade certified and made together with local communities from environmentally-friendly materials such as canvas and natural rubber.
veja-store.com

AND ALSO

bottines.nl / ethletic.com / muroexe. com / nisolo.com / ofktfootwear.com / olsenhaus.com / rombaut.com / werner-schuhe.de

Hats and Glasses

Dick Moby

Dutch (sun)glasses brand, by surfers that want to fight plastic pollution. The black frames are made of acetate waste, the coloured biodegradable and the cleaning cloth from recycled PET bottles.
dick-moby.com

Pachacuti

The modern, classic Fairtrade hats (m/f) by this British label are made using traditional techniques, but in contemporary colours and styles.
panamas.co.uk

BEAUMONT ORGANIC

Yellow 108

American brand with hats and accessories (m/f/c) of recycled materials: fedoras, hats and caps, sunglasses and interior items.
yellow108.com

AND ALSO

ballo.co.za / gobi-amsterdam.com / iwantproof.com / neubau-eyewear. com / quazidesign.com / sticksandsparrow.com.au / two-o.com / vinylize.com

---

SECOND-HAND

There are an enormous amount of great second-hand shops, here a small selection.

Designer-Vintage

Buy and sell authentic second-hand designer items from major brands.
designer-vintage.com

KALO / Klädoteket / Kleiderei / L'Habiblioteque / LENA the fashion library / Sabina & Friends

Innovative fashion libraries in Copenhagen, Gothenburg, Cologne, Paris, Amsterdam and Stockholm. For a fixed amount per month, you have access to an endless wardrobe (f), from sustainable brands, young designers or vintage items (also for sale).

kalokopenhagen.dk / kladoteket.se / kleiderei.com / lhabibliotheque.com / lena-library.com – see also p. 065 / sabinaandfriends.se

REWEAR

Brings designer-lovers together (f): you can borrow clothes, shoes and bags from luxury brands out of someone else's wardrobe (worldwide).
rewear.co

The Next Closet

Well selected and broad collection of designer items, that you can also sell yourself.
thenextcloset.com – see also p. 060

Vestiaire Collective

One of the most well-known sites for second-hand high fashion and designer items (f/m/c). Gems from fashion houses such as Stella McCartney, Chanel and Gucci, verified for authenticity.
vestiairecollective.com

AND ALSO

beyondretro.com / buffaloexchange. com / ebay.com / etsy.com / glamcorner.com.au / unitedwardrobe.com

Do-it-yourself

bemorewithless.com/project-333 / clothingexchange.com.au / loveyourclothes.org.uk / offsetwarehouse.com / sewnatural.eu

---

INFORMATION

Clean Clothes Campaign

Aims to improve working conditions in the global garment industry. Pushes companies to take responsibility, supports workers, demands good legislation and gives tips to consumers. Website has lots of information, and actions to participate in.
cleanclothes.org

Ecouterre

Eco fashion blog with news, innovation, designers, tips and more.
ecouterre.com

Fashion Revolution

International organisation that wants to change the fashion industry,

founded by forerunners Orsola de Castro and Carry Somers in the wake of the Rana Plaza factory disaster on April 24th, 2013. Annually organises activities on that date; on the site, you can find information and tips. Publish a Transparency Index about major players.
fashionrevolution.org

Fur Free Alliance
Makes people aware of the animal cruelty caused by fur, works to ensure that people no longer buy or wear fur and politics take measures against the industry. Tips, info and a list of fur-free brands and stores.
furfreealliance.com / furfreeretailer.com

Good On You
Australian app that rates the sustainability of over 1,000 fashion brands. Also offers deals on labels that score well, the possibility to approach brands and a blog.
goodonyou.eco

Magnifeco
Blog, podcast, book and events about eco fashion and sustainable living. Brand profiles, emerging designers and innovative developments.
magnifeco.com

Make it last
Stylish Swedish sustainable fashion blog, focusing on timeless quality, redefining modern luxury and smart choices.
makeitlast.se

Mochni
Well-curated blog with brand profiles, interviews, do's and don'ts, green beauty guide and ingredient list, travel guides, a glossary and more.
mochni.com

Sustainably Chic
Stylish, comprehensive blog about sustainable fashion, eco lifestyle and clean beauty, full of lists, tips and profiles (bags, care, living, kids, etc.) and an overview of other blogs, podcasts and publications.
sustainably-chic.com

Wardrobe Crisis
Clare Press is Australian *Vogue*'s sustainability editor-at-large, ethical fashion advocate and journalist; has written various books on the subject and hosts podcast series Wardrobe Crisis.
clarepress.com

AND ALSO
anniinanurmi.com / consciouschatter.com / ethicalwriters.co / garbagepilestyle.com / mygreencloset.com / peta.org/living/fashion / remake.world / sustainabilityinstyle.com / theecoedit.co.uk

Certification and organisations
apparelcoalition.org / bcorporation.net / bkaccelerator.com / circle-economy.com / ec.europa.eu/environment/ecolabel / eco-age.com – see also p. 021 / ecofashionweek.nz / ecofashionweekaustralia.com / ethicalclothingaustralia.org.au / ethicalfashionforum.com / fairmined.org / fairtrade.net / fairwear.org / fashionforgood.com / global-standard.org / greenfashionweek.org / oeko-tex.com / made-by.org / naturtextil.de / redressdesignaward.com / responsiblemining.net / thecircle.ngo / wfto.com

>> More? The chapter 6 guide features websites and initiatives with information about a sustainable lifestyle.

GREEN KIDS

Stores

BÖF
Copenhagen + webshop (Den)
Wide selection of timeless basics from small, independent brands. The international webshop is categorised according to material.
boefboef.com

Mamaowl
webshop (UK)
Beautiful children's fashion made of organic materials.
mamaowl.net

Brands

Disana
This brand was one of the first to receive GOTS certification for their products, and produces in Germany. Washable diapers, and children's clothing made of organic cotton and mulesing-free wool.
disana.de

ManyMonths
Finnish label with woollen basics that grow with your children: the Adventurer size fits from 1 to 2.5 years old.
manymonths.com

Milk and Masuki
Childrenswear with graphic animal prints for kids from 0 to 8 years of GOTS-certified cotton. Also offer other sustainable children's brands in their webshop and physical store in Bowral, Australia.
milkandmasuki.com

Mini Rodini
An ode to the creativity and imagination of children. Made of sustainable materials and the Swedish brand is member of Fair Wear Foundation.
minirodini.com

Nature Baby
Shops and webshop in New Zealand with complete range of clothes, care products and furniture for the little ones.
naturebaby.eu

nOeser
Every Dutch nOeser collection is made from organic cotton, and in addition to the plain basics, there are beautiful prints, often animal themed. Almost everything is unisex.
noeser.eu

POPUPSHOP
Cool Danish children's clothing (and swimwear), much in grey and black and featuring photographic prints. The organic cotton is grown in Turkey, where the clothes are also made. They now have a GOTS-certified collection and bright swimwear for women too.
popupshop.com

Renting children's clothes
Don't buy, but rent – it's possible in increasingly more countries, such as via vigga.us (Den), happykiddo.be (Bel) or bebethreads.myshopify.com (UK).

INTRODUCTION

I started pretty late with facial care. I was well into my twenties when I first thought it might be a good idea to perhaps do something for my skin. It hadn't really occurred to me before, it just hadn't seemed necessary. Asking a friend for advice, she recommended Weleda. A stroke of luck then, that I got started with one of the most sustainable brands out there (since, I've tried and liked others too).

377

billion euros we annually spend on beauty products

But why, at that particular moment, was I suddenly struck by the need to take care of my skin? I was getting older, of course – but did I see that myself? And where did the urge to do something about it come from? Did I read somewhere that I needed it? And how did I link getting older to care products, and that they'd help? I'm still not absolutely sure this is always the case, if all those creams actually do what they claim. The problem is, of course, that there's no way to test this, unless you've got a twin brother or sister that doesn't use anything. So for now, I'm playing it safe. In general, I have the impression that natural ingredients benefit my skin. But I also want it to just be okay to get older.

Synthetic substances don't do anything anyway – many of them are made of petroleum and contain no active properties. They might feel nice to apply, but they close off your skin and dry it out, meaning you have to keep using (and buying) more and more. And that has everything to do with one of major issues of personal care: it's an industry. And not a small one either. Everything's focused on making you feel bad, ugly, old, wrinkly, fat and frumpy. So you buy products to change that. It's an incredibly commercial business, in which people are getting rich thanks to your low self-esteem, doubts and insecurities.

40.4

billion of this on men's cosmetics and personal care

I try to fight that. 90% of the time, I only use lipstick and nothing else. No foundation, blusher, corrector, primer, contouring, mascara, eyeshadow, eyebrow pencil. I try to accept myself as I am. This doesn't make me better than someone else, because I very much understand that you would use it. I'd really like to myself sometimes. Because is it easy? No, not at all, particularly in the fashion world. I often feel that I'm not good or good-looking enough, and even don't attend parties or events sometimes, because I think I can only go if I have a full face of make-up. And then *that* makes me feel bad. But I don't want to be the only one in photos with bags under my eyes, without the healthy glow and flawless skin. Behold the great contradiction and struggle. Because this isn't right, of course – if you stand for something then you should also walk the walk. But at the same time, I'm also vain, I want to be beautiful and for everyone to like me. I don't always shave my armpits, because that doesn't really

In a society that profits from your self doubt, liking yourself is a rebellious act

feel right to me either. That hair just grows there, it belongs there, why should it go? And even more importantly, why should women remove it, and not men? But every now and then I'll put on a top with sleeves when I actually wanted to wear that jumpsuit without. Because I don't want to be labelled as an activist, I don't want to embarrass my partner, or sometimes simply because I don't dare. And then I'm not really free – which in turn really annoys me about myself.

Most of us experience this. The pressure to look a certain way is huge. It's about skincare and make-up, but also your body shape. Just a reminder: you weren't put on this earth for the sole purpose of a thigh gap or flat stomach. Or to be very skinny, ultra-fit or whatever else. It helps to sometimes remind myself of this. Looking good is great, but not at the expense of everything. Because there's always something: skinny, bushy eyebrows, fit, hourglass, plucked eyebrows, curvy. It's never right, and you have the body you have – this is what you've got to work with. If you're naturally slim, it'll be difficult for you to achieve an hourglass figure (unless you get fat injected, always a possibility of course). And I just can't accept that we live in a society where this isn't okay. The time I've spent during

my life worrying about my body – what a waste! When I look at old photos, I think: girl, you were gorgeous! Not fat and just fine. I deal with this a lot better now, although such feelings still get to me sometimes.

So this goes way deep. Interestingly enough, often a lot more so for women than for men. But certainly not only women – more and more is emerging about the pressure men feel about their bodies. They too must look toned, clean-shaven (or not) and like a metro man (or not anymore). And this is just as tough as what females face and can lead to just as many problems. Traditionally though, the focus has primarily been on women. They must be beautiful. The 'beauty norm' almost always plays a part in how we are judged and treated. Women still earn less than men, are being judged continuously on their appearance and outfit and have been the targets of cosmetic companies for a long time. The influence of models and the way in which women are objectified in adverts, magazines and the media is undeniable. There's not enough variety, in size, age, colour and background – the ideal that we have to match up to is ridiculously limited. So let's stop that.

Easier said than done. Fortunately, for this chapter I was able to interview beauty experts, make-up artists, models and innovators. In the field of scent, for instance. From a young age, scent has played an important role in my life. But I've only been aware of this for a few years now. And I'm not talking about regular perfume, or about synthetic mixtures of substances that are often too heavy or fake smelling. No, I mean the healing effect of sniffing lavender. The happy potency of rosemary. Pick some, put it in your pocket, rub it between your fingers now and again and register what happens. Instant happiness. This book is written on scent energy (okay, and chocolate, chai lattes and sweet encouragements). We smell all day long, but we rarely realise it. It directs, reminds and warns us, attracts and repels us. So, don't use skincare products or make-up if you don't want them or need them, and even ignore everything in this chapter. But do me one favour, and *do* do more with scent. It can improve your life, give you energy, and make you feel good about yourself. And that's what this chapter (or book) ultimately is about.

168

chemicals are in the 12 care products women use on average daily (men use 6, containing 85 chemicals)

SKINCARE

EVOLVE · FRENCH GIRL · DR. ALKAITIS · TRUE ORGANIC OF SWEDEN · MADARA

Long Live your Biggest Organ

Our skin is the body's largest organ. On average, it covers a surface of 7m², and per 1cm² contains about 11 metres of blood vessels, 45 metres of nerves and 10 million cells. What?! Wow. The skin protects us, eliminates waste via sweat and sebum, and ensures our body can breathe. What kind of skin you have, what it looks like and how long it stays in good condition is largely down to genetics. But you can help. Particularly by making sure it doesn't dry out and oxidise, or in other words, perish. Your skin acts as a gateway for the transition from the outside world to our inner one. And while we're increasingly concerned about the food we put into our body, we don't yet do the same about what we put on it. Even though, for a large part, this is similar: your skin absorbs what it's fed. From what you apply on your skin, 60% ends up in your blood. It's said that if you can't eat something, maybe you shouldn't be rubbing it into your skin. High time then, to have a good look at how we take care of our precious armour.

Synthetic? Chemicals? Toxins? No.

Regular care and make-up products on the market contain a lot (in total, around 12,000 different) of chemicals. The reason for this is simple. They're cheap. Much, much cheaper than natural substances with healing properties. The glossy brands you see in magazines often spend more on advertising than on ingredients. The lower the costs, the higher the profit. Synthetic substances close off your skin – maybe you recognise the layer that vaseline-type products leave behind (and what lots of people like, especially on the lips it's addictive). Or they dry out your skin, so you need more and more. The biggest junk in regular care-products are substances associated with cancer, birth defects or fertility problems, substances with hormonal influence on our growth and recovery, persistent compounds that don't break down in our body or in nature, and substances that cause allergies or weaken our immune system. Now don't immediately start thinking: help,

During her lifetime, a British woman spends on average over 38,000 euros on facial care.

I've been using day creams for over twenty years, I'm mortally ill. This is intended as support, so you can make healthy choices, and become aware of the kinds of things you're putting on your skin. Here's a simplified and abbreviated list. Watch out for:

01 / Perfume or fragrances

These are general terms that can contain all kinds of things. Phthalates, for example, used to make plastic (such as your shower curtain) softer, but in fragrance to bind them to your skin and keep them smelling longer. They disrupt the hormone balance and are linked to infertility.

02 / Preservatives

(because if something contains water, it can culture bacteria or mould). Also an umbrella term that can mean lots of things. For example:

— Formaldehyde: which is in many products and linked to cancer.
— Parabens: ensure a longer shelf-life by killing yeasts and fungus. Associated with infertility, cancer and a strong, female, hormonal effect. Parabens get into your blood via the skin and even though there may only be a tiny amount per product, add it all up and you're applying quite a bit. Citric acid is, a natural alternative, for example.
— Phenoxyethanol: a preservative, just like parabens. Often in products loudly claiming to be paraben-free, but it comes from the highly-toxic phenol and causes many allergic reactions.
— Triclosan or triclocarban: both anti-bacterial and associated with fertility problems.

03 / Mineral oil, paraffin or petroleum jelly

These are petroleum-based oil, wax and grease. They completely seal your skin, meaning it can't breathe and dispose of waste substances. Underneath this sealed layer, your skin continues to dry out more and more, and doesn't produce sebum or fat to keep it elastic. Because your skin no longer self-regulates, you increasingly need more of the product. Vaselines and lip balms are usually made of this – recognise that feeling of having to keep applying? Products of petroleum are the cheapest to make, which is why, for example paraffin is widely used. Vegetable oils, such as nut, olive, sesame, argan or sunflower are natural alternatives.

04 / Silicones

The somewhat chicer variant of mineral oils, with almost the same effect. Can be found in luxury products, but they close off the skin like petroleum-based products.

05 / Foaming agents such as SLS and SLES

These provide the foaming effect of shampoo, gels and soap, but also dissolve your own fats, cause hair loss and in combination with other substances, can be carcinogenic. A bi-product of SLS and SLES, dioxane, also increases the risk of cancer. So what makes your hair foam can also make you lose it.

06 / Solvents such as PEGs *(add number)* and propylene glycol

PEG is polyethylene glycol, an emulsifier that ensures other substances blend. The higher the number, the bigger the chance of an allergic reaction. Carcinogenic substances are released during production. Propylene glycol is another solvent used to mix. Antifreeze in your car is also glycol, and the effect is drying and degreasing.

The Think Dirty app scans your personal-care products, tells you about the ingredients and rates how damaging they are. It now contains over 800,000 products, hopefully soon from all over the world. The Campaign for Safe Cosmetics also has a lot of information.

---

07 / Synthetic dyes and fragrances

These come from petroleum and can be harmful. They stay behind in your skin and there can cause all kinds of things, including discolouration. If it's in a perfume you really, really like, then spray it on your clothes or hair.

Fortunately already less common, but what really shouldn't be in your creams and gels, are these toxic substances: BHT/DBPC, butyl acetate, coal tar, ethanolamines, ethyl acetate and lead.

NATRUE

German certification for natural cosmetics, with brands such as Weleda, Dr. Hauschka and Lavera as members. Has three phases: a product can be certified natural, partly organic and completely organic.

BDIH, Cosmebio and ICEA

German, French and Italian certifications for natural products, also partly organic.

COSMOS

Collaboration between the major certification bodies for organic and natural cosmetics, to achieve more standardisation. Founded by BDIH, Cosmebio, Ecocert, ICEA and the Soil Association. Organic is the standard, and no animal testing, nanoparticles or genetically modified ingredients.

USDA Organic/Canada Organic

Certification of the United States Department of Agriculture. If a product has this label, at least 95% of the ingredients are organic. If at least 70% are organic, the product may be labelled 'Made with Organic' (no genetically-modified ingredients). Canada has a similar label: Canada Organic.

Australia has many different organic certifications, including NASAA and Australian Certified Organic.

>> You'll also sometimes see the EU Ecolabel, read about this on p. 054.

>> More information about many certifications (including Nordic Ecolabel or BioGro New Zealand) can be found on the Eco Label Index website.

What the Certifications Say

Choose certified organic and natural as much as possible. But, there are also very good brands or products without certification – because they can't afford it, for instance. Keep using your common sense and read the ingredient list to see what you're applying (the ingredient it contains most is mentioned first). Here are a few of the certifications you can look out for.

Ecocert

French certification organisation, specialised in natural products. For cosmetics with the strictest 'natural and organic cosmetic label', 95% of ingredients must be natural and a minimum of 10% must be organic (this also includes water, which can't be certified and is the main ingredient of most products – up to 60%). This doesn't automatically mean that the product is also made ethically.

Soil Association

British certification with the strictest demands for personal-care products. The ingredients must be 100% organic, or 95% or 70% (represented by different labels). The rest then can't be toxic or genetically modified and must be vegetable based and harmless. If an ingredient's available organically, then it must be used. Doesn't necessarily say anything about ethical trade.

A Fresh Start

If you feel you're dependent on products or addicted to make-up, try using less for a while, or even nothing at all. In a month your skin will be completely renewed, so the substances you've rubbed into it have disappeared. Start afresh. What do you actually need? Only cleansing, and if you really have a dry skin, perhaps hydrating using a little moisturiser, this may be enough. Admire and preserve your natural beauty. You can also care for your skin from the inside out. Rich omega 3 fats contribute to a smooth skin, glossy hair and strong nails, and drinking enough water ensures less

**Dutch women spend 5.3 hours per week on personal care /
Men 3.9 hours / Women do it primarily for themselves, while
men predominantly find it important for others**

dehydration. Prevention is better than a cure, so try to figure out why you have that spot (stress, unhealthy eating, lack of sleep?). We've the tendency to plaster it with all sorts of things. Your skin loses overview and balance from all those lotions, serums, creams, masks, gels and tonics. Intervene less, radiate more – you can always give it a go.

It Costs More, Yet Less

Sustainable personal-care products cost more than standard brands. No doubt about it. But at the same time, they don't. This is why:
> Synthetic products really don't work, they contain few or no active ingredients. In fact, they dry out

KESTER BLACK

your skin, so you continue to use more. You pay little, but actually too much, and just keep spending.
> Natural products are more expensive, but more powerful. So you need less.
> With regular cosmetics, the price of environmental pollution and what it really costs to make (and to clean up) is not included, sustainable cosmetics are more likely to do this.
> We nearly always use too much. Whatever you do, don't use products you don't need and in any case, less: our skin can't absorb it all.
> Do you really need a separate day cream, night cream, eye cream and neck cream, or is it just a marketing trick?
On average, women use more than twelve personal-care products a day. Do we really need all of these? That spot will disappear more quickly of you don't cover it. Without lots of make-up, our skin can breathe, and you'll become more comfortable with the way you look. Can you, and do you dare, go without that 'mask'? I think so. There's a natural beauty inside everybody... The profit made by the cosmetics industry is based on your self-image and idea of happiness. Make sure you're in charge of that.

Cruelty-Free, of Course

In Europe, selling products that have been tested on animals is banned. Cosmetics tested on animals in other countries aren't allowed into stores either. International rules are not always as stringent or equal, so be careful. It's totally unnecessary to use mice or monkeys to test our products.

There are quite a few brands that don't have any problem with this, and do use animals outside of the EU, for example. If a brand wants to enter the Chinese market, it's obligatory that it's tested on animals. Pressure from China is huge, because the market is enormous and money beckons. Brands such as MAC, who first proudly displayed an animal-testing free statement on their website, have succumbed to this.

The international Humane Cosmetics Standard can be recognised by 'The Leaping Bunny' logo. Only for brands that are 100% animal-testing free.

> Animal protection organisation PETA has a good list on their website of brands that don't use any animal testing (and an iPhone app with urgent actions against animal cruelty). They have their own logo for products: also a rabbit, but then with ears shaped like a heart.

Don't want to use any animals at all to make yourself beautiful? Then look for the ever-broader assortment of vegan products. Remember that vegan does not automatically mean natural or organic, and vice versa. Avoid:
Glycerine: can be vegetable-based, but also often comes from animal fat – check the label.
Keratin: from animal bones, hair and hooves.
Collagen: from fish, mostly in anti-ageing creams.
Lanoline: from oil from sheep's wool.
Silk: spun by caterpillars, particularly put in expensive products.
Carmine: red dye made from crushed lice (also called E120). ⟶

'Pay attention to your diet, your lifestyle and your mind, how you think. Meditate, for example, work out and say what you want to say. Don't turn yourself into a walking time-bomb. This'll help the way you look. I'm angered, for instance, by all the marketing money that's used to paint a dishonest picture of what skincare could mean for people. They believe and fall for the lies, resulting in them not only feeling unhappy, but their skin becoming worse too. The fakeness of the cosmetic industry bothers me, there are so many lies. We don't live in a journey, we live here, it's now! So if you don't dance right now, sing or have fun, then you never will. Because in your eighties it's too late. Don't worry about getting from A to Z, but engage with letters B and C and be in the moment. Enjoy what you have and take good care of each other.'

Alexander Dikkes, natural skincare expert

> Also be careful with hair and make-up brushes. They're made from animal hair more often than you might realise.

> Want to be certain? Choose products featuring the Vegan logo (with the sunflower).

Plastering Yourself with Plastic

Plastic is in a vast number of personal-care products. Strange but true. Who wants that on their face? It wouldn't sell if it was featured on the label. And so they don't, or disguise it in names you don't recognise. The pieces are tiny and called microbeads. In the chapter about fashion I've already written about microscopically small pieces of plastic that come out of polyester clothes in the wash and pollute the water. This is also what happens with these microbeads. So not only are you plastering your skin with plastic, it also ends up down the drain, in the sewers and eventually the sea. Fish and birds eat the particles, beaches clog up. The particles are particularly widespread in scrubs and peels, but also, for example, in shampoo and toothpaste. Major brands such as Estée Lauder and Revlon like to use them in their products. It probably goes without saying, but: don't use microbeads.

> Avoid products with polyethylene, nylon, polypropylene, polyethylene terephthalate and polymethyl methacrylate.

> Have a look at the Beat the Microbead website, and download their free app. You can use it to scan the barcode of products to see if they are 'free', there's a list of good brands and products and lots of information about (un)safe personal care.

> From 2018, the UK has banned the production and sale of microbeads in 'rinse-off' products such as soap and toothpaste (it's still allowed in make-up and sunscreen that you don't rinse off, after powerful lobby from the industry). Hopefully it will soon be extended and other countries will follow suit.

Microbeads are Mega-Bad

– Every time you use a personal-care product, 5,000 to 95,000 microbeads are released. The particles accumulate in the fish that we eat (and in plankton, their food).

– Aquatic animals often don't see the difference between food and plastic. Some birds also eat plastic because to them, it smells like food. In a study, microplastic was found in more than a third of the 670 fish examined, with one fish containing 83 pieces.

– When microbeads break down, harmful, toxic substances are released: they can cause hormonal abnormalities and neurological diseases. Especially if substances have been added during production, such as flame retardants: they all leak into aquatic life.

– Microplastics in toothpaste are 100 times smaller than in scrubs. They're found on almost every beach and in every ocean around the world, and on ice caps at the North and South Pole.

– They sink to the bottom, so there's a lot we can't see. The ocean contains 5,000 billion floating pieces of plastic, weighing in total more than 250,000 tonnes. According to UNEP, microplastics are the ocean's most harmful pollutants.

ABEL

80,000

The American NGO Environmental Working Group
has examined roughly 80,000 products, whether they
contain toxic substances, to what extent and the
subsequent dangers. Their Skin Deep Database checks
cosmetics, sunscreen, nail varnish, hair products, perfumes
and skincare for men and women – try looking up your
favourite brands. The Good Guide website does something
similar, for personal-care products, food, household
products and children's goods.

Fairy Tales, Fables and Greenwashing

All kinds of claims are also made by the personal-care industry. Don't fall for them:
— An increasing number of brands are proud to declare they don't use something, for example that they're paraben-free. This can also be to distract from another, unfriendly ingredient they use instead. So keep checking the label.
— View words such as pure, natural, hypoallergenic, healthy and green with some reservation. Non-regulated terms, easy to splash over the packaging, and can be indicators of greenwashing.
— Is one ingredient featured prominently on the packaging? Check its position in the ingredient list: what's in it most should be at the top. Is the spirulina, rosehip, aloe vera or green tea at the end of the list? This is called angel dusting: boasting about something that's barely in it.

I Love Sunshine

Oh my, the sun... We can't live without it and you just feel how glorious it is to have those rays caressing your skin. We need vitamin D from the sun, to feel good and healthy and to grow bones and muscles. It's also in eggs and oily fish, but this doesn't help vegans of course. The big star provides us with most of our vitamin D. A shortage leads to weaker muscles and bones, but also a downturn in our mood. It can certainly be behind a winter dip or depression. But this doesn't mean we should all start sunbathing for hours on end. Burning is an absolute no-go, and sun rays age your skin, cause wrinkles and in the worst case, cancer. This is what you need to know:
— SPF stands for 'sun protection factor'. The sun protection factor protects above all against UVB rays (for 'burn'). There are also UVA rays, that cause ageing ('age'), so preferably choose a product that works against both. UVB is stopped by glass, UVA usually not.
— Your body makes vitamin D as soon as you're in the sun. For most of us, fifteen to thirty minutes of rays on our hands and face daily (without sunscreen) is enough. Your skin doesn't endlessly keep making vitamin D, so it's not a case of 'the longer the better'. Slowly creating a good pigment protection layer (that beautiful tan!) against the

sun is important. So also in autumn and winter get outside as often as you can.
— A high factor doesn't mean that you can stay in the sun a lot longer. So, don't go baking in the sun with factor 50 for twice as long as with 30 – that's not how it works.
— UV is also in the light you pick up when you're sat in the shade. You can burn on a cloudy day too.
— It can be tempting to go for a cheaper, lower factor (and bronze up nicely), but don't use lower than 30, and definitely not if you've got pale skin.
— In any case, you don't use enough. Almost all studies show that everybody applies too little to achieve the factor on the packaging. I don't like the feel of it either, but it has to be done.
— Standard sun products contain a chemical filter, and therefore lots of chemicals. Your skin absorbs them and they get into your bloodstream. Some filters even trigger a reaction when they come into contact with the sun, and cause free radicals that can be very harmful (which also happens when you burn, so what's the point of these products?). Don't use sunscreen containing oxybenzone, nor those with avobenzone, benzophenone and octyl methoxycinnamate.
— Go for brands with a natural (physical) sun filter such as zinc oxide or titanium dioxide, which not only work best, but also take care of the skin. Some will leave a white film, so test on your skin first.
— In the heat of the day you're better off not going in the sun anyway. I avoid between midday and 2, others even say between 11 and 3.
— Also a good idea: wear a hat and clothing to protect your skin.
— Burnt anyway? Drink enough water to stay hydrated, and treat your skin with cucumber, yoghurt or (homegrown) aloe vera.

>> *Choose brands with natural filters and better ingredients, such as Biosolis, COOLA, Eco Cosmetics, John Masters Organics, Raw Elements.*

Less Packaging, More Storing

Do you recognise this – that you buy something and think: goodness me, plastic foil, a bow, stickers, a cardboard and plasticised box, a glass jar with plastic labels and large lid, a paper brochure and a construction to hold the box in place? Wow.

MERAKI / DR. ALKAITIS / OWAY / COOLA / EVOLVE / KESTER BLACK / MUKTI / LESS IS MORE / TRUE ORGANIC OF SWEDEN / MÁDARA

WE'RE APPLYING, BUT WHO'S SUPPLYING?

Nearly every certification, and much of the information relating to natural cosmetics, concerns the ingredients. Makes sense, as this is the part that actually goes into your body. But sustainable is also: made with respect for people. What about them? What are the conditions and what's the reward for farmers and workers making organically-certified products? Some organic certifications, such as Ecocert, also make demands of production of resources and the end product. But often these subjects aren't at all mentioned. It would be really good if certification bodies and brands would take this a lot more serious. There are brands that explicitly work fair trade, such as cocokind, Dr. Bronner's and FAIR SQUARED, and Weleda also provides some information about this. The more, the better.

A good example of this is the murky flip-side of 'shine' in cosmetics. The glossy effect of shampoo, for example, is created by mica. This is a collective name for 37 minerals, from the Latin word micare, which means to sparkle. It reflects and breaks light, and is used to give paint, car lacquer and cosmetic products a pearlescent effect. Mica is sourced from rocks, often by children. There are estimated to be 20,000 children working in mines – worldwide, but particularly in India and China. Danger of collapse, deadly lung diseases, working in the sweltering sun. They don't go to school and work long hours. Terre des Hommes campaigns against child labour and exploitation, on their website you can see how you can help.

The less packaging, the better it is for the environment. Makes sense. And then preferably also made of recycled, environmentally friendly or biodegradable material. But at the same time, you also want to keep products for as long as possible of course, so you don't have to throw them away. This balance, pretty much:

— Don't buy too many products at the same time. If you first use what you have, you don't have to throw anything away.

— Choose smaller, airtight packages you can't keep for so long. Often, these don't contain harmful preservatives. Or opt for bulk that stays good for a while when closed, and refill. Also cheaper.

— Don't save natural products for too long anyway. They'll lose their powerful effects and bacteria can get into them as they don't contain chemical preservatives.

— But also don't care too much about expiration dates. If it still looks and smells okay, then it's fine. It's something that needs to be on the packaging, but completely depends on your own common sense. There's far too much being thrown away unnecessarily.

— About the POA ('period after opening') – that's that picture of the open pot with for example 6M or 12M on it. This means you can keep it for this many months after opening. As a guideline, fine, but don't keep to it rigidly. Mascaras last about three to six months, creams six months to a year, sunscreen and cleansers a year, powders two years, lipsticks two to three years, the same as deo and soap.

— A pot is easier to empty and reuse. A tube not so easy and needs to be thrown away – but the

'Less is more. Don't use cotton wool but apply everything using your hands. Wash your hair less frequently. In most cases, shower gel's rarely needed, the skin can take care of itself. And if you use products because they make you feel good, then do choose clean and sustainable brands. Why wouldn't you use sustainable, healthy cosmetics? In the end, it's no more expensive, better for your health and all the other rubbish is really a waste of money. For regular products, the price of environmental pollution and the true costs of making them are not calculated. People often don't realise that actual costs aren't included in such a low price. In addition, these synthetic ingredients do nothing at all, except dry out your skin, which only makes you buy and spend more. Sustainable care-products contain ingredients that work. So you can throw away a tenner on something that doesn't do anything and then keep spending because you need to keep applying. Or you can invest a bit more in something that actually works.

If you spend a short amount of time in the sun unprotected, morning or late afternoon, your skin can produce vitamin D and its own sun protection. The skin thickens, and melanin comes to the surface. This also tans you. Alternatively, you can use natural filters, such as zinc oxide and titanium dioxide, or a non-harmful synthetic filter like octocrylene.'

Caroline van Eeuwijk, owner of sustainable beauty salon and shop C. Cosmetics in Amsterdam

opening is much smaller and you don't touch the product with your fingers, meaning it lasts longer. Choices!

— Try cutting a tube in half if nothing more is coming out – you'll be surprised how much is still in it.

— A growing number of brands have packaging-free cosmetics, like the solid shampoo by Lush or crystal deodorants.

— Avoid aerosol cans with hairspray, deo or after-shave, they contain harmful propellants. A pump is nicer to use anyway, or a roller or stick.

— Do you like to use cotton wool? Try using it on both sides, it works fine. And preferably choose organic and/or Fairtrade cotton. You can also simply wash your face with your hands, or with a washcloth or biodegradable konjac sponge (made from the Asian porous root vegetable).

Do-it-Yourself

I should actually do this more often too. We don't have to buy all those masks and scrubs, they're easy to make ourselves. Just with what we have in the fridge. Why not give it a try? Cheaper and fun:

01 / The tip from make-up artist Lou Dartford (see p. 101): 'A model once gave me a great recipe during a shoot, to use at night if you've suddenly got spots. Mix garlic, coconut oil and heather honey and apply as a mask: it really works!'

02 / Aloe vera plant at home? Cut off a leaf, break or cut open and rub the liquid on burnt or scraped skin.

03 / Dry skin? Mix a mashed avocado with a tablespoon of honey, apply and rinse off after 10 minutes. Mixing two tablespoons of yoghurt with a spoonful of honey ensures soft, glowing skin after only 10 minutes.

04 / Sugar, salt and used coffee beans are great for scrubbing. Mix a few spoonfuls with organic olive oil and rub over your body. Pop under the shower, and you'll be as good as new. Also great for dry, rough hands.

>> British botanist James Wong wrote the book *Grow Your Own Drugs*, full of natural recipes (eye gel, soap or sunscreen) for a range of ailments, or for relaxation – made as much as possible of kitchen-cupboard ingredients.

MAKE-UP AND HAIR

11

days per month
is what
an American
woman on
average spends
on her hair
(and in terms of
money, annually
almost 47,000
euros)

Eye of the Beholder

So I don't wear that much make-up, but am very aware of being kind of an exception to the rule. I only use a little bit of powder if I'm going to an important event or having my photo taken. I occasionally wear mascara, and when I do, I use lots as my eyelashes aren't particularly long which means, understandably, that I like them to look gigantic. What you'll almost always see me with though, is lipstick. And so that has got to stay on; once it's gone, immediately there's nothing left of my face. Therefore I like a lipstick that lasts, otherwise I have to constantly

keep reapplying. That really requires chemical substances. What's more sustainable: a regular brand that you only use once and lasts for a long time? Or a sustainable brand that you have to reapply four times a day and is finished quickly? For your body, the second, for the environment I'm not so sure. So for now I alternate between these two strategies.

01. Regular make-up contains an enormous number of chemical substances. Some are associated with cancer, hormonal disruption, allergies – exactly the same as with personal-care products. If you apply them to your lips, you swallow them, and on your eyes or nails they get into your body through your skin. Not the best idea (also not for the environment).

02. A study demonstrated ten years ago that two-thirds of the red lipsticks examined contained lead. I like to wear red lipstick. Hopefully there's now been slight improvement, but still. Check out your favourite brands online in the Skin Deep Cosmetics Database or Good Guide.

03. Choose natural and preferably organic brands: there are lots in the guide at the end of this chapter.

INTERVIEW

LOU DARTFORD

Lou Dartford (1979) is a British make-up artist and beauty blogger, who only uses sustainable products. She's worked for magazines such as *Grazia*, *Nylon* and *Wonderland*, and for artists including Tiny Tempah and Birdy.

Is it easy to find sustainable professional make-up?

'It was very difficult, but it's becoming increasingly easy. I think because the demand is growing and because green technology is constantly developing. The products can now compete easily with conventional brands. The current boom in clean health and beauty is also pushing it into the mainstream. The brands aren't so easy to find in regular stores yet though, most of them you must buy online or in independent boutiques or health food stores. Hopefully this'll soon change. And not everything's available: waterproof needs synthetic ingredients to make it water repellent, and neon colours don't exist in the natural world. So you'll sometimes have to compromise.'

What do we have to pay attention to when buying personal-care products and make-up?

'Read the product labels, just as you would do with food. The longer the list, the bigger the chance it contains things you don't want to be in there. In any case, watch for parabens, phthalates triclosan, SLS, SLES, mineral oil, paraffin and anything that comes from petroleum'.

Which make-up brands do you recommend?

'RMS Beauty, Dr. Hauschka, Weleda, Vapour Beauty, W3LL PEOPLE, Inika, ILIA, The Organic Pharmacy, Therapi Honey Skincare, Pai Skincare, Tata Harper, Absolution (the best organic lipstick!) and Neal's Yard Remedies.'

Who are your heroes?

'Make-up artist Rose-Marie Swift has worked with all the big names. She's founder of RMS Beauty, an organic make-up line. I can listen to her for hours. Imelda Burke is also a big hero of mine. She's a major influence on the green beauty revolution. About eight years ago she launched her Content Beauty boutique, at a time when there were very few sustainable brands. Now, her shelves are brimming with cool, cutting-edge products. It's *the* place for anyone who wants to learn about natural care-products.'

Lou's top sustainable skincare and make-up tips

> Choose brands with minimum, environmentally friendly, or refillable packaging

> Go for glass as much as possible and recycle your pots

> Choose organic and fair-trade cotton-wool and buds and recycled tissues

> Mousseline wipes are great to cleanse your skin (and can be used often), washable cotton-wool is also handy

> Try a product before you buy it, so that you don't have to throw it away if you don't like it

> Choose make-up and hairbrushes made of sustainable wood or bamboo instead of plastic $\longrightarrow$

Lou's London hotspots

01 / Neal's Yard Remedies 'Wonderful organic beauty brand, with a wide range of herbal and homeopathic remedies, tea, tinctures and other wellbeing products.'

02 / The Gate 'Really lovely vegetarian restaurant.'

03 / Riverford at The Duke of Cambridge 'Organic pub with delicious food and drink.'

04 / The Keep 'Sustainable boutique full of things I'd love to have in my wardrobe!'

05 / The MaE Deli 'Cafés of the food blogger Deliciously Ella, with the most amazing healthy, vegan food.'

06 / Content Beauty 'An amazing organic-beauty boutique. They've got a really good webshop, but if you're in London, you really should visit the store. It may be small, but has a huge, well-selected range of sustainable products. They also provide facials and acupuncture.'

Natural Beauty

This part is dedicated to Alicia Keys. She's cool, feisty and a hero. Of course, she's a great singer (I've lost count of the number of times I've sung *'New Yohork, concrete jungle where dreams are made of'* at the top of my lungs – sorry neighbours...). But a while ago she hit the headlines because she'd decided to stop using make-up. Because she no longer wants to feel insecure, no longer wants to hide behind a mask. Because she wants to be able to be herself and feels more liberated and powerful than ever without make-up. She hopes to kick-start a revolution, in which everyone with #nomakeup can share. Of course, you can think: okay, but Alicia Keys is beautiful. And you'd be right. But without make-up, she looks very different to the Alicia Keys you're accustomed to. And you are beautiful too. And so am I.

Alicia wrote a statement about this on the Lenny Letter website, a feminist platform created by ground-breaking actress and writer Lena Dunham (do go and have a look).

More celebrities share this frame of mind. Leandra Medine, from the well-known fashion and lifestyle blog Man Repeller, doesn't wear make-up. Because she's lazy, she says, and because she's satisfied with the way she looks, and accepts the wrinkles, bags and anything else that's part of her. Magazines are reluctantly joining the movement – which certainly already existed before Alicia Keys 'converted', but was given a major boost by her. *Glamour* interviewed Mila Kunis, who appeared without make-up in an (unedited) photo. Great quote from Mila: *'I don't wear make-up. I don't wash my hair every day. It's not something that I associate with myself. I commend women who wake up 30, 40 minutes early to put on eyeliner. I think it's beautiful. I'm just not that person.'* Almost all the images you see in magazines have been manipulated quite heavily after the shoot, with Photoshop or other programmes. There are appeals for this to always be mentioned alongside the photos, so that everyone realises they're not real. But for the time being, quite the opposite is the case, and it's pretty unique if there's a statement somewhere that a photo hasn't been photoshopped. Back to Mila Kunis: *'I hate it. There was a company that I did a photo shoot for once that manipulated the photo so much, I was like, "That's not even me." Like, what's the point? You wanted my name, and then you wanted the version of me that I'm not.'*

The More Hair, the Better

I cut my hair quite drastically some time ago. And that while I've spent my whole life wanting more hair. I was always one of those people that almost never went to the hairdresser, because then I always got upset so much had to be chopped... Now that it's shoulder length, it's a bit thicker – although still couldn't be described as thick. It is, and will always be, lanky – and now and again resembles a flat pancake on my head. Regular cuts are a good idea, and not washing it too often. You can do these more sustainable things:

Wash less frequently

Your hair doesn't actually want to be super-clean. This makes it dry, brittle and lacklustre. And greasy: we wash our hair every day because it's greasy, but it becomes greasy because we wash it every day. Washing strips the grease, making your scalp overcompensate and produce even more grease. Try to wash less frequently for a while, and your hair will come more into balance. Beach hair, just out of bed hair: basically all trends that propagate washing less for better, fuller hair. Still a bit greasy, but you don't want to wash it? Bring on that ponytail or topknot!

Wash sustainably

Regular shampoos, conditioners and styling products are also full of toxins and chemicals. You massage them through your hair and skin, rinse them out towards the sea or spray them on your scalp (and so inside of you). $\longrightarrow$

I LOVE
YOUR HAIR!

Try something else

Rinsing with water only seems to work very well for some hair types, or using products such as vinegar, soda or oil. The internet is full of suggestions – olive oil masks to moisturise, for instance.

Non-toxic dyeing

Want to dye your hair? Avoid the standard products containing toxins, such as ammonia, peroxide, formaldehyde, phenyl diamine and coal tar. There are few alternatives that truly achieve the same result (maybe natural henna), so you could consider dyeing less often (deep breath). Is that grey really that bad?

Use less

Nowadays, we're using five or six hair products a day, including mousse, gel, prep, spray, wax etc. Less is better and none is best, something like that.

Natural brands

Choose brands such as Intelligent Nutrients, Oway, John Masters Organic or Less is More (and find a green hairdresser) – see the guide at the end of this chapter.

KEVIN.MURPHY

Nails and Varnish

If someone has a top tip for strengthening nails, then I'd love to hear it. I've had brittle nails that break easily my entire life – it doesn't matter what I do: change my diet, take vitamins... This is why I like to wear nail varnish, as it looks better and the layer reinforces them a bit. It's probably not the best thing for your body: even if you choose brands that don't contain certain substances, you're still applying something that sticks so well it stays on for days. While you shower, do the washing up or work out. Nail polish can't actually be made completely without synthetic ingredients (yet). Just because there are less toxins in it, doesn't mean it's natural (and the substances may also end up in you or the environment). So if you go for it (my favourite is sky blue), keep this in mind:

— Make sure it's at least '5-free' (and preferably 7 or 10-free): that it contains no toluene, DBP (dibutyl phthalates), formaldehyde, formaldehyde resin and camphor (and no parabens, but that's already quite the norm).

— Don't apply out of habit: your nails also need rest (and you'll then of course use less).

— Make sure you have a good base, making it less easy for the substances to enter your bloodstream. Your varnish will stay on longer, too.

— Keep your nail varnish in the fridge, it'll stay applicable for longer. Mix with a basecoat or topcoat if it's become too thick.

— Choose better brands such as Floss Gloss, Kester Black or Kure Bazaar (see the guide for more).

Free tip. Healthy eating, drinking enough water, sleeping well, little stress and lots of laughter is said to have the best effect on your appearance. Nothing shop-bought can compete.

Let's focus on
the pay gap, not the
thigh gap

APPEARANCE

The Pressure is Huge

Standards about how your body should look are constantly changing – from curvy in the fifties, to heroin-chic in the nineties and nowadays, healthy and fit. From make-up looks with extremely thin, or alternatively bushy eyebrows, and from long, wavy, thick hair to extremely short pixie cuts. From large and muscular to thin and lean for the men. Actually, it's never right, it shifts super-fast, and worst of all: it's specifically intended to make you feel you're not good enough. The message is: you don't look like you're supposed to look, only when you buy our products will you belong. As long as you're not happy with yourself, it's okay, because then you remain vulnerable for the message that you can fix this by buying (clothes and accessories), buying (creams and make-up) and buying (diet products and cosmetic procedures).

The outside is perhaps easier to tackle than the inside. There are ample examples of women (and men!) who discover, after plastic surgery for example, that it hasn't done much for their self-esteem or acceptance. Contentment comes from the inside-out. Of course, it helps if you feel you look okay, but it would be great if we no longer let this depend on the prevailing norms or what companies think we should be. It's time to win back our beauty, and to celebrate diversity. For me, all of this is certainly a reason to choose sustainable care-products that base their adverts more on what their products can do for your skin than on what you should look like.

Models and Us

The personification of many of these issues. Models are inspiring, beautiful and yet also controversial. The influence of models and the way in which people are idealised in advertisements, magazines and the media is undeniable. There's not enough variety, in size, age, colour and background – the beauty ideal is frustrating and limited. Size-zero models tell us we should also be like them. Not literally of course, but figuratively. There are all kinds of protests, but the defence from the fashion world is often that clothes look better on a person who resembles a coat hanger. This is true to a certain extent, in the sense that many people will agree with it. Only, this view of beauty is also a learned, culturally determined opinion. There have been times (and those will come again) we thought very differently about this. Of course, models also think about this. And naturally, some concern themselves with their role in society, with what they want to be and to contribute, and how they can use their fame for something good. There's also more and more openness about the world behind the perfect picture. They post before and after photos on social media showing exactly what make-up and editing does. Models such as Adriana Lima and Romee Strijd give interviews, opening up about their ideal, and not so ideal, lives. That they themselves never look like this and are simply really good at knowing what their good angles are and how they should turn their bodies. That they are just as insecure, how difficult it is to always be judged on your appearance and still try to be happy with yourself. More and more is happening:

> Some magazines ban ultra-skinny or too young girls. *Vogue*, for example, has drawn up a 'health pact' in which they promise not to book models that appear to have an eating disorder or are under 16. Models must be able to eat healthily behind the scenes and their privacy must be respected.

> Models in France now need a doctor's certificate stating they have a healthy weight before they can step onto the catwalk. This has been French law since December 2015. Their body mass index (BMI) must be compatible with modelling: those who book a model without such a statement, risk a fine of 75,000 euros and a prison sentence of up to six months. Media that publish photos of photoshopped models must also accompany them with a label stating that they have been manipulated. Leni's Model Management is one of the first agen-

cies to promote another version of beauty. Leni Renton wants to create a healthy body image, without being a plus-size bureau. She's also committed to the introduction of rules in the field of digital editing.

> New Amsterdam agency The Movement Models was set up to stretch traditional beauty standards, and cast characteristic and cool personalities; Australian Rïin Models to represent dark-skinned models. We need many more people of colour on covers and runways, such as the amazing Alek Wek, Jourdan Dunn, Liu Wen, Rob Evans, Chanel Iman etc. There's still much to do in terms of diversity, ethnic background and age. Older women wonder why clothes meant for them is shown on models that could be their (grand)daughters. They don't identify with what they see, which isn't smart, because on average, it's a wealthy target group. And why do we see young, blonde girls 99% of the time? As if nothing else exists, and as if they are the only ones who have money to spend. Fortunately, older models like Veronica Webb, Maye Musk and Daphne Selfe are the new stars – hopefully their number will grow. Also, powerful regular-size (or plus-size, as they're maddingly called in the industry) models are conquering the fashion world. Succesful changemakers such as

Robyn Lawley, Philomena Kwao, Ashley Graham, Iskra Lawrence, Tara Lynn, Precious Lee and Zach Miko (this includes men too!) bring much-needed diversity and raise their voice. The 'body positive' movement, pioneered by amongst others Katie Willcox, is strong and important.

> The Model Alliance was founded by model Sara Ziff. She brings together models, agencies, casting directors and scientists to campaign for fair treatment and equal opportunity in the model and fashion industry. The website contains many resources and calls to action, about issues such as healthcare, sexual harassment and child models. Platform The Model's Health Pledge promotes safe and good working conditions for models. They can report abuse and find information about for instance food and business. Some fifty fashion companies have now joined, including modelling agencies and magazines.

Model, fair-trade fashion ambassador and my good friend Rebecca Pearson supports colleagues and new models with her platform and blog, Modeltypeface. She writes very openly about the modelling industry, about their rights and her own experiences. She's often invited to talk about body image in the media – this is her story (overleaf).

REBECCA PEARSON

Rebecca Pearson is a sought-after British model. She's shot for *Vogue*, *ELLE* and *Glamour* and worked for the likes of The Body Shop, Nivea, People Tree and L'Oréal. She's also a writer and runs the blog Modeltypeface, with tips for models and information about their rights. She's an outspoken opinion leader on body image and has commented about this issue in media such as BBC News, Sky News and *The Telegraph*.

You're a model for sustainable brand People Tree and ambassador for fair trade. Why is this important to you?

'When I started modelling for People Tree, I saw that ethical fashion can be stylish, flattering and even sexy. I can vividly remember my first shoot. It was a long day with an endless change of outfits, but I was excited by each and every item. I then accompanied the brand to Bangladesh, where we drove through the horrific Dhaka to their factories. There, the workers get a fair wage and conditions that everyone should be able to expect. I now have a personal connection with the label 'Made in Bangladesh'. I can buy clothes from a brand on the regular high street, and envision the slums, the homelessness, the begging, the filthy factories and despair, or I can imagine workers in a clean, safe factory where men and women are paid equally, have childcare and benefit from community initiatives. Many people are oppressed by the industry I work in: I'm directly connected to them. As someone with a conscience I have to raise my voice and help to bring change from within.'

What's the effect of fashion images and advertisements on the way we feel about ourselves?

'I think that sometimes, when we see an advertisement, we see ourselves in place of the model. There's a sense of illusion and escapism, but there can be a sense of alienation when the dominant image is that of a young, thin, white woman. I think strides are being made: catwalks and magazines are slowly becoming more ethnically diverse. But there is a narrow beauty ideal. The older I get, the more empathy I have for everyone who says adverts have a negative effect on their self-esteem, because they feel they can never meet such a one-sided ideal.'

Do you think the models used are too thin or too young?

'Models are becoming younger and thinner. It's crazy, because the people with money buying the clothes are older. I do think it's strange to use a young teenager to sell clothes to adult women. And yes, there's pressure to be thin in modelling – and that translates to the rest of the world, where the diet industry makes billions on a global scale. I've met lots of models who have a messed-up attitude to food and their body because of the pressure they've felt ever since they were scouted. But I'm also careful when talking about weight. Growing up, I was often taunted about being too skinny, and lots of models that I know are naturally thin with a healthy appetite. How people talk about weight often sets women (and men!) up against each other, and people comment on photos with "disgustingly thin" or "real men prefer curves", without thinking about the consequences of those words.'

What would help to make fewer people feel bad, ugly or not thin enough?

'This is such a huge, personal question. I think campaigns featuring a larger variety of age, body shapes and ethnicity would help. But we also have to look at why it's such big industry to make so many people feel bad about themselves. We have to buy-buy-buy, and therefore believe what we've just bought is already "out", and we'd only feel prettier, thinner and cooler when we buy the latest. Since getting into fair fashion, I've slowed down: I'll buy one or two dresses that flatter me and last – and I don't care if they're the latest trend, because they make me feel great and bring out the best in me. It's nice to get off that carousel, I think many people would benefit from doing the same.'

Do you have a motto?

'"Manners are free" is probably my ultimate. I truly believe that if we would treat each other with good manners, the world would be a better place. Our fast society makes it easy to ignore the mum with a pram/the elderly/the person behind us to hold the door open for. Imagine if we helped everyone! But we don't, because we're tired, in a hurry, swept along in a big crowd during rush-hour or because we're not taught to.'

What are your favourite skincare suggestions?

'I love green brands with a solid ethos. But my top tip is: look in your kitchen cupboards and learn what can help your skin – from the outside and from within. Drink lots of water and eat healthy fats such as linseed, olive oil and tahini, they help your skin radiate health. Yoghurt, coconut oil, aloe vera and honey also work well as face masks. I use a konjac sponge to cleanse, they're biodegradable, made of vegetable fibres and cleanse your skin gently but effectively, while helping to neutralise the pH values.'

What are your favourite sustainable tips?

'Don't spend any money for an entire day. Can you do it? What was impossible, and what was easy? Maybe you made your own coffee, instead of buying a disposable cup with a plastic lid. Or walked or cycled somewhere and discovered that you actually didn't need transport. You might have made your own lunch, from leftovers in your fridge, rather than buying a packaged sandwich. Or waited until you got home or to work for a drink, instead of buying water that's been bottled somewhere on another continent. Tiny tweaks can lead to a gradual lifestyle change if you realise that these choices save you money and make your life more fun and meaningful.'

Rebecca recommends

Destination

'Daylesford Farm in England. It's an organic farm with an incredible spa. They make wonderful beauty-products, ridiculously tasty food, there are yoga lessons, relaxing massages, and you can go for stunning walks in the surrounding countryside.'

Store

'I always pop into Earth in Kentish Town. I could spend hours there! Wonderful organic treats and ingredients, household products and a few great beauty brands. And it's not too pricey, the staff are really friendly and there's a large discount section. I like to visit Oxfam's Vintage site and Beyond Retro's for second-hand clothes. I love vintage and it's a great way to reduce landfill.'

Male, Female, Mix, etc.

Everything in this section may sound as though it's about women only. But nothing's further from the truth. Men also experience pressure about their appearance, feel too thin or too fat, not muscular enough or too toned. They've got to be a metroman, or are too much so and have to return to their primeval self with a beard, lots of meat and tattoos. And this is just as tough and can lead to as many problems as women face. Increasingly more adverts are aimed at men, there's still a large amount of money to grab there. Men also suffer from eating disorders, body issues or aversion to their appearance. Less is known about it and they probably don't talk about it as much, but it's there – and it's important we acknowledge and pay attention to it.

Being good-looking or attractive remains a strange phenomenon. Whether we're male, female, or without label. In general, women still earn less than men for the same work. Bizarre, particularly as it seems to matter less and less in society whether you're male or female. Not everyone can identify with that gender division, and rightly so. Gender neutral toilets are being introduced, forms where you can fill in your sex as 'X', on public transport we're greeted with 'dear travellers' (instead of ladies and gentlemen), department stores are abolishing the distinction between boys' and girls' clothes. In Germany, Ireland, Denmark and Norway, 'inter' or 'diverse' are officially recognised as gender. The LGBTQ movement is growing in strength, androgynous is okay and homosexuals, lesbians, transgenders and bisexuals are not only being accepted, but also valued for what they have to offer society. At the same time though, homophobia seems to be rearing its ugly head more, men holding hands are being beaten up, and the internet filled with human rights' violating abuse. Even more reason to force change, because being able to be yourself, to not suffer from oppression or a limiting ideal picture should apply to everyone. Regardless of sexual preference, rigid aesthetic norms or feelings about yourself – fluidity is freedom. Just like the fact that colour or background has nothing to do with beauty, and the rigid ideas surrounding it are ready to be torn apart. More about this in chapter 6, but for me, sustainability is respect for our world and for each other. Full stop.

Colour Blind

I'm still angry. A while ago, I walked into a chemist. Near the make-up, I overheard a conversation between a young woman of colour and a shop assistant – also dark skinned, coincidentally. The woman was beautiful and had one of the darkest skin tones I'd ever seen. She was looking for a foundation and asked the shop assistant if she had anything for a non-white skin. I looked around me. Everywhere, I saw products that I could use. Twenty different creams, in six different shades, from ten different brands. Shelves upon shelves full. Make-up colours that suit a light skin. Shampoo for Caucasian hair. More choice than anyone could ever need. But nothing for her. The assistant pointed to a concealer: 'This one, perhaps, it's in mocha?' she asked. Mocha?! That's the colour I go if I've sunbathed for a while. I felt more uncomfortable by the second. This store was making me feel as though I'm more important than she is. As

if I need all those different products or would demand all that space. Guilt, shame, anger. I'm not more important at all. I wish I had the power to clear out half the place to make space for things for her. The assistant told her she didn't have anything else unfortunately and took off. I approached the young woman – and said, 'Sorry. This is terrible. I'm just so embarrassed that there's nothing here for you. And so very much for me.' She replied that she really appreciated that, but she was used to it. That she can never find anything for her skin or hair. And that if she finds something, she never has a choice. We talked about how ridiculous that is, from an equality perspective of course, but also from a business point of view: how stupid to miss out on so many potential customers. I told her I felt rather powerless on the one hand, but that it's people who make this happen, so we should also be able to change it. I promised her they'd in any case lost me as a customer, and I'd also discuss it with my friends and network. I left the shop in a militant mood, first passing by the checkout to tell them I wouldn't be coming back until their assortment was more inclusive. Of course, this is something I've definitely noticed and questioned before, also in other areas, but the combination with the conversation hammered it home even more. I now look at this in every store and make it a point of discussion. It may not be my struggle, but on the other hand it is. Because it also says something about me, about the world I want to live in and how I want to spend my money (more in chapter 6).

AURÉLIE CHADAINE / LAURA BONNEFOUS

SCENT

Scent has a major influence on the way we experience the world. It's hugely important to me. For you too, probably – although you may not realise it. What you smell determines nearly everything: what you taste, where your attention is focused, how you feel, what you find attractive (and who). The power of scent is incomparable. And there's so much more to find out about how on earth it works. Why is it that something you smell can immediately bring back a flood of memories? Can pull you in to a store or make you buy a house (if you like freshly baked bread, at least)? Can make you feel calm, energised, happy, hungry, in love, like a kid again or at home... The influence of our nasal organ on our brain is massive, albeit slightly mysterious.

INTERVIEW

JUNIPER RIDGE

Hall Newbegin (1967) is founder and 'Chief Wilderness Freak' of Juniper Ridge, and wilderness perfumer.

How did Juniper Ridge come about?
'I grew up in Portland, Oregon. I spent my summers hiking and backpacking around the lakes and mountain tops – this is home to me. I've always wanted to bottle that feeling of a summer day in the Pacific Northwest.'

What do you do?
'Juniper Ridge is a group of nature-loving wilderness perfumers. We make perfume on the trail, around camp fires. We work with wild plants, as it's the only way to capture the beauty, solitude and silence of the places we love. We know you can't replicate the wildflower explosion at Big Sur in spring with junk ingredients and artificial fragrance. The only way to bottle this place is to go out and harvest it yourself. Our passion is collecting plants, soil and tree sap, so that we're able to capture the essence of a particular place. We distil aromatic fragments from incredible locations like the Mojave Desert.'

How does a wilderness perfumer differ from a conventional one?
'I've never really viewed myself as a perfumer, because I'm so disgusted by what passes for perfume nowadays. If spending time in the mountains, enjoying the intoxicating scent of freshly-cut cedar branches and conifers and the way the sunlight warms the forest floor make me a perfumer, then I am one, I guess. It's so easy to forget, but we're animals and see nature through our nose. Enjoying scent doesn't just belong to me, or the twelve folks that work here, or the handful of "perfume noses" in the world. Scent doesn't only exist in the perfume department of large stores, it happens when you're eating, drinking coffee, gardening, walking to work. If you pay attention. And please, do pay attention, because your nose has so much to give you. It's such a rich world, and it's there for all of us. The goal of a wilderness perfume is simple: put the real scent and sense of calm of a certain place into a bottle. Sounds easy, but wow – it's not. It's cost me more than fifteen years to learn what I know. We use no synthetic ingredients, but instead century-old traditions such as steam distillation, tinctures and enfleurage. Nobody does this anymore, since it's so much cheaper and easier to use fake stuff. But wear a wildcrafted fragrance, and you'll experience the difference.'

Why is smell so important to us?
'Our senses, particularly smell, connect us with our ancestral past. Using your sense of smell, you

engage a deep and age-old part of yourself. We have a deep connection with nature. The superior health benefits of hiking in the woods compared to going to the gym have been clearly researched. You also feel very different, right, when you've been outside rather than at the gym? All those studies that show being in nature has such an above-average positive influence on our blood pressure and hormones don't come as a surprise to me. The wilderness never fails to work wonders, perks you up and awakens emotions and memories. We usually don't even realise it's happening. Smell everything. Inhale your surroundings. Beauty is everywhere. My mind is racy and anxious, just like many other people's. But when I smell, I don't do it as a casual hobby, but as a survival mechanism. It's what brings me back to my body and gives me back perspective: yes, everything will be okay. I need this and wouldn't know what to do without it.'

Do you have a hero?

'My heroes are freaks and outsiders. I feel drawn to people who aren't afraid of ignoring rules and traditions and say: "I can do this better, my own way." Steve Jobs, Alice Waters, Neil Young, Gary Snyder, James Freeman of Blue Bottle Coffee. These people aren't scared to be crazy and change things.'

Hall's hotspots

'There's a huge amount of innovation and creativity going on in places such as Los Angeles, Portland and Brooklyn. My favourites are Tanner Goods in Los Angeles, Standard & Strange in Oakland (a store whose motto is "buy fewer, better things", what could be more sustainable than that?), The Perish Trust in San Francisco, Asher Goods in Seattle, Beam & Anchor and Danner Boots in Portland and Westerlind in New York. Berkeley Bowl Grocery Store is the best organic grocery store in the country, if not the entire world.'

JUNIPER RIDGE / COLIN MCCARTHY

Perfume is Power

When I talk about scent, I don't necessarily mean perfume, and certainly not the conventional stuff. Just like the rest of the cosmetics industry, perfume is big business. For (luxury) brands it works as a flagship and generates lots of profit. Unfortunately, an expensive bottle doesn't mean it's also good quality: most of the money often goes on marketing and exclusive distribution. A 100 euro-bottle may only cost 1 euro in terms of ingredients. This is because of the synthetic, chemical fragrances. A synthetic, replica rose-scent costs around 2.50 euros per kilo, an essential oil from the actual petals around 8,500 euros. That's why. The price of essential oil is also connected to the amount of plant or flower that you need to extract the scent from. For example: for one kilo of essential oil, 550 kilos of lavender are needed, 3,300 lemons or even 22,000 kilos of rose petals. The scent is distilled using steam and captured in oil – this is then essential oil. It's a laborious process that as said requires lots of natural raw materials, making it more expensive than synthetic substances. About one-tenth of all materials now used to make perfumes are natural, the rest synthetic. Not great news for your skin and the environment.

114

Annually, we spend nearly 31 billion euros on perfume.

01 / To conserve a perfume longer, it often contains preservatives, such as formaldehyde, parabens or phenoxyethanol. Not our favourites.

02 / To bind the fragrance to your skin it may contain phthalates or other substances that have a hormone disrupting and fertility-weakening effect, both in women and men.

03 / The scents are often heavy and smell 'synthetic', meaning quite a few people get headaches or don't like perfumes at all. Natural fragrances, essential oils and perfumes are less likely to have this effect, so you might want to give them a try?

ABEL

Frances Shoemack (1984) is founder of Abel, a natural, modern perfume brand.

What makes Abel different?
'Natural ingredients in the world of fragrance are a rare thing! And totally natural perfumes even scarcer. When we launched our first two fragrances they were the only 100% organic certified perfumes in the world.'

What should we look out for when we buy beauty products?
'The industry is full of greenwashing, and "perfume" is one of the vaguest labels out there. It's used to describe everything, from organic essential oil to the thousands of synthetic compounds used nowadays as scent in the beauty industry, most of which aren't even tested for safety. There's often no way of knowing exactly what kind of "perfume" is in your product, we're one of the few communicating the complete ingredient list. Do some research, ask questions and find products that you trust. There are good online databases and apps that have done the leg work for you.'

What else do you do to make your life more sustainable – and what not?
'I'm far from perfect but have an 80/20 rule: if most of what I do is good, then I need to make sure I enjoy the things I do that are less good. I avoid plastic, grow my own herbs and some vegetables, have plants in the house instead of flowers, only buy what I need and from brands I trust and know are doing their bit. I buy second-hand where I can, and only new things that last. I love to travel and coming from New Zealand, I do clock-up a fair amount of airmiles. And I don't always keep to what I've said above (but hey, 80/20, right?).'

Do you have a motto?
'Will it matter in five years' time? By asking myself this, I limit my worry to only things that really matter. Simple but effective!'

What are your favourite skincare tips?
'As with so many things: less is more. Find a few shades of lipstick (or nail varnish or something else) that you like and really suit you, and wear them until they're finished. I often see make-up collections in bathrooms that are so vast they scare me! >> Don't let yourself be talked into anything – whether it's the hairdresser convincing you to buy a complete set of shampoos and conditioners, or a shop assistant giving it her best shot to sell you the complete line, when you only need moisturiser. And always try before you buy. >> If you use body oil, whether it's a good brand or coconut oil from your pantry: apply to wet skin straight from the shower and a little goes a long, long way. >> Don't be afraid to not use something if you don't need it. There are products for literally everything! I can't remember the last time I bought or used a hair product: the little residual body oil left on my hands is enough to keep it under control. >> You are what you eat: I'm sure a good diet and lots of water does more for your skin that anything you can buy.'

Frances recommends
'COOLA sunscreen is wonderful. I use their BB cream as foundation in the summer. ILIA make-up, especially their lipstick. RMS's mascara, foundation and cream blushers, and their beautifully-scented face oil. I love reading *Smith Journal*, *Kinfolk*, *In Praise of Slowness* and *Cradle to Cradle*. The Raaka Chocolate team is so passionate about what they do, and the tour through their small factory in Brooklyn was so inspiring.'

Frances' sustainable guide to New Zealand

Kowtow – 'Inspiring, ethical fashion label: they're really finding that elusive balance between style, quality and ethics.'

The Lab Organics – 'A total gem of a store in Melbourne, filled with the best natural beauty brands and lovely things for your home.'

Lonely – 'Fashion label that has a delightfully refreshing take on showcasing their garments, empowering women around the globe by (truly) celebrating every shape, size and colour the coolest way.'

Okewa Rainwear – 'Ethically, New Zealand made raincoats, stylish enough that I wear mine as my everyday coat. The perfect addition to a capsule wardrobe.'

Nature Baby – 'A bit of a Kiwi institution this one, their range of organic cotton kids clothing and accessories is vast, practical and beautiful.'

Ecostore – 'Another Kiwi institution, these guys are pioneers in making accessibly priced eco-household products (that also come beautifully packaged).'

Little Bird – 'NZ's wholefood scene is up there with anywhere in the world, but for me, a trip to Auckland is never complete without at least one meal at the now-famous Little Bird. So good, my sister brought them on the plane so we could snack on them the morning of my wedding at my parents' farm!'

01 / JUNIPER RIDGE:
CHRISTMAS FIR
CABIN SPRAY

Essential oils can be stimulating or calming, and are good for your body in many ways: anti-inflammatory, as antioxidant or against infections. You can inhale them via a burner or vapouriser, in a steam bath or by rubbing it in an oil or cream on your skin. Eucalyptus is good for colds, flu, wounds and bites. Tea tree sanitises small wounds and spots, lemon is disinfecting and invigorating, lavender is really relaxing and great if you can't sleep, and rosemary helps concentration. Aromatherapy is as old as mankind itself and be very effective in influencing how you feel. Choose oils that are certified organic and watch out if they seem very cheap, they could be synthetic anyway.

Why not try a natural scented candle, burning some oil, lighting some Palo Santo wood (unique smelling wood from the South American Palo Santo tree, attributed to having mystical properties), spraying a mist or having dried lavender or rosemary at home – it might work for you too?

02 / ABEL:
RED SANTAL

This is the scent soundtrack of this book

01 / Abel: Red Santal
02 / Aveda: Chakra spray no. 3
03 / Good Candle Brooklyn: Spruce/Cedar candles
04 / Juniper Ridge: Big Sur trail resin/Backcountry Cascade Forest cabin spray/Christmas Fir cabin spray
05 / Palo Santo wood (Fairtrade certified)
06 / P.F. Candle Co.: Campfire/Lavender candles

PERSONAL CARE

DR. BRONNER   HUMBLE BRUSH   JOHN MASTERS ORGANICS

Showering and Soaking

A relaxing bath, showering and lathering... wonderful. But soap can contain substances you'd rather not have on your skin – and that don't *really* clean you (nothing new there). SLS and SLES are used in shower gel and soap for the foaming effect, but can cause eczema and allergies. DEA, that makes products creamier or less acidic, can also cause irritation and in studies has been linked to cancer. There are better ways:
> Use soap, deodorant and perfume with natural ingredients – preferably certified organic.
> Choose solid soap now and again instead of shower gel. It's making a comeback, costs less water to produce and less plastic for packaging.
> You can probably use less: in general, we're accustomed to smothering ourselves with more soap than we need, particularly liquid.
> Turn off the tap when you're soaping your hands, body or hair. So easy, and really makes a difference.
> Why not wipe your hands dry on your hair when you've washed them: no need for a paper towel and your locks get some extra va-va voom when you tousle them with the moisture.

Teeth

This is a difficult one. My dentist strongly advises to use brands such as Colgate or Sensodyne, to clean and protect my teeth optimally. I'd like to find reliable information about how much better they are than natural toothpastes. Because there are quite a few alternatives, without foaming SLS and SLES and triclosan for instance. There are also doubts about fluoride – that it's toxic, causes bone problems and even tooth decay (!). In Sweden there are warning stickers on the tubes, but it's not considered dangerous enough everywhere.

– Brands including Weleda, Urtekram, Tom's of Maine, Dr. Hauschka, Kingfisher, The Humble Co. and Davids sell (more) natural toothpastes. But you can also make it yourself from baking soda and coconut oil. You'll find all kinds of recipes on the internet. There's also solid toothpaste (on a stick) or in powder form, to save on packaging, such as by Lamazuna or Lush.

– We get through a massive number of toothbrushes – about 3.6 billion a year, it's said. That's a huge amount of plastic in our trash or oceans. You can look for a toothbrush that's more natural, from BamBrush, Brush Better or Humble Brush for example, made of biodegradable bamboo. Goodwell+Co makes good-looking brushes that only need their biodegradable head replaced, and even a more sustainable non-battery powered toothbrush.

– Brushing your teeth with the tap running? Surely not?

Deo

You sweat an average of one litre per day, but this can be ten times more on hot days or when working out. Sweat is one of the biggest taboos we face – nobody wants to walk around with soggy armpits or reeking of perspiration. While it's actually very good for you: it carries away waste materials, and without sweating, you'd overheat. Many deodorants contain aluminium chloralhydrate to stop the sweat; this closes the sweat glands, so the moisture can't come to the surface. That can be very irritating (so hold off on such deo after you've shaved your armpits). They also often contain parabens for a longer shelf-life, and artificial fragrances.
> You're better off with deodorants that counteract the odour, than products that seal the skin (so you don't sweat). Choose salt crystals, for instance, from Salt of the Earth or Crystal.
> Instead of an aerosol with propellants, go for a stick, roller or pump.
> Cutting your armpit-hair short, or shaving it off (if you don't have such fundamental objections to this as I do, of course) can also help, just like airy, breathable clothes.
> Don't use disposable razors, it's such a waste. Preferably go for the ones with replaceable blades, or even better, a long-lasting shaver. Looking at shaving creams, avoid the standard chemical-laden can – choose a natural brand or use soap or shower gel.

Intimate

The vagina's very sensitive and the most absorbent part of our body. So what happens down there is extra important: we don't want toxins, chemicals and any other junk. Cotton is normally grown using pesticides and chemical additives (see chapter 1) – and it's also used to make our tampons and sanitary pads. Pretty crazy, isn't it, that we think it's quite normal to stuff all of that inside of us? A woman uses thousands of tampons or panty liners in her life. Great they're there, but they also create a pretty large mountain of waste – and we know the environmental pollution that cotton causes. Menstruation's not much fun at the best of times, and all of this doesn't make it any better.
> Buy tampons and sanitary towels made from organic cotton and corn starch, like those by Yoni or Natracare. Use nothing containing bleach, perfume or plastic, and preferably not made of regular cotton.
> There are also washable cotton sanitary towels – I've never tried them, but just like washable baby-nappies, they could be better to use than you'd think. American brand THINX makes great washable underpants: genius! No more tampons or towels needed.
> You can also insert cups that collect your menstruation. Quite a few women are rather enthusiastic about them, so it may be worth a try. You can find lots of brands and stores online. ⟶

INTERVIEW

YONI

Wendelien Hebly (1982) is co-founder of Yoni: tampons and sanitary towels made of organic cotton and nothing else.

Why Yoni?
'We believe that women should be able to choose what products they use in and around one of the most absorbent areas of their body: their vagina. Therefore, organic cotton and no plastic, perfume or pesticides. And we do our best to get these on regular shelves. People are becoming increasingly aware of the impact our products have on the planet. It's strange to consider there's no ingredient list on most tampon, sanitary towel and panty-liner packaging. With us, what's in the box is on the box. We believe that people should be able to make conscious decisions – so they need to know that there's a choice, and alternatives must be available.'

Do you have a life motto?
'When was the last time you did something for the first time? My partner and I ask ourselves this a lot, and I love it! It helps you keep your eyes open for new things.'

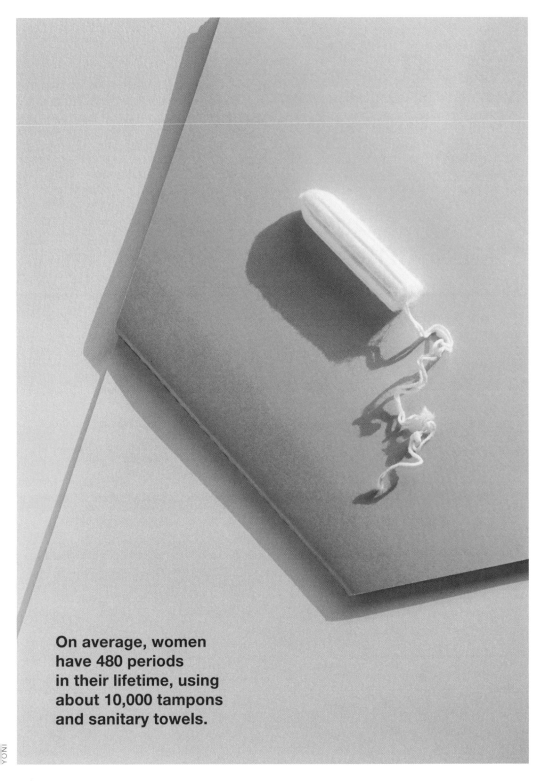

On average, women
have 480 periods
in their lifetime, using
about 10,000 tampons
and sanitary towels.

YONI

> If possible, don't use cleaning products for your vagina, and certainly no regular-brand soaps that aren't natural. This might upset your internal balance and isn't necessary – in general, it'll manage.

Of course, this also concerns the male intimate parts. Be careful with condoms: although most are made of rubber, this doesn't necessarily make it A-OK. Rubber is a natural, renewable product from the rubber tree. But the workers on the rubber plantations often have it rough, are poorly paid and have to work hard and long. Additionally, artificial fragrances and flavours are often added to condoms (who actually likes this?), and the lubricant can be pretty chemical.

> Make lovemaking extra enjoyable with Fairtrade rubber condoms, from FAIR SQUARED, for example – they also compensate for their CO_2 emissions. > Of course, you can also go for the most natural methods (besides abstaining, but doesn't make many people happy) such as pulling out early or based on your temperature when ovulating – but be very careful, these don't always end well.

GREEN KIDS by Laura de Jong

HURRAW! BALM

Less is More
Buy and use as few baby-care products as possible. Unnecessary, your baby's fine as it is. Bathe as little as possible, once a week is plenty. Then you won't have to apply so many products because the skin's dried out.

Hospital Bag
To be sure, fill your 'get-away bag' with natural products. Your baby may get his/her first bath in the hospital, where there aren't natural products usually available.

Coconut Oil
Life saver. Full stop. Buy an organic coconut oil in a glass jar. Yep, the sort you can also cook with. Preferably without the scent removed, so one that still really smells of coconut. Functions as cream for the bottom, bath oil, massage oil and against thrush.

Rubber Dummy
Some children get a lot of comfort from a dummy. Nothing wrong with this, but I don't like the idea of a plastic dummy. Hurray for dummies made of natural rubber by Hevea, Natursutten and Ecopacifier.

Washable Nappies
A baby uses an average of 5 disposable nappies per day. That's 700 kilos of nappy waste per year. A sustainable choice? Go for washable nappies. There are also washable wipes: soft cotton or bamboo with a little water. That's all you need. And you can wash them with the nappies. Still prefer disposables? Avoid preservatives such as phenoxyethanol and parabens.

Sun
Wet clothing lets through more UV rays. Special UV-resistant clothing is recommended for children, such as from POPUPSHOP. The protection offered equals factor 50. Apply mineral sunscreen to exposed body parts every two hours.

GUIDE

STORES

AUSTRALIA AND NEW ZEALAND

belle & sage
webshop (NZ)
Selection by an experienced make-up artist, who wanted to find professional alternatives to all those chemicals. Make-up, personal-care, hair, wellness (oil, chocolate), fragrances and a good blog.
belleandsage.com

Flora & Fauna
webshop (Aus)
Wide choice of personal-care, make-up, hair and teeth products and brands, but also kitchen accessories, supplements, food, fashion, scented candles, books, gifts and much more. You can return jars, bottles and packaging.
floraandfauna.com.au

The Lab Organics
Melbourne + webshop (Aus)
Large selection of well-curated brands: hair and make-up, skincare, fragrances, accessories, etc. In-house make-up advice also available in the stylish store.
thelaborganics.com.au

Tonic Room
Auckland + webshop (NZ)
Wide range of skincare, make-up and hair brands, products for mother, child, men and your home, supplements, books and much more. Consultations and treatments are offered in the store, from massages and facials to herbal medicine and mindfulness.
tonicroom.co.nz

AND ALSO
beautifulbecause.com.au / bellanaturally.com / eveorganics. com.au / fairlings.com.au / iamnaturalstore.com.au / naturallysafe.com.au / nourishedlife. com.au / ohnatural.co.nz / shopnaturally.com.au / theapothecarystore.com.au / thelowtoxfox.com.au / vanillabloom.co.nz

EUROPE
Alice&White
Stockholm + webshop (Swe)
Well-curated products for your body, face and hair, women, men and children, for travel, gifts, home and more.
aliceandwhite.com

Amazingy
webshop (Ger)
Wide choice of personal-care brands and make-up, but also products for children, mothers, pets, and bottles, bags, books etc.
amazingy.com

Belladonna
Berlin + webshop (Ger)
Products for your hair, face, body and bathroom, but also fragrances, gifts and treatments.
belladonna-naturkosmetik.de

Big Green Smile
webshop
Large range of natural and organic care products, make-up and lifestyle products. Has a British, French, German and Dutch/Belgian site.
biggreensmile.com

Content Beauty
London + webshop (UK)
Good and extensive selection of care products, make-up and lifestyle brands (sent free of charge to Europe). Treatments also available in-store.
contentbeautywellbeing.com

Ecco Verde
webshop
International webshop with many brands and over 10,000 articles.
ecco-verde.com / ecco-verde.de / ecco-verde.fr / ecco-verde.it / ecco-verde.se

Jolie
Helsinki + webshop (Fin)
Well-curated store for personal care, make-up, body, men, gifts, wellness, interior etc. There's also a natural spa with treatments.
kauppa.jolie.fi

LoveLula
webshop (UK)
Large selection of skincare, make-up and hair brands (sent free worldwide).
Also extensive vegan range and gifts section.
lovelula.com

Natural Skincare
Limerick City + webshop (Ire)
Store (called Alchemist Earth) and webshop with large variety of brands: skincare, bath, make-up, women, men, child, fragrances and much more.
naturalskincare.ie

Naturisimo
webshop (UK)
Make-up, personal-care, hair products, scents, supplements, homeopathy, men's care, but also fashion, interior fragrances, bags, gifts and more (sent free worldwide).
naturisimo.com

Naturligt Snygg
webshop (Swe)
Comprehensive, green beauty store offering many brands, but also an information platform with reviews, blogs and news.
naturligtsnygg.se

AND ALSO
nourish.ie / ruohonjuuri.fi / tiare.de / vanzeebeauty.com / violey.com

UNITED STATED AND CANADA
Clementine Fields
webshop (Can)
A strong selection of brands for your face, skin, hair, kids, men, water bottles, aromatherapy and more.
clementinefields.ca

Credo
Boston, Chicago, Los Angeles, New York, San Diego, San Francisco + webshop (US)
Broad range of eco-friendly/cruelty-free brands: skincare, haircare, make-up, fragrances etc. Organise in-store events, and some also have a spa. The website provides lots of information about ingredients and clean beauty.
credobeauty.com

Follain
Boston, Nantucket + webshop (US)
Well-curated range of skincare, make-up, haircare etc. Offer 'clean consults' and regularly have pop-up

stores in cities such as New York.
follain.com

Pharmaca
stores + webshop (US)
Wide choice of beauty, hair, body
products, supplements, homeopathy and more. With blog and online
search according to 'condition'.
pharmaca.com

The Detox Market
*Los Angeles, Santa Monica, Toronto
+ webshop (Can/US)*
Many well-selected brands for natural
skincare, make-up, hair, fragrance,
wellness etc. Website features lots of
information and stores regularly host
events.
thedetoxmarket.com /
thedetoxmarket.ca

AND ALSO
aillea.com / aylabeauty.com /
capbeauty.com / citrinenaturalskin.
com / ecodivabeauty.ca / levertbeauty.
com / lilou-organics.com /
lurkmade.com / ondabeauty.com /
petalandpost.com / pureandsimple.
ca / shopfigandflower.com /
thegreenjunglebeautyshop.com

*>> Many health-food stores sell the
larger care and make-up brands such
as Dr. Hauschka, Lavera, Sante and
Weleda.*

*>> Chains such as Holland & Barrett,
Boots (part of their Botanicals line) and
The Body Shop (the Nutriganics line is
certified organic and a number of products contain Fairtrade ingredients) also
sell, besides regular products, natural
and organically-certified brands – care-
fully check the ingredients on the label.*

*>> On the websites of larger brands
you'll find beauty salons who work
with their products.*

BRANDS

Many of these brands are sold in the
stores featured in this guide, and/or
have their own webshop.

Skincare

Antipodes
Stylish, organically-certified brand

from New Zealand with an extensive
range of plant-based skincare products and make-up.
antipodesnature.com

Bulldog
British brand for men. No microbeads,
synthetic fragrances or artificial colours,
cruelty-free (and a favourite of Mr
Eyskoot). Products for your skin, body
and facial hair, deodorant and more.
bulldogskincare.com

Burt's Bees
Care products and make-up from
the US, made from animal-friendly
recovered bees wax and plant-based
and essential oils, herbs and minerals.
Products for your face, nails, men,
baby, feet etc. The brand supports
the bees and reports about their sustainability policy. Do now sell in China,
where animal testing is mandatory.
burtsbees.com

CONTENT BEAUTY

cocokind
Organic and Fairtrade-certified
(affordable) personal-care products,
made in California. Every product
contains less than five ingredients,
and coconut oil is an important com-
ponent. The lovely fragrances come
from organic essential oils, and if you
return an empty jar, you receive 50%
discount on that product.
cocokind.com

Dr. Alkaitis
Personal-care brand for face, hair
and body – organically-certified, wild
harvested and biodynamic, handmade in California.
alkaitis.com

Dr. Hauschka
German brand – the certified
make-up and face, hair and care
products contain natural ingredients
and biodynamically-grown healing
plants.
drhauschka.com

ELDE
Norwegian natural/organic and vegan
personal-care products and make-up
brand (that first sends you free samples to try).
eldecosmetics.com

Éminence
Extensive skincare line from Canadian
organic brand, popular with celebrities including Alicia Keys, Jennifer
Lawrence and Madonna, only sold
in their own spas. For every product
bought, they plant a tree.
eminenceorganics.com

Esse Probiotic Skincare
Innovative organically-certified brand
that works with pre and probiotics
and microbes to feed the good
bacteria in our skin. Buys directly
from African women's communities
to stimulate fair trade.
esseskincare.com

Evolve
British handmade and largely organic
brand (showing which percentage
is natural and which organic), with
products for face, hair and body.
evolvebeauty.co.uk

FAIR SQUARED
Fairtrade, organic and vegan German
brand for men and women, with
products for face and body, shaving,
sun and condoms.
fairsquared.info

French Girl
Modern, certified organic (and vegan)
personal-care, make-up, hair products and oils, made in Seattle, with
a French sense of style.
frenchgirlorganics.com

H&M
The Conscious Beauty line is natural,
partly organic and vegetarian, with
creams, masks, hair products, lip
balms and (perfume) oil. Look for the
Ecocert certificate, as most of the
H&M range is not natural.
hm.com

Herbivore Botanicals
Natural, vegan and stylish skin- and haircare products, made with ingredients mainly from America.
herbivorebotanicals.com

L:A Bruket
Swedish organic personal-care brand, inspired by the coast and nature, with soaps, face creams, hair and shaving products, scented candles and detergent.
labruket.se

Lavera
Extensive range of personal-care products and make-up, made from natural, and as much as possible organic, ingredients by German, affordable brand.
lavera.de

Little Barn Apothecary
American label (of two guys) with natural/organic, good-looking, locally-made (in Atlanta) face, body and hair products.
littlebarnapothecary.com

Lush
Personal-care products, soap and make-up, made of fresh fruits and vegetables and essential oils. The British brand does still use synthetic ingredients such as preservatives and perfumes. The products are vegetarian and handmade, and some are packaging-free.
lush.com

Meraki
Danish brand for skin, hair and home, with simple ingredients, junk-free and organic where possible. In addition to creams, shampoos, lotions, brushes and sponges, also sells scented candles and cleaning products.
merakishop.dk

Mia Höytö
Organically-certified brand for face and body, made in Finland.
miahoyto.us

Mukti
Extensive line of Australian, certified organic products for face, skin and hair (with native Australian extracts), as well as scented candles, make-up tools and gifts.
muktiorganics.com

Nuori
Contemporary, Danish personal-care brand for body and face, made from natural ingredients and without chemical or synthetic additives. Produces small batches and special packaging, making the products as fresh as possible.
nuori.com

Pai
Certified organic, vegan British brand, with facial products and body care for women and children.
paiskincare.com

Province Apothecary
Innovative Canadian brand, derived from allergy research. Certified organic, made in small batches from local and seasonal ingredients and aromatherapy.
provinceapothecary.ca

Pure Nuff Stuff
Natural where possible, organic and fair trade, with as few ingredients as feasible. They make (in the UK) small quantities, to keep the products fresh – for your face, body and hair.
purenuffstuf.co.uk

Rudolph
Organically-certified brand: the Danish founder discovered the amount of harmful chemicals in her body from beauty products after taking a Greenpeace test. Face, hair, fragrances and a good sunscreen.
rudolphcare.dk

Santaverde
Vegan and certified organic German personal-care brand, with creams and anti-ageing products based on aloe vera.
santaverde.de

Sóley
Personal-care brand with organic ingredients and Icelandic herbs, plants and volcanic clay, based on knowledge passed down by Soley's great-grandmother. For your skin and hair, but also scented candles and tea.
soleyorganics.com

Sukin
Australian brand with extensive collection of affordable, natural and vegan products for face, body, hair and baby.
sukinorganics.com

Trilogy
Broad range of natural or organic personal-care products made in New Zealand, especially known for its rosehip oil.
trilogyproducts.com

True Organic of Sweden
Organically-certified personal-care products, with a limited range and environmentally friendly packaging. Makes All You Need Is Me, the eco-variant of the '8-hour cream' that is often used by make-up artists.
trueorganicofsweden.com

Weleda
Major Swiss brand with certified organic personal-care products, soap, toothpaste and shampoo, some from their own medicinal herb garden. The website features lots of information about the ingredients and what they do.
weleda.com

AND ALSO
africaorganics.co.za / angelalangford.com / badgerbalm.com / bubbleandbee.com / bjorkandberries.se / cowshedonline.com / emerginc.com / estellethild.com / graydonskincare.ca / greenpeople.co.uk / herbfarmacy.com / karmameju.com / livinglibations.com / lucyannabella.com / madaracosmetics.com / martinaorganics.co.nz / nafha.eu / patyka.com / renskincare.com / ringana.com / sisterandcoskinfood.co.uk / sanctumaustralia.com / skinessence.ca / surfacecares.com / susannekaufmann.com / swbasicsofbk.com / thejojobacompany.com.au / theorganicpharmacy.com / therubscrub.com / therapi.com / thisworks.com / truemindfulbeauty.com / zenology.com

Sun

Biosolis
webshop
Natural and organic sun products: sunscreen, after sun, children's products and self-browner.
biosolis.info

COOLA
webshop
Extensive collection of largely certified

organic sun products from America, with sprays, lotions, kids and sports products and after suns.
coolasuncare.com

Eco Cosmetics
German vegan, organic brand, with a range of sunscreen: for children, snow, aftersun, but also make-up with sun protection, skin, hair and dental care.
eco-naturkosmetik.de

Raw Elements
Cruelty-free American brand with 95% organic ingredients, set up by a lifeguard who wanted to stop the pollution of our skin and environment. Broad spectrum protection, which doesn't harm marine life and the ocean, in plastic-free reusable packaging.
rawelementsusa.com

AND ALSO
greenbeaver.com / lovea.fr / thankme-later.com

Make-up

Absolution
French certified face care, body and cosmetics brand, with, according to make-up artist Lou Dartford, the best organic lipsticks available.
absolution-cosmetics.com

freshMinerals
American make-up brand with vitamins, antioxidants and a sun-protection factor, made from a mix of natural minerals and pigments.
freshmineralsusa.com

Hurraw! Balm
Vegan, organic, raw lip balm from the US, in many colours and flavours.
hurrawbalm.com

Hynt Beauty
American make-up brand, natural, free from synthetic or chemical substances and vegan.
hyntbeauty.com

ILIA
Largely organic, American make-up brand, with natural dyes and without chemical additives. Favourite lipsticks of model Rebecca Pearson and Frances Shoemack from Abel.
iliabeauty.com

Inika
Vegan and certified organic make-up from the UK, with an extensive line and tools for face, eyes and lips.
inika.co.uk

Kjaer Weis
New York label from Danish make-up artist Kirsten Kjaer Weis, who discovered in her work how bad conventional make-up can be for your skin. Most is certified organic, with a refillable packaging system to reduce waste.
kjaerweis.com

Rituel de Fille
American cruelty-free make-up brand, set up by three sisters inspired by the magic of natural pigments and ingredients. Eye make-up in strong colours and lipsticks that stay put.
ritueldefille.com

RMS Beauty
Organic, raw and 'food grade' cosmetics from famous Canadian make-up artist Rose Marie Swift (she's been in the business for 35 years and worked for all the big magazines and names), who started her brand when tests showed that her blood contained toxic concentrations of heavy metals and loads of pesticides and other chemicals. Extensive line that's the favourite of many professionals – see also p. 101.
rmsbeauty.com

Sante
German make-up and personal-care products, from exclusively plant-based ingredients and oils. Most are gluten-free and/or can be used by vegans.
sante.de

Tata Harper
Vegetarian and organically-certified American brand, locally-made in Vermont. Extensive line of facial care, aromatherapy and make-up.
tataharperskincare.com

Vapour Beauty
Cruelty-free and make-up brand (70% organic, 30% natural) from the US, made on solar and wind energy, in recycled packaging with vegetable ink. Designed to be applied without brushes or other tools.
vapourbeauty.com

W3LL PEOPLE
Extensive line of natural and cruelty-free make-up with organic ingredients, made in small batches in Austin, America.
w3llpeople.com

AND ALSO
hiro-cosmetics.com / janeiredale.com / lilylolo.co.uk / mineralogiemakeup.com / occmakeup.com

Hair

Aveda
Established in 1978 by environmentalist Horst Rechelbacher in America, to create a brand based on plants and aromatherapy, in close collaboration with the indigenous peoples who grow the ingredients. His business grew, and he sold it to Estée Lauder to start a new adventure: Intelligent Nutrients (see below). Aveda uses mainly natural, and where possible organic substances in their hair, facial and body care products, make-up, fragrances and tea. Recycled packaging and use of wind energy.
aveda.com

Intelligent Nutrients
The new brand by Horst Rechelbacher, that he wants to take as far as possible. Uses 'food grade ingredients': if it's good enough to put on your skin, you should also be able to eat it. Many hair (such as shampoos, conditioners and styling) and skincare products, and scents. Everything is made from certified organic ingredients, they support groups in Africa where some of the ingredients originate, and their farm in Maine uses sustainable energy.
intelligentnutrients.com

John Masters Organics
American hairstylist Masters spent years in the business, but started to worry about the amount of chemicals he worked with. His products are certified organic and harvested in an environmentally-friendly way. Specialised in hair, but also offers face and body care for men.
johnmasters.com

Kevin.Murphy
Natural and cruelty-free hair brand in

recycled packaging. Australian stylist Murphy worked with big names and magazines (and according to *Vogue*, even invented the beach look), before creating a line with shampoo, care, dyes and styling products. kevinmurphy.com.au

Less is More
Organically-certified Austrian brand, with shampoos, conditioners and styling products. Made the All-in-One Wash gel & Shampoo especially to help refugees, by giving away lots at Vienna train station, and donating the proceeds to aid organisations. lessismore.at

Oway
Italian brand using biodynamic methods, to for example distill essential oils from herbs and plants. Supports worldwide communities who source their natural, certified and raw ingredients. Specialised in hair products, for washing, styling and colouring, but also offers facial and body care products, tea and aromas. oway.it

AND ALSO
beehonestcosmetics.com / davines. com / mr-smith.com.au / oliebe.com / rahua.com / urtekram.com (this big Danish brand also offers personal-care products and has an extensive food line)

>> Hairdressers and salons
On many brands' websites (such as Aveda or Intelligent Nutrients) you can find where their products are used.

Nails

butterlondon.com (British, in many colours, also make-up) / flossgloss. com (American, award-winning, cruelty- and 7-free) / idunminerals. com (Swedish brand in good colours, also make-up) / intensae.com (vegan brand in many colours) / kesterblack. com (Australian 10-free, vegan, cruelty-free, locally made) / kurebazaar.com (French brand with cool colours, up to 85% natural) / pacificabeauty.com (US vegan, 7-free, also skincare and make-up) / pritinyc.com (pioneer from NY, works with major names and Fashion Weeks; also for kids) / shopncla.com

(strong, 5-free, made in US) / sparitual.com (vegan from US) / zoya.com (American brand with large collection, also for lips)

FRENCH GIRL / AMELIA HOWDEN

Scent

Abel
One of the pioneers in the field of sustainable perfume. 100% natural, developed by New Zealander Frances Shoemack. Collection of five modern (unisex) fragrances, also in sample and travel format.
abelodor.com – see also p. 116

Haeckels
Natural perfumes, care products and interior fragrances, handmade in the UK. Each scent exactly references a place (the name is the GPS location) and is made of plants and herbs collected there.
haeckels.co.uk

Honoré des Prés
Stylish French perfume and eau de toilette without chemicals and synthetic substances.
honoredespres.com

Juniper Ridge
webshop
Wilderness perfumes from the US. Sustainably harvests plants, bark, moss, flowers and herbs and extracts the scents in traditional ways (lots of information on their blog). Makes small batches – also scented balms, interior sprays, incense and tea.
juniperridge.com – see also p. 113

Mandy Aftel
Sometimes called the godmother of natural perfumes. Natural scents, elixirs and tea and perfumes to eat or cook with, made by hand and in small runs in California (where she gives workshops).
aftelier.com

AND ALSO
ayalamoriel.com / doterra.com / hiramgreen.com / oneseedperfumes. com

Washing and deodorant

Dr. Bronner's
Fair trade and organic brand from the US with soap, haircare, lip and body balms, baby care, toothpaste, coconut oil and cleaning products.
drbronner.com

Salt of the Earth
British deodorant line based on salt crystals that counteract the odour, both in solid and spray form, with and without odour, and also for feet.
crystalspring.co.uk

STOP THE WATER WHILE USING ME!
Natural and biodegradable soap, hair, child and care products, that also ask something of you: to turn off the tap while washing. The German brand refills packages and donates to their own Good Water project.
stop-the-water-while-using-me.com

The Ohm Collection
Natural, powder deodorant, made from sodium bicarbonate. The Dutch brand also offers facial and suntan products.
theohmcollection.com

AND ALSO
agentnateur.com / smplskin.com / soapwallkitchen.com / thecrystal. com / welovetheplanet.nl

Teeth

AloeDent
Natural toothpaste and mouthwash without fluoride, with aloe vera. At many chemists.

Brush Better
Australian toothbrushes, made from

sustainably-sourced bamboo and biodegradable (including the packaging). Offers a subscription service to get a new one in time. brushbetter.com.au

Davids
Stylish, natural toothpaste, made from American ingredients, without fluoride or SLS, vegan, family-owned and in more sustainable packaging. davids-usa.com

Goodwell+Co.
More sustainable, good-looking dental products from the US, such as biodegradable toothbrushes (of which you only need to replace the head), natural toothpaste and better floss. Also the inventors of the first powered toothbrush without battery, made of durable material. thegoodwellcompany.com

The Humble Co.
Swedish brand with dental care and brushes, that tries to keep money in the local community. The bamboo handle of the Humble Brush is biodegradable (as well as the packaging). They're working to find alternatives for the nylon head. For every brush you buy, they give one away in a developing country. thehumble.co

AND ALSO
bambrushes.com / kingfishertoothpaste.co.uk / lebonandlebon.com / thebamboobrushsociety.com / tomsofmaine.com

Intimate

FAIR SQUARED
Condoms made of Fairtrade certified, vegan and natural latex. fairsquared.info

French Letter Condoms
UK webshop with condoms and care products from FAIR SQUARED, and intimate care, lubricants and massage products made from vegan, natural or organic ingredients. frenchlettercondoms.co.uk

Natracare
Organically-certified, ethical British brand with biodegradable tampons,

sanitary towels and incontinence products made of organic cotton, without chlorine or plastic. natracare.com

THINX
Cool, taboo-breaking American brand that makes washable underpants for your period – no more need for disposable products. Have their own foundation to give girls and women worldwide a safe place to learn about their bodies and rights, and change the narrative about menstruation. shethinx.com

YES
British brand with certified organic, plant-based lubricants and intimate products. yesyesyes.org

Yoni
Cool brand of sanitary towels and tampons made of organic cotton without harmful chemicals. yoni.care – see also p. 120

INFORMATION

Lou Dartford
British make-up artist who only uses sustainable products, and blogs about her work. louisedartford.com / louisedartfordgreenbeauty.com – see also p. 101

Modeltypeface
Blog and platform by Rebecca Pearson, with lots of information about the modelling world, their rights and issues such as body image. modeltypeface.com – see also p. 109

Websites
healthyisthenewskinny.com / lennyletter.com / manrepeller.com / modelalliance.org / peta.org/living/beauty / rinmodels.com / themodelshealthpledge.nl / themovementmodels.com / thinx.org / wayofgray.com

Certifications and information
beatthemicrobead.org / cosmebio.org / cosmeticsdatabase.com / cosmos-standard.org / crueltyfreeinternational.org /

eceae.org / ec.europa.eu/environment/ecolabel / ecocert.com / ecolabelindex.com / goodguide.com / icea.bio / kontrollierte-naturkosmetik.de / natrue.org / peta.org / safecosmetics.org / soilassociation.org / thinkdirtyapp.com / usda.gov/topics/organic

---

GREEN KIDS

Personal care

Énamour
Minimalistic skincare for the whole family. Packaged in glass bottles and made in Montreal. enamour.co

Natural Birthing Company
Vegan-friendly care during pregnancy, post-delivery and while breast-feeding. Developed by midwives and made in the UK. naturalbirthingcompany.com

AND ALSO
babyscent.com.au / greenpeople.co.uk / heveaplanet.com / lovekins.com / naif.com / purenuffstuff.co.uk / sukinorganics.com / weleda.com

Nappies

Waterwipes
No flannel and water on hand? These wipes are a good alternative. Only contain water and a drop of grapefruit seed extract. waterwipes.com

AND ALSO
applecheeks.com / bambinomio.com / bambonature.com / boutiquebummis.com / blueberrydiapers.com / bubblebubs.com.au / bumgenius.com / cheekywipes.com / ecoriginals.com.au / honest.com / imsevimse.com / naty.com / planetwiseinc.com / thirstiesbaby.com / totsbots.com

03

FOOD

INTRODUCTION

7,500

the number of animals
a meat-eater consumes
on average during
his/her life

30%

of worldwide energy
consumption is used
by the food sector
(which is responsible for
22% of greenhouse-gas
emissions)

It shouldn't be so complicated, really. Our body runs on food, we put some in and off we go. Piece of cake. But it's not that simple of course. There's a lot more involved in the choices we make all day. Do you eat a lot, or little? Often or occasionally? Do you eat everything, no animals or no animal products either? Sugar, e-numbers, carbohydrates? Grown far away or locally, but then in a heated greenhouse? And why do you eat? Are you hungry, or just peckish? And what's the difference, in fact? And once you've decided on all that: actually how sustainable is your salad, steak or snack? What's the influence of what you consume on your health, but also on the world around you? So many questions… Enough to make you lose your appetite.

I've got a major sweet tooth. If it was down to me, I'd breakfast on pancakes, lunch on chocolate and dine on pie. I don't, of course (and writing it down makes it suddenly sound a lot less appealing), but you get my drift. Generally speaking, I snack too much. I know it's stupid, because it's not going to make me look better or get healthier. But sometimes it's stronger than me. Why? Knowing that something's not good, and then doing it anyway. Allowing short-term satisfaction to beat long-term rationale. Wanting something tasty now, and therefore perhaps be overweight, have diabetes or who knows what later. I've never been happy with my double chin and thighs slash hips slash behind, and diabetes runs in the family. So, I need to be careful and do my best to programme myself differently. At the same time, I also try to be more relaxed and feel less guilty (I'm getting older and wiser). I saw a post on social media in which a girl said she'd rather be a little curvier and happier, than more toned and stressed. Amen. I'll always be vulnerable to comfort through food – and that's also part of me.

Funnily enough, some people would probably call me a health freak when it comes to food. I don't want poison in it or people and animals to have been exploited for it. Strawberries or green beans that have been pumped out of the ground with the help of pesticides just don't taste as good either. And I don't understand why I'd put something in my body that contains chemicals and suffering. Organic products are easier to find than fair trade, while sustainable food also means the people who grow and produce it are treated well. Just as with care products, the social aspect deserves a lot more attention. Because we're all human beings, and there's increasingly more of us. About one hundred years ago there were two billion people on the planet, thirty years ago five billion and now more than seven billion. The world population's growing faster and faster (an extra billion in the last twelve years!) and is also becoming older. So,

You are what you eat. So don't be fast, cheap, easy or fake.

more and more food is needed. And this comes from all over the globe. We used to cultivate it ourselves, or your neighbour did. Now, there's an all-year-round supply of mangos, beans and bananas in the shops, while they may not even grow where you live (and not in every season anyway). This causes food miles: lots of fuel, CO_2 emissions, energy to heat greenhouses, plastic for packaging.

1,3
billion tonnes: the amount of food we waste worldwide – a third of the entire production

We then go on to waste about a third of all food produced annually. (Meanwhile, people are starving...). Because we buy more than we can eat. Because we're lazy and don't store it properly or for too long. Because we don't look at what we have in our cupboards before we hit the shops. Because supermarkets don't think fruit and vegetables look pretty enough or buy more than they can sell. Because cultivation isn't well organised or over-production is stimulated. Whatever the reason, it needs to stop. Just like all the other non-sustainable aspects of our food. I'm afraid I'm about to tell you that eating meat and dairy is extremely bad for the environment. Sorry in advance. But I think you actually do want to know.

17
million oil barrels worth of energy are needed to make the plastic water bottles that Americans use in one year (which you could run 1 million cars on for a year)

Because fortunately you can make a difference. By making other choices. Looking after yourself. Using common sense. Shopping smarter. And you're not the only one: there's an unstoppable movement happening around food. We're more advanced in the field of sustainable food than for instance fashion or personal care. Organic products are available in increasingly more supermarkets, there's growing attention for cut-price chicken and other animal suffering, and no-one thinks you're crazy for buying fair-trade bananas. The number of health-food shops is on the rise, just like the number of food-blogs. Becoming more sustainable is possible, even if you haven't got that much to spend. Healthy eating is hot, and luckily, enjoying food is too. So, time to get our teeth sunk in.

EATING AND BUYING

The Impact of your Food

Everything we eat is made. Food costs energy, water and sunlight to grow, or electricity and resources to be produced in the factory. And then plastic to be packed, fuel to be transported, energy to be frozen. Making our food uses much more energy than we get back in return. It guzzles fossil fuels, including to produce it, heat it or cool it down, or to make pesticides and artificial fertiliser. What we eat has an enormous impact on the world. Emissions, pollution and packaging, but also exploitation of animals and people. Fortunately, some change is happening: agriculture is being modernised, food scandals trigger progress and we're becoming more aware of the impact of our choices.

>> There's increasing attention for the actual costs of the products we use, such as chocolate, vegetables and meat (but also, for example, T-shirts). The organisation True Price conducts research into the social costs that remain hidden: the impact on climate, water, biodiversity and the costs of living wages and decent working hours. Importer Nature & More provides information about this with its organic pears, pineapples and oranges, and compares regular vegetables or fruit with the organic counterpart. They want to show that lots of conventional vegetables and fruit are too low-priced, because the costs of for instance negative environmental impact and fair pay aren't included. Organic food is therefore not too expensive, but regular too cheap. Shouldn't there even be higher taxes on products that hugely impact our planet (such as meat)?

20% to 30% of the environmental impact Europeans cause through consumption is food related (particularly meat and dairy).

KHUMKUMMEH

133

Shop Near and Now

The best you can do to reduce the impact of your food is to buy locally and in season – preferably organic. The closer your food is grown, the less energy it costs to get it onto your plate. Simple. We've gotten used to being able to buy anything we fancy, day in day out. But raspberries, tomatoes and mangos in cold months just doesn't make sense. To me, a bit like patio heaters (put on a coat, grab a blanket, make a bonfire or go inside). This fruit has covered hundreds of kilometres or been grown in energy-eating greenhouses. The further the fruit and vegetables travel, the more you need to do to it to keep it fresh and ensure it ends up on the shelves okay. Preservatives or pesticides, and plastic to package. And that's both less healthy for us, as well as the environment. Luckily, there's plenty of fruit and vegetables that occur locally in the winter (or summer) and are really delicious.

> Search online for a vegetable and fruit calendar to see what's in season near you (for example,

Eat Seasonably (UK), Eat the Seasons (UK/US) or Seasonal Food Guide (Aus)).

> Farmers' markets and farm shops are great, maybe you can find some local ones – even better if they're organic.

> (Re)visit the market and ask for products from the area. Often surprisingly cheap too.

> How delicious is a ripe, freshly-picked strawberry? Local fruit often has more flavour than prematurely harvested, frozen and then later defrosted water bombs.

> Buying in season really saves money – because then there's an abundance. Just like buying locally: we have to pay for all that transport, of course.

> Enjoy the seasons! I always look forward to mandarins, which we only have in the autumn. They're also at their most delicious at that time of year.

These Apps Make Sustainable Eating Easier

(Check which are available in your country; more and more are coming up, you're bound to find substitutes)

Ethical Barcode – Scan products for information from NGOs about climate change, animal testing, GMOs, working conditions, LGBTQ rights, organic production etc.

EWG's Healthy Living – 80,000 foods, 5,000 ingredients and 1,500 brands; you can scan barcodes and search by product. Products are rated based on nutrition, ingredient concerns and degree of processing (app also includes the Skin Deep care-product database).

Farmstand – Discover the best local food from over 8,700 farmers' markets worldwide.

Good Guide – More than 75,000 products (food, personal care, household) analysed on composition.

Best Fish Guide / Good Fish Guide / Seafood Watch – Information about (more sustainable) fish, and businesses that sell or serve it (in NZ/UK/US).

The Climatarian Challenge – App from Australian organisation Less Heat Less Meat, getting you started with 8,000 carbon points and deducting your CO_2 emissions per meal.

Too Good To Go – Free app that fights food waste: stores, restaurants, cafés and hotels daily sell their surplus food for a fraction of the price ((Bel/Den/Fr/Ger/NL/Nor/Swi/UK).

Become a Farmer

It can't of course get any more local than growing your own food. You don't have to have an enormous garden or green fingers to do it. Our garden gets a lot of sun and is about 70 m², large enough for a vegetable patch. And so we eat garlic, rocket, chard, lettuce, Indian cress, broad beans, apples, blackberries and raspberries from our own garden. Not everything's as successful, but that's just how it goes. But – in my defence – it's mainly due to the slugs. Nurturing your own food, from seed to green bean, is both exciting and relaxing. It's quite a bit of work, particularly keeping your garden weed-free. But I know few better ways to help switch off for a while. Fortunately, even if you don't have a garden, you only need a tiny bit of space to grow your own fruit or veggies.

» Many plants can be grown in pots, such as tomatoes, beans, grapes and strawberries. Herbs are also easy enough, like parsley, chives and (above all) mint. Lettuce and rocket are quite willing too, and garden cress and garlic. Sprout vegetables such as alfalfa and bean sprouts grow easily and contain a very high concentration of nutrients. You can buy a small (organic) plant, swap cuttings or sow seeds.

» You do need to have some spare time and care. Because without water, re-potting and weeding, they'll die. Limited time? Keep it small (or find a bit of community land and share the work with friends).

» Balcony, window, garden – they all have pros and cons. There are lots of websites and books that can help you, depending on where you live (and therefore how the seasons run).

» Want a garden, but haven't got one? You can rent an allotment or participate in a city-garden project. Guerilla gardening is also growing in popularity, transforming unused pieces of land into blooming vegetable patches.

SLOW FOOD

The slow-food movement is a response to fast-food addiction. Food should taste good and be made without harm to environment, animal wellbeing and health, and producers should receive fair compensation. Diversity, growing locally and contact between farmer and customer is important. You can become a member of Slow Food International, which has many local branches and organises activities.

LEMON POPPY

Around half of Europeans want more animal-friendly products in the shops. 82% think farm animals should be treated better, and nearly two-thirds want more information. Sweden is frontrunner in terms of how many people are willing to pay extra for more animal-friendly products (93%).

THE DUTCH WEED BURGER

Mark Kulsdom (1976) is chief everything and co-founder of The Dutch Weed Burger.

How do you want to change our food and the industry?

'The Dutch Weed Burger is a 100% plant-based burger concept, enriched with seaweed. We also make other products and have a restaurant. Seaweed is a plant full of nutrients, such as proteins, amino acids, minerals and vitamins. It's a source of protein that's relatively simple to grow, with virtually no waste, misery and pollution. The difference with the old, animal-protein industry is enormous. We want everyone to know and taste that plant-based food's an enrichment for your culinary world. It's a fully-stocked kitchen providing you with everything you need.'

What are your tips for people who want to eat (more) plant-based?

'Buy a few good vegan cookbooks and get stuck in. Plant-based eating is so much more than salads, lentils and beans, although these can be prepared deliciously too. Run through one with your partner or room-mate during breakfast, decide who's going to make what and compile a list so you know what you've got to get. You may suddenly end up eating soccas with fried asparagus, onion and garlic – a dish you've never made before. Allow yourself to be surprised and don't think: I must be a vegetarian from now on and can't have anything anymore. But rather, think: I'm going to eat plant-based food as often as possible. This way, you keep true to your intention and don't have to feel guilty if you don't always completely manage.'

What really needs to change about the way we approach food and animals?

'We must learn to acknowledge and appreciate animals. Many animals play a really important role in maintaining a healthy ecosystem. The ocean supplies more than 70% of our planet's oxygen.

Exploit or decimate species, as we've unfortunately been doing for the last seventy years, and you create acute danger for the continuation of our own race. Insanely short-sighted. Animals don't deserve to die prematurely in a slaughterhouse, after a life of suffering in the bioindustry. It's time to put this misery behind us. Live and let live.'

What annoys you?

'People's inattentiveness when it comes to the simple things. Like turning your moped's engine off when waiting to pick up a friend, and if you do still smoke, not flicking the filter into the gutter. It's just so incredibly dumb and irritating when people are so lazy and spoil it for the rest.'

Do you have a hero?

'My hero is Gerrit Jan van der Veen. He was a sculptor and became one of the leaders of the resistance in the Second World War. I find it fascinating when people revolt against injustice and am curious about what drives them. Gerrit was almost entirely apolitical before the war, but he felt he had to do something and went for it completely. I find that very admirable.'

$\longrightarrow$

Mark's choices

Koffie ende Koeck (Amsterdam)
'Best vegan cakes in the western hemisphere.'

Café de Ceuvel (Amsterdam)
'Truly the chillest hotspot in North Amsterdam. Completely vegetarian and a really great kitchen.'

Almodóvar Hotel (Berlin)
'A vegan hotel, how cool is that? The breakfast is very extensive, with scrambled tofu and vegan sausage.'

Oumph! and Oatly (Sweden)
'These brands are inspiring in terms of look and feel, but they also run really powerful campaigns.'

We Need Less Meat

I've not eaten meat for over 25 years, and only some fish. At the moment, I'm eating mostly plant-based. That's easier in my case, as I've never really liked meat. You did me no favours with a pork chop, steak or ham sandwich. But I quit because of the bioindustry. Large-scale companies produce meat, most of which is for export. The animals are packed into factory farms and have living space – they can't even go outside. They must grow as quickly as possible to be sold and are fed huge amounts of concentrated food over a short period of time, causing chickens to collapse, their legs unable to take the weight. They become stressed and sick because they're all so crammed together, and subsequently also transported like

that. Have you ever seen cattle transports on the road? It's heart-breaking. I once spent some time in a factory farm for an animal rights NGO, to draw attention to this animal abuse. We had one square meter, as little space as one pig in intensive industrial farming. After eight hours I couldn't move and started going slightly crazy.

Eating less meat is better for you, better for the environment and better for the animals.

» Do we really need to eat animals? Isn't that strange and awful? Does animal-friendly meat exist?

» Animal agriculture destroys the environment more than everything else we eat.

» Our meat consumption is one of the biggest causes of ever-growing CO_2 emissions and climate change.

» To make meat heavier, it's injected with water (so you pay more for it).

» Ruminants such as cows and sheep emit methane gases that are terrible for the environment: 28 times more harmful than CO_2.

» To prevent animals in factory farming from getting ill (partly because they have to live so close to each other), they're fed antibiotics and penicillin. Enjoy your meal.

» Cattle breeding causes a manure surplus, with lots of harmful ammonia and phosphorus. Fertiliser is polluting for soil and water.

» Growing animal feed costs lots of space and, for example, causes massive deforestation in the Amazon region.

THIS IS WHAT YOU CAN DO

01 / Stop eating meat
Difficult perhaps, but by far the best. Choose nuts, meat substitutes, pulses, tofu or other proteins. Not eating meat has many advantages. It's cheaper. It's healthier. Lots of people lose (a little) weight. There are all kinds of websites and books with recipes and ideas. A world of new flavours and ingredients will open up to you. Make sure the

Every year, we eat on average 34 kilos of meat per person. Australians eat the most, 90.2 kilos, closely followed by Americans. It takes a lot of food and drinking water to produce meat: for every kilo of beef, up to 25 kilos of feed and 15,000 litres of water (to grow the feed). 97% of all soya worldwide is used to feed cattle. 80% of farmland worldwide is used for livestock (and so not for growing food), and it's a leading source of our CO_2 emissions. We now globally produce four to five times as much meat as in the sixties (and on average we eat 20 kilos more per person). Emissions from 1 cow is equal to that of 4.5 cars (or driving around the earth one and a half times).

other animal products you eat are organic. The animals supplying your eggs, milk, quark, butter and honey deserve a good life. Animal ingredients are in more things than you think. In many cheeses, for instance, rennet is used that comes from calf stomachs.

02 / Eat less meat

Or in other words: become flexitarian. Also an option – skipping meat several days a week makes a real difference. You can check out Meat Free Monday for kick-off inspiration: an initiative from Stella, Paul and Mary McCartney to encourage everyone to have at least one meat-free day per week. On the website, you'll find dishes and information (to hopefully go from one day to more).

03 / Can't live without?

> Opt for an animal with less impact on the environment, such as chicken instead of beef and lamb.
> Buy as locally as possible.
> Choose organic meat. Animals kept organically

have more space, are not unnecessarily injected, get decent feed and are allowed to grow normally. The cattle feed and the ground aren't processed with chemicals and the feed mostly isn't imported from hundreds of kilometres away. It's a bit more expensive, but if you eat it less frequently, you're still spending the same. Regular meat is too cheap: the production is subsidised and the costs to society due to environmental pollution, health effects and waste management aren't incorporated. Buy from the local, organic farmer or butcher.
> Eat smaller portions.
> Never throw it away. If an animal's been killed for you, you're going to eat it too.

>> *The British Vegetarian Society has been around since 1847, and provides information about vegetarian food, recipes, organises vegetarian weeks and has its own certification, 'Vegetarian Society Approved.' There are similar organisations in many countries, and local NGOs who campaign to change the bioindustry and cattle breeding.*

More Fish in the Sea

Fish can be good for you. It contains lots of vitamins and minerals, the omega 3 in oily fish is healthy for our brains. But we're not so good for the fish. Our seas and oceans are full of unique nature and important sources of food. We can't keep using those as we're doing now. The boat and fishing rod has now been replaced by giant trawlers with nets, hauling in everything they encounter. Including everything they weren't looking for. About 40% of fish caught is bycatch, which is simply thrown back overboard – generally, dead. This also includes whales, dolphins and turtles, for example, which head for the fish and get entangled in the nets. These figures are supplied by the fish industry itself, so it could possibly be worse – there's also a lot of illegal fishing going on, which we have no insight into. Most of the species we eat are currently overfished.

If we continue like this, we'll have fished our waters empty by 2050.

Meaning they're dying out, also because the fish are unable to grow into adulthood and so are less able to reproduce. And we haven't even talked about the animal-unfriendly fishing methods – although I can't really imagine (more) animal-friendly fishing. We've already talked about plastic and the plastic soup in chapters 1 and 2: the plastic we throw away on the streets ends up in the water, decays into small pieces and is eaten by the fish. They die or are caught, and then we eat all the substances and chemicals again. The industrial haul (and transport) also causes a lot of CO_2 emissions and environmental pollution, and damage to the bottom of the sea and underwater landscape. So this must stop. And you can help (although we need to ask ourselves, as with meat: is there really such a thing as sustainable fish?).

> Don't eat so much fish. Or no fish, of course.

> You can get omega 3 fats from for instance walnuts, flaxseed (oil), chia seeds, soya beans etc.

> The World Wildlife Fund has an overview on their website, with Seafood guides per country and you can download the Seafood Watch, Best Fish Guide or Good Fish Guide app, so you can make a better choice (and can see what fish species you really can't eat because threatened by extinction).

> Choose wild fish with the MSC label. This is the fish version of the FSC certification for wood, and these fishermen don't overfish and limit damage to nature and the sea. There's criticism of this independent certification for not being stringent enough – and even if every fisherman fished according to these rules, there'd still be too much caught. The fish also often comes from far away. But it's in any case a step in the right direction. About 10% of wild fish has this certification – increasingly available in shops and restaurants.

> Ask for the most animal-friendly varieties from your local area, for example at the market or fishmonger.

> There's also farmed fish, so specially made for eating. Sounds good, as more stays in the sea. But this isn't always the case: if wild fish, for example, is caught as feed for the farmed fish. That doesn't help. If the fish are farmed in open water, this is sometimes at the expense of nature reserves, such as parts of the coastline or a lake. The cultivation can also pollute the water because, for instance, antibiotics or excrement get into it (not good for the water and the wild fish). Farming in closed containers also exists, but this then reminds me of industrial farming. Should you eat farmed fish, buy it with the ASC certification. The farms are more environmentally aware, and use, for example, plant-based feed and less antibiotics. There's also criticism of this label because the standards are too weak, but it's something; going for fish that's certified organic too is a bit better still.

> Catch your fish yourself? I find it hard to imagine how you can see the hunting down and hooking

of something alive as a hobby. There must be something that can make you happier? If you must, then make sure you know what you're doing, and get informed about animal stress, pain and (endangered) species, so you cause as little damage as possible and make a conscious decision.

72% of fish-eaters worldwide believe we should only eat sustainably-caught fish

54% say they'd be willing to pay more for certified fish

Vegans have More Fun

Just like meat, dairy has a huge impact on the environment. Sorry, but your butter, cheese, eggs and Greek yoghurt are also very damaging. They come from farm animals, so lots of greenhouse gases are released during production. One litre of milk costs 1,000 litres of water, and a kilo of cheese 5,000 litres. A huge amount of space is needed for agriculture (both for the animals them-selves and for their feed), that's not used for gro-wing food for people. But in addition to the (often hidden) environmental damage, animal suffering is a reason many people switch to a vegan diet. How logical is it to use living animals to feed us? Is it necessary? Fish may lack the cuddle factor that calves have, but animals are animals – and why should we eat them or their products? The vegan movement is growing rapidly around the world and is losing its rather more extreme image. It does have quite a few benefits.

» Eating vegan is cheaper. Plant-based products cost less than meat, fish and dairy.
» It's often healthier and a lot of people lose weight because you eat less fat. But only if you eat nor-mally and varied of course, not if you live on chips and vegan mayonnaise. Important films such as *What the Health and Forks over Knives* document staggering health benefits of a plant-based diet.
» A varied diet is crucial, this will enable you to go completely animal-ingredient free. So make sure you choose alternatives such as pulses, nuts, tofu, tempeh, chickpeas, lentils, mushrooms, beans, marrowfats, seeds, seaweed etc. Vitamin B12 you'll get less automatically on a plant-based diet, so if you for instance seem to be getting tired, you can look into taking a supplement.
» Watch out for hidden animal ingredients, such as gelatine (from bones) in sweets.
» Vegetables and fruit aren't only healthy, but abo-ve all, super tasty: plant-based cuisine is incredi-bly creative and surprising. There are all kinds of great blogs and cookbooks to give you inspirati-on, such as Lisette Kreischer (see below), Thug Kitchen, Oh She Glows, Minimalist Baker, Forks over Knives, Krautkopf, Sophia Hoffman etc.
» It's the only way to join the amazing ranks of Ellen DeGeneres, Pamela Anderson, Russell Brand, Bill Clinton, Peter Dinklage, Ariana Grande, Woody Harrelson, Anne Hathaway, Liam Hemsworth, Rooney Mara, Moby, Michelle Pfeiffer, Joaquin Phoenix, Brad Pitt, Natalie Portman, Sia, Alicia Sil-verstone and Stevie Wonder.

INTERVIEW

LISETTE KREISCHER

Lisette Kreischer (1981) knows everything about plant-based eating and puts cooking and baking without animal products on the map in the Netherlands. She shares her love of the plant-based kitchen through vegan cookbooks and projects like the Dutch Weed Burger.

How has vegan food changed your life?
'Plants grow and bloom. Cut off a piece of sea-weed, then the plant will easily regrow. At the basis, it's a very friendly kitchen. And that's also what I experienced when I began plant-based ea-ting. I started feeling better physically and men-tally, stronger, happier. Through the conscious choices, I followed the seasons and ate better.

Additionally, it can make the distribution of food in the world fairer, save water and reduce agricul-tural land, so we can create primary forests and contribute to the restoration of the oceans. What more do you want? Think this choice has little to offer in terms of taste and variety? Do not fear, my friend. This kitchen is incredibly rich. Think of the endless combinations you can make with nuts, grains, pulses, vegetables, fruit, seeds, herbs, algae, sweet, sour, salty, bitter and umami.'

What are your best tips for everyone that wants to eat (more) plant-based?

'In any case, I'd start gradually. Of course, you can go completely vegan from one day to the next, but if that's far-removed from your lifestyle, it could prove difficult. Often people then run back to their old lifestyle, while your body just needs time to accustom. So, take it easy, do some research and above all: combine and alternate. These two are essential. Be amazed by all the plant-based ingredients a health-food store has to offer. Food is more than a sum of proteins, carbohydrates and fats. Food is also memories, emotion, togetherness, sharing. Take this into account and it'll be easier. This is how I started to veganise my mother's food. I replaced the bacon in the endive mash with sundried tomatoes, and I simply left out the eggs in her famous tray pizza.'

JONATHAN VAN ALTEREN

In Lisette Kreischer's book *Ocean Greens* you can read all about seaweed and find fifty creative, plant-based recipes. For example, these cookies:

RECIPE

Chocolate Chip & Weed Cookies

for approx. 10 to 12 cookies

225 g spelt flour (or ground wheat flour)
½ tsp baking powder
50 g unrefined cane sugar or coconut blossom sugar
75 g vegan dark chocolate, chopped
1 tbsp dried sea lettuce (available online at health-food shops)
1 tsp vanilla powder (or zest from 1 pod)
pinch of fine sea salt
zest of ½ an organic lemon
50 g of pecan nuts, roasted and finely chopped
100 ml rice syrup or coconut blossom nectar
100 ml sunflower oil
1 tbsp water

Preheat the oven to 180°C. Line a tray with baking paper. Mix the flour, baking powder, sugar, chocolate, sea lettuce, vanilla, salt, lemon zest and pecan nuts in a bowl. In another bowl, mix the rice syrup with oil and water and stir this through the flour mixture. Knead well with your hands until you get a consistent dough. Make small balls, arrange on the tray and then push them down a little, but keep them fairly thick. Bake the cookies for 12 to 15 minutes until golden brown. They'll become crispy at the edges and soft in the middle. Take them out of the oven and leave to cool on the tray.

Poison in your Veggies

Okay, so you happily go and crank up your fruit and veggies intake – and then there's this. Much of what you can buy in the supermarket is grown using pesticides, insecticides, artificial fertiliser. This is done to combat insects and to also get as much revenue as possible from the ground as quickly as possible. Pesticides are associated with bee mortality and diseases in other pollinating creatures. No, thanks.

> Buy organic fruit and vegetables, grown without toxins and artificial fertiliser.
> Locally grown is also better, because the fragile products don't have to be sprayed to protect them or extend their shelf-life.
> The website What's On My Food shows how many and which pesticides are on average found on different food products, and how you can avoid them.
> Washing fruit and vegetables helps only in a very limited way to remove traces of toxins. Most is in the skin and on the inside, so don't think that if you wash it thoroughly, it doesn't matter what you buy.

Organic Matters

Organic is important for the environment and the animals. That it's better to cultivate and eat without chemicals, pesticides and veterinary medicines, seems common sense. Whether it really is healthier for us, well, the jury's still out on that. In any case, it's often tastier, because it's had more time to grown and bloom, hasn't been boosted artificially, and isn't weighted with water. Organic production produces less harvest, which can be a problem if the population continues to increase. The question though, is whether we're not currently hugely over-producing: we throw away a large part of the food we make. I'll come back to this later, but we're talking 40% of all food. No longer doing this makes fully organic production more attainable.

— Organic means without poison, artificial fertiliser and pesticides, while preserving biodiversity and soil well-being, animal welfare is of paramount importance, as few medicines as possible are administered, and 'genetically modified' is out of the question. The earth stays healthier (due amongst other things to crop rotation, resulting in fewer diseases in the soil), the animals are treated better,

The demand for organic food in Europe keeps growing, the market is worth nearly 30 billion euros. Germany has the biggest sales market, internationally in second place after frontrunner America. Within Europe, the Swiss spend the most on organic food, followed by Denmark and Sweden.

KROMKOMMER

and we don't get any traces of poison in our food. Products are not processed with synthetic or chemical flavourings or preservatives. Look for the EU Organic Label, Soil Association or Ecocert-label, the USDA or Canada Organic certification, and many more (see also p. 090). Always keep an eye on whether it's independently verified, and that they're not just making the claims themselves.

— Organic doesn't automatically mean healthy. It can still contain lots of sugar or fat. Organic doesn't per definition mean local either. It can still come from far away, for instance imported tropical fruit such as bananas, mangos and pineapples. And it's not always more CO_2 neutral, because for example a cut-price chicken swells from chick into chicken in a few weeks, and so has less time to emit gases. But all things considered, the advantage, for the animals and the environment, is greater than this disadvantage.

— Not all farmers or brands think it's necessary or can afford to have certification. A label is handy for us of course, but it's definitely possible to be a sustainable farmer without. It can help to get to know the people who make our food, make personal contact or delve into the stories, and then make your choices. Good can be done in all kinds of ways.

— There's also biodynamic, which goes further than organic. Here, the entire agriculture and cattle production is connected as one, and everything's processed as such. The animals' excrement is used as fertiliser for horticulture, and the fruit and vegetables that can't be sold feed the animals. The moon cycle, seasons, water, earth and air are also part of this system, produce of which can be identified by the Demeter logo.

What is Healthy?

Healthy eating's a good idea. But, what's healthy? There are many opinions about that. Lots of things in packets or sachets are heavily processed and contain chemical additives. It's probably better to eat as few harmful substances or genetically manipulated foods as possible, and at any rate, have less packaging waste. Your body performs on food, the higher the quality of what you put in it, the bigger the chance that it'll function well.

— The less ingredients in something, the better. So, go for a short list. What's in it most (based on weight) is at the start, least at the end.

— The website Food Info (don't be put off by the design) provides information in different languages about ingredients, food production, and what everything exactly means, for example E-numbers. You often don't want them, but they're certainly not always bad (some are natural, like E162: beetroot red).

— Read the label and don't let yourself be charmed by terms like 'pure' and 'natural' on the packaging.

— Use your common sense. Famous (food) writer Michael Pollan says: don't eat what your grandmother wouldn't recognise as food. Preferably not ready-to-eat products every day, microwave meals or multipacks of crisps. This really saves on environmental and health impact (and money).

— Cooking yourself, with fresh ingredients, is fun and tasty and if you do it smartly, healthier and cheaper.

— It doesn't all have to happen at once. Start with what seems doable and take it from there.

— Do you eat gluten-free, lactose-free, raw, paleo or another diet? Then you'll certainly know a lot more about that than I do. But I hope you find what's in this book useful, and it helps make your food more sustainable.

— There's all kinds of inspiration to be found on social media via hashtags such as #wholefoods, #healthyeating or #eatclean on Instagram. There's a wealth of websites with recipes, interviews and informative blogs about ingredients. And there are of course plenty of cookbooks and even more blogs about healthy eating. In the guide is a list of my favourites, but here's a bit more about a few of them:

Green Kitchen Stories – I've never made so much from a blog or a cookbook, with such delicious results. The Swedish duo David Frenkiel and Luise Vindahl create simple and healthy vegetarian dishes, based on vegetables, fruit, whole grains and natural ingredients. Whatever I try, it's often surprising and always flavoursome. True heroes – also see p. 148.

Deliciously Ella – British blog (and books) about plant-based, unprocessed and delicious food. She also has her own range of snacks and two amazing delis in London, where you really must go for lunch if you happen to be there.

The Forest Feast: Simple Vegetarian Recipes from My Cabin in the Woods – Says it all, right? The photos of Erin Gleeson's house in the woods

(blog, socials, books), accompanied by those beautiful dishes… Life goals.

My New Roots – 'Whole food lover' Sarah Britton creates holistic, inventive, predominantly plant-based recipes. She wants us to experience a different world of flavours, and in her second book, *Naturally Nourished*, she uses everyday ingredients to do this.

Thug Kitchen – Eat like you give a fuck. The funniest vegans out there, who aim to verbally abuse you into a healthier diet. It works!

— Find out what really works for you, get informed and take some information with a grain of salt. Superfoods for instance can be amazing, but sometimes also expensive and even a waste of money. A British data journalist has collected the best studies about the health effects of nearly one hundred food products. He created seven categories, from 'not proven' to 'strong proof' and put these into a clear graph. The 'strong proof' category contains barley (for cholesterol), garlic

(blood pressure), oats (cholesterol) and olive oil (cardiovascular disease). Below these are a few in 'good' or 'promising', but most are in the 'no definite', 'little' or 'no proof' category. Check out the 'Snake oil superfoods' section at the Information is Beautiful website if you want to know more.

— Don't get carried away. Being too concerned with being clean or healthy is often less good for you, increases stress and reduces pleasure. The 80/20 rule is often recommended, where you eat healthily most of the time, and ease up for the remainder.

— At the same time, do whatever you want to do. If you want to eat clean full-time, go for it. Don't let anyone put you in a corner, and don't be put off by people that think you're no fun. Live and let live.

Fair Trade: Long Live the People

I say it often: there needs to be much more attention for the people who make our things. Whether it's our clothes, skincare products, furniture, books or food. Why would we want to have products that people were exploited for? And how is it even possible we can buy them? Fortunately, things are happening to change this. You might be familiar with the blue-green Fairtrade International logo. The organisation works in many sectors, but is biggest in food, such as coffee, bananas, chocolate etc. It's a development model, so the products with a certificate are on their way to fair trade, but not always yet where they should be. With your purchase you support them to get there.

— Daily, we eat all kind of things that don't grow near you, but in distant (developing) countries – mangos, coconuts, tea, you name it. These foodstuffs are often cultivated under bad conditions on plantations or in small communities, where the local population, sometimes children and often the environment, are exploited. Fairtrade certification concerns a fair price, sales guarantee and good working conditions. The farmers receive a premium for the community (for education, for example). A trusted, long-term relationship is essential, so they can work together towards improvement.

— There are also environmental rules, although less stringent than with organic. These products often come from far away, so consider that there'll be pollution due to transport and CO_2 emissions. Can you buy something that has an organic and Fairtrade certification? Even better.

— In supermarkets and chains, you might also find food with the Rainforest Alliance logo. This is also certification for (mostly) environmental, social and economic sustainability (so a better choice), but less strict than organic and Fairtrade.

Food on a Budget

Organic and/or fair-trade food is more expensive. Quality too. That's just the way it is. But you can also eat better if your budget's limited.

> Try shopping at the end of the day. Many shorter shelf-life products are then reduced, which can easily save you half. I do this regularly and it often yields a dish I haven't eaten before too.
> Keep your eye on offers from health-food shops and supermarkets anyway. But buy only if you're really going to eat it, because getting tempted and then not using it is a waste, not just of the products, but for your wallet too.
> Online you'll find lots of websites with suggestions for meals made of cheaper ingredients, such as Budget Bytes or Cook for Good.
> Especially buy those products you eat most often organic and/or fair trade, and alternate with regular or local products – a way to make your money count most.
> Buy less, but better. Most of us still buy more than we can chew and sometimes throw food away. If you put that cash into organic, Fairtrade and/or local food, it'll really make a difference.
> Save (more expensive) sustainable meat and fish for special days, making it exception-al (see what I did there?).
> Buy food with a long shelf-life in large quantities: more is often cheaper.
> Visit an organic farmers' market or local market. It's often cheaper than in shops, particularly at the end of the day.
> Some organic subscriptions offer great deals, because you're helping guarantee sales you get discounts.

GREEN KITCHEN STORIES

Luise Vindahl (1985) is nutritional therapist and – together with David Frenkiel – founder of popular vegetarian food blog Green Kitchen Stories.

Why did you and David start Green Kitchen Stories?

'We started it around eight years ago, as at that time we couldn't really find any modern, healthy, vegetarian recipes, such as they are almost mainstream today. David is a vegetarian, but I'm not – I'm focused on healthy, balanced food. We were eating very differently but wanted to combine healthy and vegetarian. It wasn't there! If you went into a café, you couldn't just order avocado on rye-bread. David was an art director and really interested in blogs. It started as a hobby, to collect the recipes we created. We wanted to combine them with amazing pictures and a story, which was quite different from what was out there then. And that's the way we still do it. People recognise and like to follow the stories. It's very personal, we write from our heart and create what we like. It's a mirror of our lives, but as we've grown, we've separated work and personal a bit more, especially now we have kids.'

Your work has become very popular – why do you feel it fulfils such a need?

'We really believe in quality. If you do your work well, it shows. There are a million food blogs. Many make the same recipes. We want to stay original and creative. I focus on where my passion and energy come from and try not to look at others. Doing what you are good at makes your work better, more true and real. This social media era is new for all of us, where everything has to look good. Instead, we focus on feeling good. I don't eat food because it looks great, but because it makes me feel great. What we do comes from real life, and it's useful. Everyone is cooking, eating and wants to feel better and make better choices. Many people e-mail us to thank us because they feel better. We're living in a society where everything is available all of the time, and we can't choose, we have too many options. Trends can make people change and get them for instance to try chia pudding more often. We aim to turn the trend into mainstream and make healthy eating normal in these times of abundance.'

Why do you do what you're doing?

'I have a passion for finding balance in my life, but also to guide other people to find it. Everyone deserves to feel good, not just people who have the money to buy green smoothies in a café. That's why we still have Green Kitchen Stories as a free website. We also add options in our recipes, so you can choose if ingredients are more expensive. Healthy food is for everyone. With only a few adjustments you can create a lot more balance in your body. I love teaching about the self-healing body. You can do so much with so little. Take a walk instead of the bus, stairs instead of the elevator, green smoothie instead of cola. It's not difficult, but you need to make a decision every time, and it needs to become a habit.'

How can we combat the need to always want more?

'Social media makes this so hard, it keeps telling you, you need new things. You can use the same jacket you had last year, you don't need a new coat. I suffer from that too, we desire so much. We just made the decision that very soon we'll start a project to stop buying new things for three months. It sounds like a long time, but it should really be a year. Of course it is possible! It's only things.'

What else do you do, and don't you do, to make a difference?

'I try to do a lot, but don't succeed all the time. With clothes for the kids for instance, I aim to buy sustainable brands, they last longer so I can pass them on to other kids. I recycle lower-quality clothes and bring them to delivery points. And I of course really try to think about food waste. I cooperated on a campaign to stimulate using what you think is waste in another recipe, or to eat it for lunch the next day. We created recipes for that, and for instance also use the water from the chickpea can – that's handy for vegan recipes. I bring a glass jar when I order a coffee to go. I try to feel proud about it instead of embarrassed, because people do sometimes stare at you when you hand it in... I aim to buy unpackaged items, but then when I go to our summer house, I make a Nespresso coffee. I am not proud of that. All those metal capsules! Now and again I buy to-go baby food in a squeeze package, I'm not proud of that either. But I don't worry about being perfect, I don't have time for that. I'm an optimist, I focus on my goals and actions. I try to create sustainable habits, instead of worrying about all the things I don't do or do wrong. Being negative doesn't help.'

Do you have a life motto?

'Never give up your dreams and look at life from the bright side. This is so important! We can create so much darkness, and that's so easy to get stuck in. I see it happening in our society more and more, and I really want to focus on the light.'

Who's your hero?

'Pippi Longstocking! She's very optimistic, strong, she can take care of herself. I have always done that, and I love that she is a free thinker.'

Do you have a favourite sustainable fashion item?

'A recycled golden ring. I only wear rings, and they are very personal and always have a history. You change during your life, and sometimes a style doesn't suit you anymore. But it's a shame not to keep the beautiful materials. There are goldsmiths where you can bring in your old jewellery and they make something new out of it. I did it for me and David, so we both have rings of our own gold and history, with each other's names engraved.'

What are your top tips and tricks?

'Challenge yourself to not buy anything for three months. Swap clothes with friends who have the same size and style. Hand clothes and items in to recycle, or sell them online, for instance through Blocket or Tradera. I would really love to sell at flea markets, I very much enjoy the social side of it, and I want to teach my kids they don't need new stuff.'

Luise's top tips

Stedsans in the Woods – 'A sustainable restaurant and hotel in the middle of the Swedish woods. Simple luxury in nature. The food is cooked over an open fire and you sleep in beautiful Bedouin tents. Take a swim in the lake or get warmed up in the floating wooden sauna.'

Stikkinikki – 'Freshly made organic and vegan ice-cream made with real ingredients – they have lots of shops in Stockholm.'

Johan & Nyström – 'Direct-trade coffee with their own roasting company and cafés in Stockholm.'

Kalf & Hansen – '100% organic and sustainable, freshly made Scandinavian to-go food.'

Mini Rodini – 'High-quality kids' clothes, sustainable production and fun design.'

Mumbaistockholm – 'All jewellery is handmade from recycled gold, with only natural gemstones and certified conflict-free diamonds.'

Gårdsnära – 'A website that helps you find local produce from small farms in Sweden.' ⟶

This soup is spectacular paired with the beans, but if you decide to serve it without you can add some lemon and chilli flakes to make it a little more pungent.

1 tbsp cold-pressed coconut oil or olive oil
2 small leeks, rinsed and finely chopped
2 cloves garlic
1-2 tbsp fresh ginger
2 tbsp fresh thyme, chopped
600 g potatoes, peeled
1 litre vegetable stock
1 large bunch / 150 g large-leaf fresh spinach, rinsed and thick stems discarded
sea salt, to taste

Spinach & Potato Soup (with Spicy Chermoula Beans)

Green Kitchen Stories
serves 4

Serve with
1 avocado, sliced
yogurt or coconut yogurt
Jalapeño Chermoula Beans
hemp seeds, drizzle of olive oil

Heat oil in a large sauce pan on medium heat. Rinse and finely chop the leeks, peel and crush the garlic and grate the ginger. Add them to the saucepan along with the thyme and sauté for a few minutes until soft and smells fragrant. Peel the potatoes, cut them into quarters and add them to the saucepan along with vegetable stock. Let cook for 10-15 minutes and then add spinach. Stir to let the spinach wilt down into the soup and let simmer for just a few minutes. Use a hand blender to mix the soup smooth. Add salt, taste and adjust the flavours.

Serve the soup topped with a quartered and sliced avocado, a dollop of yogurt, Jalapeño Chermoula Beans (you can find the recipe on the Green Kitchen Stories website), a scattering of hemp seeds and a drizzle of olive oil.

BE AWARE OF PALM OIL

Palm oil is in 60% of composite products, such as biscuits, lipstick, ice-cream and soap. This is bad news. 85% of this oil comes from Indonesia and Malaysia, where jungle and rainforest are constantly cut and burnt down for this ingredient. Terrible. For nature, the animals (lots of monkeys) that live in it and the people that live from it. Increasingly more sustainable palm oil is being used, although Greenpeace questions the various standards and whether they go far enough. This isn't always transparent. So, steer clear of regular palm oil and ask for the real sustainably produced version, for example via the score card of the World Wildlife Fund.

**Eat with pleasure.
Not with guilt.**

Love your Liquids

We are 70% water. Drinking enough and healthily is important for ourselves, but plenty also goes in to everything we use. Lots of water is needed to produce cotton, meat and chocolate. We must handle it sparingly, because sufficient and clean water is essential. But due to pollution and drought, this is far from normal everywhere.

In many countries the tap water is good enough to drink, and spring water no healthier. Minerals that naturally occur in water are good for your body, but they often occur just as much in regular water as in spring water. Check if this is the case in your country, and if possible buy as little mineral or spring water as you can. Instead, get a nice refillable bottle (or a thermal cup for your coffee-to-go), from for example bkr, Frank Green, KeepCup, Klean Kanteen or S'well.

Ask for tap water when you're eating out. Worldwide we buy 1,000,000 plastic bottles each minute. Americans are said to throw away about 2,000,000 plastic bottles per hour – many of which contained spring water. 91% of all plastic isn't recycled.

Dutch bottle brand Dopper emerged from a campaign to reduce the use of PET bottles. The bottle is conquering the world, two million were produced in 2016. Dopper has an app, listing publicly-accessible worldwide water-points, and supports water projects.

A cup of coffee costs 140 litres to make (tea, 30 litres). Coffee beans, tea and cocoa are often produced in poor conditions, with environmentally-polluting methods. Buy certified organic Fairtrade coffee, tea and chocolate. It's very easy to get nowadays – a number of supermarket own-brand teas and coffees are Fairtrade. I don't drink coffee, but I do love tea. My favourite brands include Clipper, Kromland Farm, Lemon Poppy, Løv Organic, Pukka and Yogi Tea (in the guide you'll also find coffee brands such as Cafédirect and Equal Exchange). It really matters that your tea is (fair and) organic. Lots of pesticides are sprayed on tea plants and the leaves aren't washed. So you're pouring that straight into your mug. Coffee is just as heavily drenched, so it's definitely worthwhile to go for organic there too.

You can use the remains of your cup of coffee or tea for all kinds of things. Scrub pans clean with coffee grounds or sprinkle it in the garden or balcony pot to try and keep away snails and cats who don't like the smell. It's also great as scrub, mixed for instance with honey and coconut oil or avocado (check out the brand Rub Scrub). Rub a used teabag over your hands if they stink after cutting garlic or onion. Empty your used teabag over plants as feed or coffee grounds as fertiliser.

Scandinavians drink the most coffee per year worldwide: the Finnish in the lead with 12 kilos per person (about 10 cups a day!), then the Norwegians and Icelanders. The Turkish, Irish and British drink the most tea. Coffee is one of the most popular drinks, often drunk more than water and soft drinks. This helps developing countries, as it's their biggest source of income after oil.

Most soft drinks contain heaps of sugar. In cola, six or seven sugar cubes per glass. In Red Bull even more. Wow. In juice too, but then because of the fruit. Still sugar. There's a growing number of sustainable alternatives, such as Bionade, ChariTea, fritz-kola, LemonAid and organic, local juices. Tastier and better (even though they still contain sugar, but at least the juice is made of better ingredients).

Tap water can be 1,000 to 10,000 times cheaper than spring water, and produces 500 times less CO_2 emissions. A quarter litre of oil and 3 litres of water is needed to make a bottle of spring water. Every year 2.7 million tonnes of plastic are produced for water bottles.

We use an enormous amount of water without even having to turn on a tap (the Dutch, for instance, 1.5 million litres a year). This is 95% of all the water we consume and is particularly down to agricultural products like cotton and food. To make a sandwich, about 40 litres are needed, for a bar of dark chocolate, 2,400 litres.

Grocery Shopping, Sustainable Style

At most supermarkets you can find increasingly more organic and fair-trade products. But it's still only a small percentage, so you may not be able to get everything you're looking for. Ask when you're missing something – the more people that do, the more obvious it'll become that customers want it. At the same time, chains often put considerable pressure on their suppliers to reduce prices, instead of using their relationship in a positive way and buying only ethically made goods. The number of health-food shops and independent businesses that have the most wonderful fruit, veggies and a wide range of all kinds of other specialist groceries is rising fast, so there's

hopefully one near you. They don't squeeze farmers, often have lots of expertise and direct relationships with the people who supply the products. In the guide you'll find some (web) addresses. If you want to throw away less, you can consider a reusable bread bag, your own nets for fruit/vegetables, jars for dry food, and so on – available from zero waste (online) shops.

DON'T GET TALKED INTO IT

Be careful with greenwashing and claims such as natural, green, healthy, superfood, pure – those kinds of things. The more people wanting to buy sustainable and healthy food, the more money there is to be earned. And the more brands and stores want to claim that they are it or have it. Food watchdog Foodwatch (active in a growing number of European countries, already in the Netherlands, Germany and France) has lots of information about this and hands out an 'award' for brands that talk rubbish. Milk-strawberry flavoured snacks, for example, containing only 0.03% strawberry powder (and 667 times as much sugar).

Don't Feel Like Cooking?

More and more organic, vegetarian and vegan cafés and restaurants are popping up, and 'normal' restaurants more frequently offer vegetarian and vegan options. Lots is changing in the catering industry, with increasing emphasis on authentic, local and fair trade – though it's always smart to look beyond the claims alone.

— Online you'll find all kinds of lists of sustainable restaurants and cafés. The Happy Cow website is full of vegan and vegetarian options worldwide, or search on vegetarian/vegan/organic + place.

— In the app ResQ, restaurants and caterers can offer leftover meals at a discount. You can reserve them online, pay and pick up. Currently mainly has participants in Scandinavia, but the number's rising rapidly.
— Asking questions in restaurants also really helps, it lets them know it matters to their customers. For example, what dishes are in season, whether the fish is sustainable, whether they know where the meat comes from, if you can have tap water – those kinds of things. Chefs and waiters with a passion for food and ingredients will take pleasure in telling you all this or find out for you.

— Ask for a doggy bag if you can't finish everything. A waste to throw it away, and wonderful to already have lunch for the next day. Luckily, less and less people see asking for this as a taboo. Make sure that your saved food is safely stored in the fridge within two hours (don't freeze it!), and you eat it the following day. Otherwise you can throw it away anyway.

The top tips from Jop van de Graaf, Dutch co-founder of organic salad bars SLA

People 'Michael Pollan for his mega contribution to the awareness of "real eating" in the extremely dark world of industrial food. I'm fan of his motto "Eat food. Not too much. Mostly plants."'

Stores 'Acne Store in Stockholm. I buy clothes twice a year and that's when I'm in Stockholm in this store.'

Brands 'Loving Earth from Australia: delicious buckwheat granola. Unoco offers wonderful raw coconut water. Gkazas is an organic olive oil from Greece we always use at SLA. Bocca Coffee is organic and just as tasty (maybe even more so) than the non-organic options.'

Eating-In Rules

Eating at home saves on money and emissions, and is also plain comfortable or fun. Cocooning is in, with games, movies, Netflix and of course, food.

— If you cook with fresh ingredients, so without packets and sachets, you know exactly what's (not) in them – in terms of preservatives, pesticides, additives. Better and often tastier.

— Get together with a group of friends and take turns eating at each other's homes: preparing food for more people costs less energy (and leftovers) than when everyone cooks separately.

— Experiment with cold dishes. We're often used to our evening meal being warm, but why actually? Again, saves energy.

— Make something from leftovers or ask your guests to bring theirs and create something new with them.

— On your own? It's always tricky buying for one – good luck finding a quarter of a cauliflower or small amount of tofu. Cooking for multiple days or people (for example, a fixed day per week) can help, this also saves money. Do you have food left or do you want to eat with neighbours, at home or on a trip? Via websites such as Josephine, Meal Sharing or Olio you can share meals (also if you're not alone, of course).

STORING

Don't Waste Anything

We throw away huge amounts. Per year we waste a third of all edible food produced. In particular, lots of rice, pasta, bread, milk and dairy, cake, biscuits, vegetables, potatoes, fruit and meat. Daily, a small country like the Netherlands alone discards 10 million slices of bread. Unbelievable. Supermarkets only want cucumbers and bananas as straight as arrows, perfectly round tomatoes and ideal carrots. Anything that doesn't fit on the shelves or doesn't look flawless is refused and destroyed. Insane, right? I prefer a strange pear, and it's just as tasty. In rich countries we dump about as much food per year as is made in Sub-Saharan Africa. There's an incredible amount of hunger in the world. If we stop throwing food away, we can really do something about that. This also reduces environmental impact. Lots of produce makes a huge journey before you can put them in your shopping basket. Rice from India, bananas from Columbia or tea from Sri Lanka – that's quite a bit of kerosene and CO_2 emissions. Cultivation also of course costs natural land, labour, energy and water. All for nothing if we don't eat it afterwards. Stopping food waste helps to combat climate change, and of course saves money. Let's go.

Buying

» So, buy less. Only what you need, can eat or can store. Afraid of having too little, nearly all of us buy (and cook) too much. How often is there really nothing in your cupboards? Exactly.
» Check what you still have. Nothing's so wasteful as four open packs of rice and three half-full cans of coconut milk.
» Make a list. Only be tempted to buy things that aren't on it if you'll eat it straightaway or can save it.
» Plan your meals in advance and buy/cook for several days.
» Eat something first. Shopping on an empty stomach is famous for stimulating over-buying.
» Pay attention to expiry dates, but use your common sense. Many products feature such a date to avoid claims, and they're often far too short or even unnecessary, such as with pasta, rice and flour.
» Do go for those lovely, crooked cucumbers and double carrots; the more often we buy these, the more we'll persuade shops to just put them on the shelves.
» Do you buy in bulk to use less packaging material? Great – but be careful with products that don't have a long shelf-life.
» At the shop, don't always take the item from the back of the cooling, especially if you're going to use it well before the expiry date. Who manages to make a carton of (oat)milk last for more than a couple of days anyway? Grabbing one that'll last for over three weeks may feel like a victory, but is actually a loss if the one at the front won't be bought and therefore thrown out.
» Shopping for the same day? Then choose the product with the earliest expiry date. And keep an eye out for reduced stickers, of course.
» Do you really want to make a stand against the system of throwing away and excess? Then dumpster diving might be something for you. This involves rummaging through the bins of shops and supermarkets for good, discarded food - you can find lots about it online. $\longrightarrow$

A third of all food produced worldwide is thrown away before it reaches us – at a value of around 550 billion euros.

Consumers in Europe and North America waste on average 95-115 kilos of food per year. In Sub-Saharan Africa and parts of Asia this is 6-11 kilos.

Some 842 million people worldwide don't have enough to eat. If a quarter of all the food that's now lost or wasted could be saved, they could be fed from it.

Supermarkets waste lots of food. In the Finnish app Froodly you can find food that's 'at date' and is being offered cheap. More than a hundred supermarkets have joined, and that number's growing. Danish NGO store Wefood sells 'out of date' supermarket food that would otherwise be thrown away and is such a success that a second store has opened. LOOP restaurant in Helsinki serves dishes made of supermarket food-waste (like Instock in the Netherlands) and OzHarvest Market in Sydney is the first Australian rescued-food supermarket.

So, another way is possible. Denmark managed to reduce its food waste by 25% in five years. The organisation Stop Wasting Food was very important in this: on the website you can find lots of information and inspiration.

Researchers expect us to reach tipping point in 2022, when sustainable food production will have a substantial turnover share of 15%. This is the point where consumers will start following the behaviour of others and from which there's no way back.

>> Still bought too much? Via websites such as the German Foodsharing you can offer or collect leftover groceries. They've already saved 12,225,572 kilos – online you can maybe find similar initiatives near you.

>> Leftover vegetable, fruit and kitchen waste? Compost it in a compost bin/heap or worm hotel (and then use it to grow some greens).

Cooking

> Make portions you and your family can finish. Something left anyway? Don't throw it out! Put in the fridge in sealed containers for next day's lunch or as basis for an easy meal.

> Cook for several days at once and freeze it, saving time another evening.

> Start your own 'out of date dinner club' and cook with expired products. Clear out your fridge and kitchen cupboards, comb the supermarket looking for reduced stickers and smile nicely at your baker and greengrocer. Using ingredients that would otherwise be thrown away you can prepare a delicious dinner. Do it safely though, and use your common sense.

> There are plenty of websites and cookbooks with tips for dishes with leftovers, or how to use over-ripe fruit (in smoothies) or vegetables (also in smoothies), for example. Internet is your friend – you'll find inspiration, storage tips and leftover recipe ideas on the various Love Food Hate Waste websites (Australia, New Zealand, Canada and United Kingdom, but the information is handy for everyone). On the SuperCook website you can enter the ingredients that you have leftover or in the cupboard, and you'll get suitable recipes.

Food

> Logical, but still: only open packaging if you're certain it's going to be (fully) used soon.

> Pre-cut vegetables spoil faster than normal ones. So, eat these first.

> The stems, of broccoli and chard for example, are often also edible, and the leaves of leeks. Seriously delicious, don't discard them.

> Learn from your own eating habits and leftovers, or those of your dining companions. Adjust recipes to what you really eat (and enjoy).

> Go for nice containers, glass jars or food wraps (such as Apiwraps or Honeywrap) instead of cling film or aluminium foil. And of course, a cool lunch box.

> Do you have pets? They'll also be pleased with your leftovers – but check they can have them! Chocolate (not that you ever have it left…), onion, garlic and grapes can be very dangerous for dogs and cats.

INTERVIEW

KROMKOMMER

Chantal Engelen (1983) is co-founder and owner of Dutch rescued-vegetable brand Kromkommer ('Crooked Cucumber').

Why Kromkommer?

'According to estimates about 5 to 10% of all fruit and vegetables in the Netherlands is wasted because of their looks. Hundreds of kilos of too-small peppers, two-legged carrots, twin tomatoes that don't meet standard requirements. Not right, surely? Containers full of good vegetables are thrown away before they even reach the store. But fluctuations in production and lack of communication within the chain also result in vegetable surpluses that are then destroyed. We make sure these veggies get back onto your plate in various ways, for example through our own soup brand and campaigns.'

What are your best tips to combat food waste?

'Buy quantities that suit what you need: if you choose bulk packaging only to throw part away, then you're ultimately spending more. Don't buy fresh produce too far in advance, otherwise opt for frozen or canned goods. Also pay attention to your water consumption when cooking. Vegetables can be cooked in a small amount of water, and with the lid on the pan they can steam cook nicely. Make sure you have a stock of long-lasting products (e.g. pasta) in your kitchen: those can be used to make dishes with leftovers from previous meals. Do you want to know how much food has been produced, consumed and, above all, wasted worldwide in the time you read this? Visit the World Food Clock online.'

French supermarket chain Intermarché has been offering non-perfect fruit and vegetables since 2015. But they go even further: they've also started a trial to sell misshaped biscuits – missing a corner for example, or looking different from the rest. Annually, thousands go into rubbish bins, while they're just as good and tasty. Let's hope it doesn't stay a trial, I want crazy cookies too (and they're cheaper as well)!

Store Smarter

Clever storage really helps in tackling all that wastage (and obviously saves money). Uncertainty about whether it's still edible is the main reason we throw away food. Therefore, some special attention for this important topic.

Expiry Dates

Look at, but don't pay too much attention to the expiry date. There's a deadline on it, but you decide whether it's still good or not. Smell it, and if it appears to be edible, it probably is.

– 'Use by' is for perishable goods, such as meat, fish, fresh juices. The date signifies the last day you can still use it safely. But if you do something with it, so bake, grill or boil it, it'll be okay in the fridge for two more days.

– 'Best-before' indicates that a product is in any case fine up to that date, but there's a pretty big chance afterwards too. The manufacturer simply can no longer guarantee quality, so it may discolour a little or lose some flavour. But usually it's still fine to eat.

– Put the products with a best-before date in sight, so they don't disappear at the back of your cupboard. Check the status regularly.

– The Save the Food website (and the Love Food Hate Waste websites) show how to best save food (and rejuvenate it if possible). Also, recipes for leftovers and handy tips on how to stop food waste.

Fridge and freezer

» Set your fridge to 4°C, this is the best temperature. Many fridges are too warm.

» Leftovers can be stored in sealed containers for a couple of in the fridge. Make sure warm dishes have cooled before putting them away.

» Raw food, particularly meat and fish, should actually stay separated from already prepared products. Containers help protect against drying out and bacteria.

» Have you opened something and need to keep it cool? In an airtight container you can preserve it for a few days longer.

» Sour and oily foodstuffs or food with lots of sugar, such as jam, can be kept cool for a few weeks.

» Preferably don't store bread, honey, potatoes and basil in the fridge. It'll become dry, lumpy, tasteless or perish.

» Organise your fridge smartly, putting what needs to be eaten first at the front.

» It's warmest at the top of your fridge, coldest at the bottom. So: butter, cheese and eggs at the top. (Do eggs have to go in the fridge? Yes! I didn't

know this either. Why don't they do this in the shops then?). At the bottom, the things quickest to perish, such as meat, fish and leftovers. Fruit and vegetables are best in the vegetable drawer – they emit warmth, which can escape through the drawers. But don't put tropical fruit and tomatoes in the fridge; they don't like it.

» It's warmer at the front of a shelf than at the back, so take advantage of this. The front row also suffers the most from the door opening. Just like the products in the door itself, so put things here that can cope with it, like jars of pickles etc.

» Freezing something? Mark it with the date (and maybe what it is).

» You can't refreeze something you've defrosted: all the bacteria's still in it (they were just taking a nap).

» Freezing fruit is great for smoothies, soup is easy to freeze and dough does well too. If you freeze it in portions, you can pop it in the oven when you need it. Egg whites left after separating? They too don't mind the freezer, after a while you'll have enough to make meringues. We often have coconut milk left over, as a tin is far too much. Can also be frozen, just like cake and muffins, hummus, (herb) butter and lemon zest.

Fruit and vegetables

> Most types of fruit and veg are best kept in the fridge. Except aubergines, bananas, courgettes, cucumbers, bell peppers and tomatoes. These shouldn't be cold, but also don't love the blazing sun.

> Picked fruit and vegetables aren't dead, they continue to live. The cold from the fridge delays ageing, which is good. Too long and too cold isn't, so keep an eye on them.

> If your bananas ripen too quickly, it helps to wrap the stem of the bunch in aluminium foil. This can keep them for up to five days longer.

> Everything near bananas ripens faster as they emit the gas ethylene. Handy for avocados or tomatoes.

> Potatoes, cabbages and bulbs don't like the fridge, but prefer dark, cool places. Cut open? Then they do need the fridge.

Packaging

> The less the better. Buy fresh food if you can and choose products with the least packaging – for example, preferably no enormous multipack bags of crisps containing lots of smaller bags.

> Bring a bag or box when shopping.

> You can hand in old frying fat at increasingly more places, it's made into biofuel (or you can buy a kit to turn it into a candle).

> Packaging-free shopping sounds pretty ideal. You go to the shop with your own containers, bags and bottles and fill them yourself. More and more shops are opening.

RECIPE

Banana 'Nice-Cream'

Got any ripe bananas left? Slice and freeze them to turn into ice-cream. Or fake ice-cream, really, because you can make it without any dairy or added sugar. For two people, you need two bananas, 250 millilitres of plant-based milk (or normal milk if you prefer it or coconut milk if you like the flavour) and three large tablespoons of peanut butter or another nut butter. Put all of this in a blender or kitchen machine and mix until creamy. Delicious. You can vary of course, by adding more peanut butter (which I normally do), bits of chocolate, biscuits, coconut, whatever you fancy. Tasty as dessert, snack, breakfast, as everything, actually.

FOOD IS PERSONAL

Diet and Sugar

I know less about many things than I'd like to, but I'm definitely no nutritionist. So I'm not going to pretend to have expertise in the area of weight loss, calorie counting or diets. It's a complex subject, your body, feeling and thinking things about it. Psychological motives, emotional aspects, habits from your youth – there's all kinds of things connected. You can be happy with your body and everything it can and does do, be insecure about how some parts look, surprised by ageing etc. This is also linked to food of course. Too much, too little or exactly the right amount, only if you're hungry or out of boredom or habit. Whether you feel positive about your body or sometimes less so, it's good to be aware of your patterns.

I've learned a few things in recent years that I'd like to share with you – for what it's worth.

— The diet industry is the only profit-making industry in the world that thrives on failure. It's said that 98% of diets yield no, or bad results. That's where their profit comes from. From your insecurity. It makes me furious! The whole industry is mirroring you an unattainable ideal, advertises an unhealthy lifestyle, makes you feel bad and earns buckets full of money. Unacceptable.

— Light products don't help you lose weight. They nourish you less, so you eat more of them. You also feel less guilty if, for instance, you eat light crisps, and so you're more likely to have more. The fats have been removed to make them 'light', which is why they're not as tasty. To remedy this, they often contain more sugar.

— Diet bars and meal shakes don't work either. They often consist of lots of sugar and few fibres and proteins. So exactly the opposite of what you need.

— Crash diets, where you for instance eat about 1,000 calories a day, don't usually work either –

you lose weight quickly, but never for long. Your body feels so hard done by, that when you start eating normally again, it's likely to store up everything, just to be sure. This is where the yo-yo effect comes from, and the fact that many people, after dieting, quickly put back on any weight lost or become heavier than they were before.

— A ridiculous amount of food contains added sugar. Stock cubes, bread, ketchup, meat substitutes, crisps, you name it. We've become incredibly accustomed to sweet food, and it's 'more-ish': you want to keep eating it. Breast milk is also sweet, so since being a baby we associate it with being delicious and necessary. And this is how brands are selling more and more food, and we are getting fatter. The sugar lobby is extraordinarily powerful, and so little has happened in recent decades. But that's slowly changing now.

— We eat a lot more sugar than recommended. Americans the most: 46 kilos per year, which is ten times more. Germans, Dutch, Irish and Australians follow. For the body, it doesn't matter if it's added or natural: sugar is sugar and nearly always works the same way inside.

— Balanced eating when you're hungry, is what seems to work best. And enjoying what you eat, because it tastes good. The 80/20 rule, where you mostly do healthy and occasionally not, is also a rule of thumb. There are all kinds of books and blogs that teach you how to do it better. Because you have to teach yourself something new, and above all be able to sustain it.

A Good Start

I love having breakfast. I once read somewhere that Bill Murray loves sleeping, because it's a time machine to breakfast. I hear ya, Bill. I can't get enough of it, but I'm also a morning person, so it has to last me a while. I like to breakfast on oatmeal porridge, but try to start the day with ⟶

GRANOLA FOR GANGSTERS

Sarah Napier (1979) is graphic designer, foodie and founder of cruesli brand Granola for Gangsters.

What's Granola for Gangsters?

'Granola for Gangsters is handmade from natural ingredients, organic and local where possible, without nasties or processed sugars. I personally quality-control every batch. Most granolas are very serious: boring packages that boast all kinds of health benefits. I want to change people's mindsets about granola and how yummy it can be, and hope to contribute to healthier diets that start with breakfast. Granola is not just for grannies (no offence to all wonderful and super cool grandmas out there), and what could be less gangster than granola?'

What about the higher price of fresh, natural products?

'I'm a firm believer that you get what you pay for – G for G is most certainly a premium product and that's reflected in the price. But what you pay for is unwavering quality, amazing flavour, a genuinely healthy product (not one that claims to be, but actually is highly processed and has a lot to hide), and you support small local business at the same time.'

Sarah's top food tips

'Brands that I admire and inspire me combine artisan products with beautiful design. Mast Brothers chocolate, or Aussie raw cake and chocolate makers Pana Chocolate. I'm an avid follower of the blogs My New Roots, Green Kitchen Stories and My Darling Lemon Thyme, for their innovative plant-based approach to modern, healthy cooking.'

something else every Sunday, like (healthier) pie, cake or biscuits. Other people prefer not to really have breakfast, and each to their own. But I've never understood why we learn to eat the most in the evening. Aren't we nearly finished then? No, I need energy in the morning and afternoon, and I rather dine slightly less. I wouldn't mind trying to eat hot or more extensively in the afternoon, work a little longer, and then eat a faster, lighter meal in the evening. Breakfast as a king, lunch as a prince and dine as a pauper, is a popular saying about healthy eating. Maybe worth a try?

INTERVIEW

CAROLINE LUBBERS

Caroline Lubbers (1979) is chocolate and cocoa expert, and the first chocolate sommelier of the Netherlands.

Why chocolate?
'It's one of the least well-known and developed products in the area of quality and tasting. Although in the West we eat lots of chocolate, we don't know much about it. The potential and quality have barely been discovered! That's why it's extra fun to work with chocolate, everyone loves it. It's also very political. All the choices and steps in the chain, from farmer to consumer, have political consequences. Chocolate's a good messenger, it's attractive and concrete. Through chocolate, I want to step-by-step bring the world market more into balance.'

What can we do to improve the industry?
'All kinds of things. Once we choose better quality and are also prepared to pay more for it, more money comes back into the chain and the farmer also gets paid better. You can develop your taste, become more demanding, with the ultimate goal of a fair price for a fair bar. More of a low quality should become: less of a high quality.'

What should we watch for when buying it?
'If you want something easy from the supermarket: look at certifications and quality. So don't chose the cheapest bar. If you want something more: go to a specialist shop or look online for which chocolate makers excel and for instance win awards, such as the International Chocolate Awards. If it's not specified where the cocoa comes from, then it's not important and therefore not a special cocoa. Don't be seduced by beautiful packaging – discover that ultimately, it comes down to the flavour.'

How can you best taste and experience chocolate?
'Quietly and with a small piece! Tasting chocolate is not something to be done hastily, but with loving attention and complete concentration. Look at the chocolate, pay attention to the shine and colour. Break the chocolate while listening to the snap. Rub the chocolate and feel the texture. Smell the chocolate and try to recognise the different aromas. Then put a small piece of chocolate on your tongue. You can bite it, but you don't have to. What now takes place on your tongue is real magic: the cocoa butter, that the flavour is trapped in, starts to melt. Slowly, the flavour is released, and the experience starts...'

EDEL WEISS 40%

GRAND CRU BLEND NO.1 80%

BEHI WILD HARVEST 66%

CRU UDZUNGWA 70%

CHUNCHO ANDINO 100%

ESMERALDAS MILK 42%

FEMMES DE VIRUNGA 55%

PIURA PORCELANA 75%

CRU VIRUNGA 70%

PAPUA KERAFAT 68%

The Swiss eat the most chocolate: about 11 kilos a year, followed by the Austrians (10 kilos) and Irish (9.75 kilos).

Chocolate Forever

Do you know that slogan 'Save the planet, it's the only one with chocolate'? I could've said that. And I'm not the only one who'd marry chocolate, right? I have the tendency to eat a whole bar at once, but I now try to enjoy small pieces much more slowly and with attention (and sometimes succeed too). The world behind our favourite candy is really complex, and a lot less sweet. About 70% of all cocoa is grown in West-Africa, and exploitation, child labour (or even slavery) and poverty are still common. Of the price you pay for a bar, in the regular industry a farmer only gets 3-5%. Why should others suffer for our snacks? And then we're not even talking about deforestation, pesticides and other harm to people and our planet. It should be made as well as it tastes – and structural changes must be made by the big brands, processing companies and (local) governments. The chocolate industry must become more ethical, the farmers must receive a fair price, and the cocoa must be grown in an environmentally-friendly way. Luckily there's a growing number of great, fair/ direct trade and organic brands on the market who make this happen, such as Loving Earth, Original Beans, Pacari, The Grenada Chocolate Company, Seed and Bean, Vivani and more (see the guide). So, choose good chocolate. (I sometimes chat with Caroline Lubbers about developing an own bar, which would be called This is Good Chocolate. Who knows, one day...).

TONY'S CHOCOLONELY

Ynzo van Zanten (1971) is 'Chief Evangelist' of Tony's Chocolonely – or the man who talks everywhere about the philosophy and values of the brand.

What's the story behind Tony's Chocolonely?
'Tony's Chocolonely came about when a few passionate journalists saw the deplorable circumstances in which children sometimes work (or are even forced to work) in cocoa producing countries and wanted to give it more publicity. Teun van de Keuken, one of the journalists, decided to hand himself in to the police as chocolate criminal, because he'd bought something he knew to involve illegal practices. He wasn't convicted, but that was the birth of Tony's. They decided to start doing it better themselves.'

How's Tony's making the chocolate industry more sustainable?
'Our roadmap towards 100% slave-free chocolate worldwide consists of three steps. First of all, we want to create awareness amongst chocolate lovers about the reality in the cocoa industry and how unevenly divided that world really is. Secondly, we want to set the right example and show that chocolate can be produced in a different, better way. We believe any producer should take responsibility for their entire value chain. Tony's does this by using fully-traceable cocoa beans that we buy directly from farmers' cooperations in Ghana and Ivory Coast, by paying a higher price for the beans so the farmers earn a living wage, by investing in long-term relationships with cocoa farmers, by training them to increase their efficiency and by helping them organise themselves professionally. And lastly, we want to inspire other companies to take action too. We welcome anyone to follow, copy, or even improve, our business model. This is also the main reason why our whole concept is scaleable; to show that anyone can follow our example.'

What should we pay attention to when buying chocolate?
'Pay particular attention to eating delicious chocolate without any bitter aftertaste. So, look critically at certifications and the origins of the cocoa beans used, and simply demand that your chocolate is made in a better way. The Dutch eat on average 5 kilos of chocolate per person per year. the average Tony's fan will be way above that, but that's not scientifically substantiated.'

What do you do besides your work in your life to make a difference?
'Phew, nearly everything and still not enough. I live very consciously, without trying to be holier than the Pope. But many things to do with sustainability actually make your life more fun. And people sometimes don't want to see that.'

What's your guilty pleasure?
'I can sing along from start to finish with some Barbra Streisand numbers.'

Ynzo's motto

'You're never too small to make a difference.'

GREEN KIDS by Laura de Jong

On the Road
Avoid having to snack unhealthily while out and about. Take a container of dried fruit: dates, mulberries, dried apricots.

Healthy Feeding
Calorie counting for children? Rather not. Look instead at the nutrients in a product. Processed 'light' food is often full of sweeteners. An avocado contains more calories, but also healthy fats that your child needs to grow. Did you know that lots of overweight people are actually malnourished? A good incentive to give as much unprocessed food as possible.

Less Sweet
We've become used to sweet food in our daily lives. There's sugar in almost everything, from bread to pasta sauce. Start with vegetables when your baby is ready for his first solids. Fruit is sweet and almost all children like it.

Take it Easy
Breast milk or infant formula is the most important source of food for the first year. So, no stress if your baby refuses vegetables. La Leche League is an international organisation for breastfeeding support. Even though there are different opinions about for instance the duration of breastfeeding (from a feminist point of view, for example), they can advise you how and when to start.

Vegan or Vegetarian is Possible
You can also eat vegetarian or vegan with children. However, children are more likely to lack certain nutrients than adults. Seek advice from a dietitian on how to prevent deficiencies.

Eating Out
Simple. Just take your child with you and see what's suitable on the menu.

NĀKD

GUIDE

There are many, many good shops, cafés and restaurants with sustainable food. Lots. This is just a very small glimpse, as it's impossible to include them here from all over the world. Search online for organic / sustainable / fair trade / ethical food in your neighbourhood, or for inspiration, check out the tips in this chapter. Are you looking for suggestions in a certain city? TripAdvisor and Time Out have handy guides. And on Instagram you can find lots of great tips: use the location function to discover the hippest hotspots or research what hashtags are common for that city.

ADDRESSES

INTERNATIONAL
Happy Cow
Vegan and vegetarian restaurants around the world, updated by the community. With reviews, recipes, information and a blog.
happycow.net

Organic Restaurants
Restaurants, markets, food trucks, food stores, farms, farmers' markets, that are completely or largely organic. Global listings.
organicrestaurants.com

VegGuide
Vegetarian and vegan restaurants worldwide – also supermarkets and cafés.
vegguide.org

AND ALSO
peta.org/living/food / vegdining.com

AUSTRALIA AND NEW ZEALAND
Australian Organic Food Directory
Sustainable shops, markets, farm shops, etc.
organicfooddirectory.com.au

Eat My Lunch (NZ)
Fresh online food service, that for every lunch you buy gives a meal to a child in need.
eatmylunch.nz

Lentil as Anything
Melbourne, Sydney (Aus)
Four vegetarian and vegan restaurants (and catering), where you pay what you can afford. Everyone is welcome to come and eat or help, especially the long-term unemployed and marginalised. Active in the community and not-for-profit.
lentilasanything.com

Little Bird
Auckland (NZ)
Raw and organic food brand, with two cafés and a juicery, offering catering, classes, recipes, meal plans, events and more.
littlebirdorganics.co.nz

Organic Food Directory (Aus)
Where to buy organic food – in the bigger cities, online and farmgate.
organicfood.com.au

OzHarvest (Aus)
Perishable food rescue organisation, collecting quality excess food and delivering it to 800 charities providing assistance to vulnerable people. The OzHarvest Market in Sydney is a rescued-food supermarket, based a 'take what you need, give if you can' philosophy.
ozharvest.org

The Cruelty Free Shop
Brisbane, Canberra, Melbourne, Sydney + online
A wide range of vegan foods: snacks, dairy substitutes, mock meats, meals etc. Also accessories, beauty and interior products, pet food, books and more.
crueltyfreeshop.com.au

The Source Bulk Foods
stores + webshop (Aus)
Chain with over fifty stores, where you can buy products in bulk. Lots of local, organic, vegan, gluten free etc., and recipes and a blog.
thesourcebulkfoods.com.au

Three Blue Ducks / The Farm
Bronte, Brisbane, Byron Bay, Roseberry (Aus)
Four restaurants serving sustainable, seasonal produce. All offer different specialities, including award winning local food, homegrown ingredients, dishes with fire and smoke, a farm shop and more. Also, catering and

cookbooks.
threeblueducks.com / thefarmbyronbay.com.au

AND ALSO
100miletable.com / aboutlife.com.au / acreeatery.com.au / eggoftheuniverse.com / mondayswholefoods.com / nakedtreaties.com.au / roadhousebyronbay.com / soulara.com.au / thegrassybowl.com

EUROPE
Brammibal's Donuts
Berlin + online (+ food truck) (Ger)
Cool, vegan and mainly organic donuts (and ethical coffee).
brammibalsdonuts.com

Daylesford
Kingham, London + online (UK)
Beautiful restaurants with a shop and their own farm, that celebrates organic, seasonal food. You can sleep in the cottages and go to the spa, or the cooking school, workshops or events. Own brand of food and drink available in-store and online, as well as interior items and gifts.
daylesford.com

Gårdsnära (Swe)
Helps you find locally produced food and drink across the whole country.
gardsnara.se

Gesunde Restaurants (Ger)
Overview of organic, vegetarian and vegan restaurants in Germany.
gesunde-restaurants.de

Hermans
Stockholm (Swe)
Vegetarian restaurant with a large garden that looks over the city (with hammocks), a creative menu and barbecues in summer.
hermans.se

Jänö
Helsinki (Fin)
Vegan kiosk and grill, run as a coop.
janokioski.fi

Paradiset
Stockholm (Swe)
The largest organic supermarket in Sweden (multiple locations), also with a good skincare department and

restaurant.
paradiset.com

Restaurant Nolla
Helsinki (Fin)
Aims to be Finland's first real zero-waste restaurant. Focuses on local and organic produce, and showing that tasty and creative food can go hand in hand with sustainability and battling waste.
restaurantnolla.com

Riverford at The Duke of Cambridge
London (UK)
Organic pub, favourite of, amongst others, Safia Minney and Lou Dartford.
dukeorganic.co.uk

Stedsans in the Woods
Hyltebruk (Swe)
Restaurant and resort in the woods, with fire as sole energy source. Brings people closer to nature: you can eat ingredients from the immediate surroundings, spend the night in tents or cabins and visit the floating sauna.
stedsans.org

The Bowl
Berlin (Ger)
Stylish 'clean eating' restaurant: organic, vegetarian/vegan, gluten and sugar free.
the-bowl.de

The Farm
Dublin (Ire)
Two restaurants, with local, organic and vegetarian, vegan and gluten-free food.
thefarmfood.ie

The MaE Deli
London + online (UK)
Great delis from the popular health food blog Deliciously Ella. Also sells own-range breakfast cereals, snacks and cookbooks, and organises events. Online you'll find lots of recipes and of course the blog.
deliciouslyella.com

Veganblog
Vegan restaurants in Germany, Austria and Switzerland.
veganblog.de/restaurants

AND ALSO
Germany: chaostheorie.berlin / letitbevegan.de / pele-mele-berlin.de / veganz.de
Scandinavia: amassrestaurant.com /

døp.dk / healthinki.fi / johanochnystrom.se / kalfochhansen. se / land-bageriet.dk / neighbourhood. dk / nimb.dk / oestergro.dk / pepstop.se / ravintolaloop.fi / restaurant-relae.dk / ruohonjuuri.fi / seyhmus.se / stikkinikki.com / wefood.nu
The Netherlands: deceuvel.nl / deculinairewerkplaats.nl / gartine.nl / hemelsemodder.nl / ilovesla.com / instock.nl / meatlessdistrict.com / thedutchweedburger.nl – see also p. 137 / villa-augustus.nl
United Kingdom and Ireland:
apresfood.com / ethicalconsumer. org/buyersguides/food / fadestreetsocial.com / goodfoodireland.ie / greenguide. co.uk / mildreds.co.uk / organicsupermarket.ie / planetorganic.com / realfoods.co.uk / theclerkenwellkitchen.co.uk / thegaterestaurants.com / thenaturalkitchen.com / vegan.london / veganlondon.co.uk / waterhouserestaurant.co.uk

THE BUTCHER'S DAUGHTER /
WHITNEY LEIGH MORRIS

UNITED STATES AND CANADA
Café Gratitude
Beverly Hills, Los Angeles, Newport Beach, San Diego, Venice + online (US)
Organic, plant-based food, which not only tastes delicious, but also mentally strengthens you when pronouncing the name of the dish: I am 'Liberated', 'Whole' or 'Original'. Also catering and a blog, and a Mexican sister restaurant: Gracias Madre.
cafegratitude.com / graciasmadreweho.com

Eat Well Guide (US)
More than 25,000 restaurants, farms, markets and other places where you can buy local, sustainable food.
eatwellguide.org

Local Harvest (US)
Website with more than 30,000 family farms and farmers' markets, along with restaurants and grocery stores that feature local food. Also: newsletters with events, catalogue with mail order opportunities and more.
localharvest.org

Organic Consumers Association
Campaigning for a healthy, sustainable and just world – information, resources and events, and a food buying guide.
organicconsumers.org/buying-guide

The Acorn
Vancouver (Can)
Award-winning 'vegetable-forward' restaurant and bar, is seen worldwide as one of the best.
theacornrestaurant.ca

The Butcher's Daughter
Los Angeles, New York + online (US)
Beautiful plant-based restaurants, cafés and juice bars – vegetarian, mostly vegan, local, seasonal, organic where possible. Delicious meals and smoothies, also catering and events.
thebutchersdaughter.com

The Goods
Toronto (Can)
Organic, local and seasonal café, take-away and catering.
thegoodsisgood.ca

Whole Foods Market (Can/UK/US)
Sustainable supermarket chain with a wide range of local and organic food, care and household products, books, gifts and much more. Also offers catering, a blog/recipes and online ordering.
wholefoodsmarket.com

AND ALSO
caravanofdreams.net / dinegreen. com / dunwelldoughnuts.com / ecocult.com (search: restaurant) / hibiscuscafe.ca / liveorganicfood.ca / nongmoorganicrestaurants.com / organickitchen.com / organicstorelocator.com / peta.org/living/food/restaurant-guide /

rawlicious.ca / rootcellarorganic.ca / stfrancisfountainsf.com / thebeet.ca / thecoup.ca / thriveorganic.ca / vitacost.com / vrg.org

BRANDS

There are many great sustainable food brands. They would never all fit in this guide, so here is a mini selection for inspiration (and more information about brands for example can be found at ethicalconsumer.org/buyersguides).

Patagonia Provisions
Pioneering outdoor brand Patagonia views bringing positive change to the food industry as extremely urgent and has started a brand supporting local and organic producers. Breakfast products, soups, grains and recipes, films and inspiration.
patagoniaprovisions.com

Just for All
American innovative start-up, that aims to change the food industry to a plant-based, fair and just system. Known for their mayo (from split peas), but also develop fake scrambled eggs, cookie batter and meat.
justforall.com

Breakfast
granolaforgangsters.com (handmade cruesli without additives, but with attitude – see also p. 162) / lovingearth.net (special and stylish cereals, and chocolate) / oatly.com (cool Swedish oatmilk brand) / rudehealth.com (vivacious plant-based milks, breakfast products and snacks)

Coffee and Tea
cafedirect.co.uk / clipper-teas.com / equalexchange.coop / hampsteadtea. com / hummingbirdcoffee.com / kromlandfarm.co.uk / la-coppa.com / lemon-poppy.com / lov-organic.com / moyeecoffee.com / mrjones.org / pukkaherbs.com / yogitea.com

Soft Drinks
bionade.de / charitea.com / drinkselo. com / fritz-kola.de / lemon-aid.de

Bottles, Cups and Storage
apiwraps.com / chillysbottles.com / dopper.com / ecofoodwrap.com /

frankgreen.com / honeywrap.co.nz / jococups.com / keepcup.com / kleankanteen.com / mybkr.com / swellbottle.com

Snacks
liviaskitchen.co.uk (nutritional, natural sweet treats) / moralfibrefood.com (great raw and sugar-free snacks) / naturalbalancefoods.co.uk (tasty, healthy bars) / propercorn.com (special organic popcorn)

LOVING EARTH

Chocolate

Cocoa Runners
Good chocolate, home delivered – you can also subscribe.
cocoarunners.com

Loving Earth
Australian locally-made brand with stylishly designed, organic and fair-trade chocolate (in many unusual flavours) and breakfast cereals. Packaging made of recycled post-consumer waste, vegetable inks and compostable plant-based wrappers. Recipes, producer information and blogs online.
lovingearth.net

Original Beans
Dutch, organic chocolate brand made of unique cocoa varieties; aim to make you taste and protect rare places on earth. Works in long-term partnerships with indigenous communities and small cooperatives to empower (female) farmers, provide a good income and create a climate-

positive chain – including planting or preserving a traceable tree for every bar sold (until now: 1,138,194 trees) and biodegradable packaging.
originalbeans.com

The Grenada Chocolate Company
'Tree to bar' brand: the whole bar is made onsite together with the local population, so all profit remains there as well. Certified organic, produced on solar energy and transported sustainably.
grenadachocolate.com

Seed and Bean
UK handmade brand with Fairtrade and organic chocolate in small batches.
seedandbean.co.uk

Tony's Chocolonely
Are on the way to '100% slave-free chocolate' and want to change the entire industry. For now, the Dutch brand offers good quality, many flavours and better conditions.
tonyschocolonely.com – see also p. 165

AND ALSO
divinechocolate.com / greenandblacks.co.uk / lovechock.com / mastbrothers.com / pacarichocolate.com / panachocolate. com / raakachocolate.com / swisschocolate.ch / vivani-chocolate.de

INFORMATION

Certifications and Organisations
asc-aqua.org / biodynamic.org.uk / centerforfoodsafety.org / choosecrueltyfree.org.au / civileats. com / demeter.net / eatseasonably. co.uk / eattheseasons.co.uk / ewg. org / fairtrade.net / food-info.net / foodmatters.org / foodwatch.org / lessmeatlessheat.org / lovefoodhatewaste.com / msc.org / nongmoproject.org / pan-europe.info / panna.org / seasonalfoodguide.com / soilassociation.org / sustainweb.org / trueprice.org / vegsoc.org / whatsonmyfood.org / wwf.panda.org

Apps
cleanplates.com / ethicalbarcode. com / ewg.org/foodscores / farmstandapp.com / foodswitch.com. au / forestandbird.org.nz /

forksoverknives.com /
goodguide.com / lessmeatlessheat.
org / mcsuk.org /
palmoilinvestigations.org /
seafoodwatch.org / toogoodtogo.com

Budget Recipes
budgetbytes.com / cookforgood.com

**Surplus, Sharing and Recipes
with Leftovers**
foodsharing.de / froodly.com /
josephine.com / lovefoodhatewaste.
ca / lovefoodhatewaste.com /
lovefoodhatewaste.co.nz /
lovefoodhatewaste.nsw.gov.au /
lovefoodhatewaste.vic.gov.au /
mealsharing.com / mythrivemag.
com / olioex.com / resq-club.com /
savethefood.com /
stopwastingfoodmovement.org /
supercook.com /
tastebeforeyouwaste.org

**Health Food, Vegetarian and
Vegan Blogs**
deliciouslyella.com / earthsprout.com /
forksoverknives.com /
greenkitchenstories.com – see also
p. 148 / iquitsugar.com /
kraut-kopf.de / lisettekreischer.com –
see also p. 142 / liviaskitchen.co.uk /
meatfreemondays.com /
minimalistbaker.com /
mydarlinglemonthyme.com /
mynewroots.org / mythrivemag.com /
ohsheglows.com / renskroes.com /
sarahwilson.com / sophiahoffmann.
com / theforestfeast.com /
thugkitchen.com

Cookbooks Top 18
*Deliciously Ella / Deliciously Ella Every
Day* – Ella Woodward

*The Green Kitchen / Green Kitchen
Travels / Green Kitchen Smoothies /
Green Kitchen at Home* – David
Frenkiel & Luise Vindahl

I Quit Sugar – Sarah Wilson

Ocean Greens – Lisette Kreischer

My New Roots / Naturally Nourished –
Sarah Britton

Plenty / Plenty More – Yotam
Ottolenghi

*Smart Carbs / 5 Weeks to
Sugar-Free* – Davina McCall

*The Art of Eating Well / Good
+ Simple* – Hemsley & Hemsley

The Modern Cook's Year – Anna
Jones

*Thug Kitchen (Eat like you give a
fuck)* – Thug Kitchen

GREEN KIDS

You can of course make your own
snacks, but ready-made can sometimes be convenient. Tasty organic
meals and snacks are available from,
amongst others: bubsaustralia.com /
bellamysorganic.com.au (Aus) /
earthsbest.com / ellaskitchen.com /
organix.com (EU) / plumorganics.
com (US)

Want to give organic bottle feeding or
non-cow based? Take a look at the
following brands. Goat milk: kabrita.
com / nannycare.co.uk. Organic milk:
bellamysorganic.com.au (Aus) /
hipp.com / hippformulausa.com /
holle.ch (EU) / plumorganics.ocm (US)

Cooking yourself? There are plenty
of recipes to be found online for the
whole family. For example, on jamie-
oliver.com/family / superhealthykids.
com / weelicious.com, and don't
forget Pinterest.

AND ALSO
llli.org

04

LIVING & WORKING

INTRODUCTION

Greed is one of the major causes of poverty. Perhaps ultimately the biggest. If we take more than our share, less remains for everybody else – or even too little. I can be quite greedy, I must admit. There are moments I catch myself taking the biggest slice of cake, the best part of the Saturday newspaper or the nicest spot by the window. Not terribly bad, and quite human, but it shouldn't become too much. Especially as it turns out that sharing often makes me happier. Giving is at least as fun as getting.

28%

is the expected growth in worldwide energy consumption till 2040 (that's like an extra China being added)

Living and working pretty much concern our entire life. Many people are either at work or at home. In between, of course, with friends, at the theatre or at school, but these places also often have a roof. Everything costs energy, central heating's everywhere, everyone has to shower, water's in everything, we all cook, use devices all day, clean (okay, that's only sometimes in my case), buy things, create waste, travel from A to B and back again or simply lounge in the garden or on the balcony, we want pets and work we enjoy – and so constantly influence our surroundings and the environment. And that's good news, because we can then also direct this the right way.

Whichever way you look at it, it's all about constantly making choices. Choices that appear minor have immediate, major influence. There's just so many of us. And we're far from all-knowing, so decisions are often difficult and sometimes nearly impossible. But don't let this stop us – debating about it is more important than mindless consumption. And that's so tempting, but we actually need to try and break the habit. You probably recognise that difference between what you think or believe and what you actually do. But that's precisely it! It's about changing our behaviour and feeling reward for the better decision. And this shouldn't be difficult anymore, as it's often more fun and gratifying than what you were doing before. I prefer cycling to sitting in the car, I feel fitter and more alert at 18.5°C than at 22, and I enjoy cooking with leftovers (because I'm just lazy). I'm sure you've got similar things.

50

devices on average are constantly using power in an American household, even if they appear to be turned off – putting 16 billion euros onto the energy bill every year

In the Paris Climate Agreement, 195 countries agreed that the average temperature on earth may not rise more than 2°C compared to pre-industrial levels, and the emission of greenhouse gases must therefore be restricted. As I'm writing this, Dutch parliament is adopting a motion to close all coal power-plants in the Netherlands by 2020. So, it's going in the right direction. But it's time to let actions speak louder than words. Here are tips to protect our shared home – the earth – from human influence as well as we can. Let's make it happen!

11.5 litres of water per minute is what you use less, if you replace your old shower head with a water-saving one

23 hours a day, our 1.1 billion cars are doing nothing

27% less often, employees with a healthy eating pattern report in sick

HOME

We Need Energy

And a lot of it too. You can safely say we're addicted to it. And then in particular to fossil fuels, that cause climate change. We really need to get rid of all this. We use too much energy, and too little renewable such as sun and wind. And this isn't just what I think, we've agreed on this internationally. The Paris Climate Agreement means zero net CO_2 emissions in 2050. CO_2, or carbon dioxide, is a gas that causes the greenhouse effect, a kind of blanket over the earth, keeping it warm here. Which in itself is good and necessary, but because we're emitting more and more CO_2, this effect is intensifying and the temperature's rising – with melting ice caps, more extreme weather and loss of biodiversity as a result. Something needs to be done about this. Everything you do costs energy: from grabbing your smartphone when you get up (to make it, to power it) to showering (to purify, transport, run, heat, drain) and cycling to work (to mine resources, produce it, and of course from you to propel it forward) – not a second passes that you don't use energy. You can maximise impact by minimising this consumption, and by generating energy yourself or using more sustainable electricity and gas.

Use Less

This makes the most sense: saves money and the environment. These are some ways to do it:

Heating/cooling
Heating and cooling cost lots of energy and can account for half of your consumption – so here you can make a considerable difference.

> Wear more if you're cold (or grab a blanket). The heating doesn't have to be turned up as high and one degree lower already equates to a saving of about 7% in energy and thus CO_2 emissions. (You can also get a warm pet, for example a cuddly dog or fluffy cat. And ask lots of friends to visit – per person, you generate about 100 watts of warmth).

> Try to wear cooler clothes rather than having to put on the aircon. It costs an enormous amount of energy and is often not great for the air and your airways.

> Your heating can probably be turned down. We're accustomed to 20°C, but 19 is also fine, and maybe even 18?

> Only heat or cool the space you're in. Close the doors. All of them, also the bedroom, bathroom and pantry.

> Turn down the thermostat (or air conditioning) when you go out – but not too low, then it won't cost as much energy to get the temperature back up.

> Switch to 15°C at night too. Do it one hour before you go to bed, otherwise you'll be heating for when you've already gone.

> Cold at night? Take a hot water bottle or warm partner to bed with you, but don't heat the room. Sleeps better too. Too warm instead? Sleep under a sheet, take everything off, open the window, but avoid the aircon if you can.

> An electric heater really uses a lot of energy.

> Buy a smart thermostat. It can turn the heating on and off at set times, and shows your gas and electricity use – and therefore where you can save money and energy.

> Bleed your radiators regularly and stick reflective foil behind them, so the heat rebounds into the room.

> Renovating? A heat pump provides the best return, followed by a good boiler.

> Invite an energy advisor for tea. It may cost a bit but can also earn you quite a bit too (and if you rent social housing, more and more organisations have free coaches).

Do something today your future self will thank you for

Insulation

Less drafts and damp in your home is great and saves money. Don't forget to ventilate if you're going to improve insulation. Tackling an average family home thoroughly can save hundreds of euros per year.

> Insulate everything you can. Cavity wall, roof and floor insulation are extremely worthwhile, as is double glazing. Don't forget ceilings and pipe-work.

> Track down drafts through holes and cracks with a candle. Get those draft strips and excluders for your letterbox and under your door.

> See if you're entitled to subsidies if you're going to insulate or save energy.

>> *Any idea how much energy you actually use? Try checking your bill, compare it with others and look at when you use the most electricity and gas. You may end up with some pretty useful insights into where you can save.*

>> *The websites The Energy Saving Trust (UK, but lots of general information), Energy.Gov (US), Your Energy Savings and Your Home (Aus) are full of tips.*

Generate Yourself

Generating your own energy doesn't just sound cool, it's possible too.

Sun

Every hour, enough sunlight falls on the earth to provide the world with energy for an entire year. The sun is a massive energy supplier. Even when it's cloudy, solar panels still supply electricity, so that's stellar. The price of good panels is conti-nuing to fall.

> You can place panels on your roof, wall, garage or shed. You often don't need a permit if it's your own home, but check to be sure.

> Panels are becoming increasingly thin and flexi-ble – they can be mounted on your caravan, for example, or a good piece of wall.

> A solar boiler heats your water and home on solar energy.

> If you have a shared roof, you can have panels placed with the other owners. Get maximum yield from the panels by using a power distributor.

> Sites such as Home Power, Renewable Energy Hub and Solar Calculator have useful information.

> No flat roof, own roof or simply don't feel like panels? There are all kinds of collective initiatives you can join, cooperatives for instance, that place solar panels on sport hall or office roofs.

> On the move? Try a portable solar charger. From WakaWaka for instance, who fuel your phone using sunlight. They also sell larger cells, for bigger de-vices. Thanks to your purchase, a family without electricity in a disaster area or crisis situation will receive a WakaWaka lamp.

Wind

I feel like in recent years it has become windier. Really, it's always blowing and there consistently seems to be a headwind when I'm cycling. Sound familiar? In any case, there's enough potential for wind energy (and not for my hair). If you have the space, then you could have a windmill. How amazing would that be! But probably not. Then in an increasing number of places you can become co-owner of a windmill, or purchase wind energy collectively through wind cooperatives. This can be pretty beneficial, so maybe worth checking out your local possibilities.

Renew your Energy

One of the easiest things you can do. Make sure your energy comes from sun, wind, water or – slightly less green – biomass, instead of coal or nuclear power stations. Best of all, is when your green electricity really originates from your own country and contributes to sustainability there. The demand for renewable energy now exceeds the supply, and as result, electricity certificates are often purchased from countries where there's excess power, such as Scandinavia. It seems like we're buying green energy, but it's only on paper – in your immediate surroundings nothing changes.

So, choose green energy from your own country, or from real investments in green sources. The electricity you buy is added to the rest and channelled to us. So you don't get your own, personal green power, but you do make the mix greener.

>> *Search on 'local' or 'national' green electricity for credible suppliers.*

>> *Sites like Renewable Energy World provide information about green electricity, and for example the Green Electricity Guide for Australia and Ethical Consumer for the UK.*

>> *You can also get green gas, which is purified biogas. And some suppliers compensate the emissions of regular gas. Since it's often a large part of your energy consumption, this might be worthwhile.*

Power to the Devices

— Where would we be without our phone, toothbrush, chargers, laptop, kettle, oven, fridge, washing machine, microwave, TV, food processor or activity tracker? Many devices still use electricity even though they're not on. Turn them off completely, not on stand-by, and pull out the plugs if you don't need them for a while. You've also got handy stand-by killers (even with remote control) and sockets with on/off buttons, to switch everything off at once.

— Don't leave chargers plugged in, this is one of the largest sources of standby power consumption (although the newest chargers leak increasingly less). I'm sometimes too lazy to do this, so I've inserted a timer, allowing my plug to only work for two hours a day – enough to charge my phone.

On the Topten website you can find the most efficient European products: household appliances, cars, lighting, office equipment and much more. Also provides links to the best appliances of 15 European countries.

— Feel the back of your television, laptop, chargers or lamp. Very hot? Then they're not particularly efficient and use lots of energy: maybe time to replace them.
— Buy devices with a good energy label, such as A+++ from the EU Energy Label. More expensive but will really pay itself back. In Australia there's the Energy Rating label, and you've also got the Energy Star label from the US.
— The biggest energy guzzlers are the fridge, lighting, computer and accessories, TV and stereo, central heating boiler, air conditioning, dryer, dishwasher and washing machine. Replacing an old version with a more economical one may make

sense – this goes for instance for a refrigerator that's seven years or older. Refrigerators, freezers and dryers in particular have become so much more efficient, that buying a new one when broken is better for the environment than repairing it.
— You're better off repairing items that cost a lot of energy to produce, like computers and audio equipment, than replacing them – the same goes for items you use less intensively (like a toaster or food processor).
— Choose as small a device as possible, that really makes a difference. Also have a look at its capacity, so you'll know how much electricity it consumes. Use efficiently – and only turn on the washing machine when it's full, for example.
— Does a device run on batteries? Rechargeable is sexy.
— Do you really need a water bed or fountain?
— Quite a bit of our consumption is also in the things themselves: what it took to get the resources, make the thing or transport it. It's more difficult to make savings here, but you can choose second-hand, things that don't come from very far away, smaller things or of course just less.
— There are energy meters that show you exactly what uses how much (and where you can get results). On websites like Energy Use Calculator you can also calculate this.
— Finished with it? Sell or donate – if the device isn't too old. Or hand it in at a council disposal point (or in the store if you buy something new), so that resources can be reused; this also applies to broken items of course.

Showering and Saving Water

I love showering... And nowhere do you get ideas as good as under that warm stream, right? This is because the combination of hot water, relaxation and the monotonous task of showering itself releases dopamine, which in turn is good for your creativity (excuses, of course). Unfortunately, warm water harms the environment 50 times more than cold water. And clean water is scarce in the world. Isn't it strange, really, that in many countries we flush the toilet with drinking water? Between 6 and 8 litres each time! Less than 3% of all our water is freshwater, and we can only access about 1% of it. The rest is stuck in glaciers, polar caps or the ground. Yet there would actually be enough for everyone, if it was fairly distributed. But many people have too little access to safe water. So, cutting down is a good idea – also because it costs quite a bit to purify and get it to us.
» Why not try seeing what it's like to shower for five minutes – or in any case, shorter than you do now? Put up a timer or learn a song of that length by heart. It really makes a difference: 22.5 kilos of CO_2 per person per minute.
» Buy a water-saving shower head: one that lets through a maximum of 7 litres per minute, that is.
» Shower together (but not twice as long as a result). We do this regularly, and it's pretty good fun.
» Aim to bath less often. Costs about three times more water and energy as a (short) shower.
» Takes a while for your water to warm up? Catch those litres and use them to water your plants or make tea.
» Renovating? Consider a shower with HRS: heat recovery system from collected shower water. Repair anything that leaks while you're at it and look into installing a grey water system, using water from the shower or kitchen to flush your toilet or water the garden. And get a rain barrel if you can.
» Get those water-saving taps or screw a filter into the head.
» Usually, your hands will get clean enough under a cold tap.
» Brushing teeth or washing hands while the tap's running? Surely not?
» Do you need to flush every time you've been to

The ecological footprint calculates how many hectares of the world you need for your way of living. On the World Wildlife Fund website, you can do the footprint test, and once your footprint's been calculated, based on your eating habits, living situation and energy consumption, you'll receive tips to minimise your impact on the environment. Shrink That Footprint also provides lots of suggestions.

The payback period for solar panels in America has already dropped to less than 12 years (and with a good scheme even to 4). In the UK it can be done within 14 years.

the toilet? I'm just asking... (if you drink lots of water or tea, you're peeing mainly water).

» Take one of those buttons on your toilet that flushes less water or put a block in the reservoir. It won't be able to fill up completely and you'll use a lot less. And there's nothing like recycled toilet paper, of course.

Cooking and the Kitchen

I prefer baking to cooking, and do most of the prep for the evening meal, while Mr Eyskoot is the one setting things on fire. But no matter how you choose to divide it, there are a few easy things you can do greener in your kitchen.

— You can turn down the gas once it's boiling: as long as it keeps bubbling, it'll cook just as quickly – especially when you put the lid on, which prevents three quarters of heat loss.

— Don't keep opening the oven to look: this can dip the temperature by 65°C. Also, use it for se-

veral dishes at a time, and/or do something else with the heat when you've finished (a yummy melted (vegan) cheese sandwich for example).

— Want to cook eggs or vegetables? Put in a pan with cold water and bring to the boil. Then turn off the gas and leave the contents to simmer on for as long as needed to cook.

— When rinsing vegetables or fruit, collect the water in a bowl and spoil your plants with it.

— Don't boil more water than you need. A kettle is more efficient than a boiling-water tap.

— Remove frozen food from the freezer the day or evening before and thaw in the refrigerator (not the oven or microwave).

— Think about what you need, then open the refrigerator and quickly close it again. Increasingly normal in shops, also a good idea at home

— Put your fridge in the shade instead of in full sun – it won't have to work so hard.

— Defrost the freezer, preferably every three to four months. Even 2 millimetres of ice increases energy consumption by 10%. ⟶

We must learn to use things and love people, and not love things and use people

— Wash up in the sink or a bowl – not under running water of course. Got a dishwasher? Lucky you! It does use about four times as much as energy as by hand, but works better if you pre-rinse as little as possible and only employ when full and at the lowest temperature.

— See if you can get your kitchen (or have it made) from environmentally-friendly materials, such as bamboo, FSC wood and LED lamps. Only get appliances with a good energy label. Renovate your old kitchen or sell it.

— Use greener pans without Teflon, PFOA or other chemical coatings, and that cost less energy to make – for example from Greenpan or Riess. Choose Fairtrade-certified tableware or brands that use more environmentally-friendly materials like bamboo or cork, such as Zuperzozial or Ekobo.

Green on the Inside

Green doesn't have to be your favourite colour if you want to decorate your home sustainably – although I do think it's nice, fresh and soothing.

Second-hand

> Go for second-hand as much as possible. In thrift shops, flea markets, car-boot sales or online (Gumtree, eBay, Craigslist, more in the guide), you can find the most wonderful items, that are much more unique than bland, new furniture. There are enough tables in the world, and they really last. It may take a bit more time, but it can also absolutely save money, especially if you search well and don't just shop in the big cities.

> Do think about what you need in advance: when shopping in thrift stores, there's a pretty big chance you'll end up bringing home 'treasures' you couldn't resist, but should've.

> Try envisioning second-hand pieces of furniture in another colour or sanded down. A bit of DIY can work wonders.

> Freecycle has more than 9,000,000 members in over 5,000 groups worldwide: they want to prevent throwing away, and give and share things for free in their community.

> All kinds of things can also be found on Facebook: pages of people giving stuff away, second-hand in specific cities and pages where you can indicate exactly what you're looking for.

> A second-hand floor is also a great option: we've taken our wooden floor from another house. And besides our bed, we didn't buy anything new at all when we furnished our home – it's certainly become better-looking and cheaper as a result.

In general

> Go for quality: items and materials that'll last.

> Look for products made of natural non-toxic materials and finishes, preferably independently verified. The Nordic Ecolabel for example, certifies furniture, floors, appliances, household products and much more. Choose artisan, independent and/or Fairtrade. Can it be reused, recycled or is it biodegradable?

> See if there's an eco DIY store in your area, like Eco Home Centre (UK), Green Building Centre (Australia) or Green Depot (America), or ask for more sustainable options in your local DIY store. The more demand, the better and faster it'll come.

> Build with second-hand wood, for example with the FSC Recycled certification. New wood? Use FSC or PEFC. Bamboo's also a possibility, it grows quickly and is strong (but needs to be chemically processed).

> Use natural paint from more environmentally-friendly brands like Aglaia or Auro (more in the guide), paint with a label such as the European Ecolabel or otherwise acrylic paint or water-based latex. $\longrightarrow$

A Dutch person uses about 120 litres of water daily, to shower, go to the toilet, wash, drink and make food.

> Go for local furniture that's made in your neighbourhood or country – you support artisans and it saves transport.

> Scouring website reviews can for some purchases be a reliable way to prevent waste, for example having to buy a new shower rail every year because it's gone rusty.

> A sustainable wooden floor, one of concrete or certified natural stone, is a good idea. Be careful with carpet: lots also contain formaldehyde, which is linked to cancer. There are floor coverings with the Oekotex label, meaning that they at any rate don't contain toxins anymore, and recycled ones – such as the special Carpet of Life carpets, made from (your) discarded clothes.

> Not everything's possible, and sometimes you must make choices. Consider what's most important to you, what you use most or what has the most impact. If your kitchen cabinets need to be renovated, it's better to paint them rather than replace them – even if you may need less sustainable primer to do so. You can't do it perfectly, and that's okay.

> Ask questions if you want to know more, the store or brand should be able to tell you if their finishes are toxic, who's produced their cupboards or chairs, what the sofa padding's made of or how easy the metal is to recycle.

> Websites like EcoCult and Green Choices provide information about furnishing, green living and sustainable DIY.

Sleeping
» Make sure you have a fresh, ventilated, cool space – that'll sleep better and it's healthiest.

» Try choosing a second-hand bed, one made of used or FSC wood or one from a social workplace.

» Almost all mattresses contain synthetic materials, like memory foam, polyester and other junk. They're treated chemically, for hygiene or fire resistance, but we can become allergic to them or get irritated airways (or worse). They're also harmful to the environment (especially if incinerated as waste), and recycling is difficult due to the mix of materials. For latex, there's the Global Organic Latex Standard, for which 95% must be certified organic. Go for a natural mattress, made of natural rubber, organic wool and/or hemp – for example from COCO-MAT or Lifekind: environmentally-friendly beds, mattresses and bedding.

» Sleep under bedding made without toxins, human exploitation or animal suffering. Go for a duvet made of collected down (not picked, but for example with the Responsible Down Standard), organic wool, vegan versions of Tencel and duvet covers made of organic and Fairtrade cotton or Tencel – such as by Bedino, Coyuchi or LOOP Organic.

» Be careful with wrinkle-free sheets or non-iron bedding: they're often treated with chemicals like formaldehyde to make this happen.

Lighting
» Replace regular light bulbs with LED ones, even if they still work. LEDs use 80 to 85% less energy.

» They're more expensive but use so much less electricity you've often earned it back within a year.

» Energy-saving bulbs last up to 10,000 hours and use about 75% less electricity than regular ones.

» Energy-saving bulbs sometimes take a while to get started and give maximum light, so place them in a room where this is okay. They often can't cope as well with constantly being switched on and off, in which case LED is smarter.

» Choose bulbs with a good energy label (see p. 177). And pay attention to the number of burning hours on the box. If one's more expensive but lasts twice as long, it's ultimately much cheaper anyway.

» The more often you turn off the light when you're not there or don't need it, the better.

» A motion sensor in the toilet, shed or attic makes sure the light's only on when you're there (make sure you adjust it so that it doesn't pick up the cat).

» Energy-saving and LED bulbs are chemical/electronic waste, so when they're broken need to go to the appropriate container or can be handed in at the shop.

Only choose plastic if there's no alternative. It's made of oil and is bad for the environment and animals (have I mentioned this?). But more is coming to light about the health-risks at home. Because you walk over floor coverings (or synthetic sports fields, or rub over synthetic textiles) it fragments into tiny particles, which enter the lungs and cause inflammation – nanoplastics can also get into the blood, brain or placenta and cause damage.

ZUPERZOZIAL

Every minute an area of forest as big as 36 football pitches disappears. Pine and spruce are less damaging than (tropical) hardwood: these species grow faster.

BLOM & BLOM

Martijn Blom is, with his brother, founder of design brand Blom & Blom.

What is Blom & Blom?

'Blom & Blom was founded by two brothers with a passion for "forgotten objects". We collect, restore and redesign original lamps and furniture from unique locations. We roam abandoned factories, forgotten laboratories or former military complexes in East Germany, looking for extraordinary lamps and furniture. The story behind our product plays an important role: every object is supplied with a "passport" providing the origins and history. We now have a large collection of unique lamps and our products can be found all over the world. We supply lamps for store interiors too. Inspired by our continuous search, we also create our own designs, where we breathe new life into ordinary materials. Each design is an expression of our mission to show the purity of the original material and how special "the ordinary" can be. Our products are designed, restored and produced in our workshop in Amsterdam.'

Martijn's inspiration

Hjertefolgerne – 'A family in the north of Norway who built a sustainable house and live entirely self-sufficiently. A secret dream (except it would be too remote for me).'

According to the 'saving paradox', more efficient technology sometimes leads to higher consumption instead of lower. Sounds strange but also familiar: if something's more efficient or economical, you tend to use more of it. Economical light bulbs lead to energy savings, but using them more often negates this by about 20% to 30%. Just like driving more in a fuel-efficient car, or cake after exercising...

Clean for Real

I'll just admit it straightaway: I don't do this that often. I prefer to tidy rather than clean. Apparently I don't find it important enough to put lots of time and energy into it, but know this certainly doesn't apply to everyone (and of course, it shouldn't get gross). So here are some green tips, because *when* we're going to clean, we don't want to inhale toxic substances or wash chemicals down the drain, that then have to be purified or end up in our water and wildlife.

— Bleach isn't clean. Bleach is dirty, harmful for the environment and it stinks. And it's unnecessary: natural vinegar and a sponge work just as well. Natural vinegar is also good to tackle smells and limescale.

— Lemon's also effective against limescale, so if you need one for cooking anyway, why not rub the taps, shower and sink with it too.

Moving house? Have a major clean out and sell or give away anything you haven't worn, read or used recently. Grab a few big crates and put everything you're surprised to come across in them. Borrow or hire used moving boxes, take old newspapers to protect fragile items and go for an electric removal van. Way to go!

— In the supermarket you'll find special cleaning products for *everything*, different products for the bathroom, kitchen, worktop, fridge, you name it, they sell it. Don't fall for it, you only buy more (expensive) stuff and packaging.

— Don't use too much product, we're usually too generous. Saves money too. If you let it soak in for a while, it'll usually work even better (and you'll need even less).

— Choose sustainable and biodegradable cleaning products (preferably certified), such as Ecover, Sonett, method, Greenscents, Faith in Nature or Better Life.

— Don't unblock your toilet with chemicals, but with a plunger (or a combination of baking soda and vinegar) and put one of those guards over the plughole.

— Much of the environmental impact of cleaning comes from heating the water. Cleaning less often is therefore very sustainable (that's my strategy), or you can use colder water. Seems to work fine with today's products.

— Prefer to get your house cleaned? Choose someone from a company that works sustainably and ethically.

Of course, cleaning also includes washing your clothes. You'll find tips for this in the first chapter – but on the next page Seepje sets a good example.

» **Making environmentally-friendly detergents yourself is easy. You need vinegar, baking soda, green soap or Marseille soap (preferably organic, or at least without harmful palm oil).**

» **Mirrors/glass/tiles: fill a spray bottle fifty-fifty with vinegar and water.**

» **All-purpose cleaner: grate 50 grams of Marseille soap, dissolve in 2 to 2.5 litres of boiling water. Let it boil for a while, or leave overnight. Add a few tablespoons of baking soda and you're done.**

» **Scouring agent: mix some baking soda with the all-purpose cleaner until it's a thick paste.**

» **Toilet cleaner or unblocker: pour a cup of baking soda and a cup of vinegar down the toilet. Leave for fifteen to thirty minutes, flush and scrub with the toilet brush.**

P.F. CANDLE CO.

185

INTERVIEW

SEEPJE

Jasper Gabriëlse (1991) is co-founder of plant-based washing and cleaning product Seepje.

What is Seepje?
'Seepje is a 100% plant-based detergent from Nepal. Our products are based on the Nepalese Sapindus Mukorossi fruit. The shell of this fruit contains a natural form of soap that's released upon contact with water. After use, they can go into the biodegradable waste. Our products are available at around 1,400 points of sale.'

How's it different to other detergents?
'Together we want to wash the world cleaner and brighter – that's what a cleaning product's supposed to do! Together: so with our team, fans, suppliers and sales points. We only use renewable raw materials, in Nepal we provide better working and living conditions, and then there are also the wonderful people with a mental and/or physical disability who pack the Seepje shells in the Netherlands. Our liquid detergents are packed in beautiful reusable bottles made of recycled milk packs.'

What's your top tip?
'Research brands, ask questions and just be incredibly curious. You'll then realise that there are quite a lot of things that can be done better and it'll feel good to act on them!'

Stop the Stuff

There's so much energy, land, chemicals and water used to make our things, particularly during their production and transport, that they end up making the largest contribution to the environmental impact of a household. Consumables such as electronics, toys, furniture, vacuum cleaners, those. So by buying, or actually deciding not to, you can have huge influence. In previous chapters we've already talked about consuming less, so here only a few pointers. Enjoy it, especially the money you save, the space in your house and head, everything you don't have to dust, that can't break, get in the way, no longer fits or doesn't have to be sent back.

— Bring a bag. You won't have to accept a plastic one, and paper's not ideal either: lots of paper is needed to create some carrying capacity, and they don't last long. So use your own, looks better too.

— Buying something new can sometimes be better, if it saves energy. For example, replacing a really old fridge (older than 7 is apparently antique) or a regular light bulb.

— Choose things that last a lifetime or have such a warranty. Rather strange actually that this isn't the norm, but it definitely isn't. In fact, quite a lot of things are deliberately less well-made. This is called planned obsolescence, where products or

The things we use daily, such as clothing and paper, cost 167 litres of water a day (eating even more, almost 3,500 litres)

parts are consciously developed in such a way that they're ready for replacement in the not too distant future. Like a phone whose battery you can't replace yourself. This is the part that often needs to be renewed first, but getting it done is expensive. So it's cheaper getting a new one (even though the rest of the thing's still working fine...). Or software updates that aren't compatible with older computers. The counter-movement is growing in strength, and you can find it online under 'Buy It For Life' for example. Webshop Buy Me Once sells indestructible brands, such as pans from Le Creuset and shoes from the Dr. Martens 'For Life' collection (repaired by the label if broken). Brit Tom Cridland developed the '30-year sweatshirt', a sweater that lasts a lifetime and has in any case a thirty year warranty. The community gives each other tips online, so maybe worth a look.

— Also support the smaller, independent, local stores and brands if you need something. It'll make the high street more diverse, and people genuinely know what they're selling and can help you. Money spent there doesn't end up in the pockets of a big earning CEO for his umpteenth yacht, but you really help someone from your neighbourhood live a good life. It's more personal, transparent and fun to give your money to a small business than a faceless chain.

— Excess stuff? There are many websites and communities where you can share and exchange. Or give them to the thrift store.

— Things broken? Get them repaired. Sweden is now halving the VAT on repairs (from clothing to washing machines), to stimulate reuse. We all want that! If something breaks very quickly, you might be entitled to repair, so ask for it. Is it old? Contact the brand to ask if they take back to recycle. More and more (fashion) brands are taking their clothes back to repair, such as Filippa K, Nudie

CARPET OF LIFE / PAM KAT

Jeans and Patagonia. And maybe a Repair Café's something for you. During these free get-togethers you learn that repairing is fun and often easy. You can (jointly) fix all kinds of things there, like furniture, tableware, electronics, toys, clothes, and so on. They're in many countries, and expertise and tools are available.

— Every year, October is Buy Nothing New month. An interesting challenge, worth giving it a shot (that month, any month, or a bit longer)?

Green and Garden

We have a garden, which is great. At least, we think so – some people think it's a lot of work. And it is. Absolutely. A balcony or roof terrace can be just as wonderful, or some plants inside. Most people in any case enjoy being around green. Green thumbs up!

Inside

— Good air quality in your home is very important. You get it by ventilating well, throwing open windows and doors, and through plants. Air-purifying indoor plants convert CO_2 into oxygen and bring water vapour into the air, improving air humidity. A study by NASA shows that some indoor plants purify the air of toxic substances such as benzene, formaldehyde and ammonia. They also create ambience, which in turn provides relaxation. Types such as the curly ferns, the areca palm or gold palm, aloe vera and the spoon plant are good to have at home for this.

— Would you like more plants? Then see if you can adopt them. Quite a few people want rid of them, and there's nothing wrong with a second-hand plant, right? Explore a bit online, for example on the German website botanoadopt, but also on second-hand websites.

— Remember the name of your plant and look up how much light and water it needs. Too much or too little is the most important reason they die, so that should be easy to prevent.

Outside

— Choose organic soil, and don't use poison, chemicals or pesticides in your garden. Certainly not if you want to eat from it, but preferably not at all. It's bad for the soil and the creatures living in your garden. Are these creatures bugging you? Try natural remedies (such as coffee grind for cats and snails or a net to stop the birds), root-proof liners for weeds or if there's really no other choice, a brand like Eco Organic Garden or Planet Natural. And a good old weed is brilliant for your biceps.

— Whatever you do, try not to use too many devices – high-pressure cleaner, leaf blower, mower: is it really necessary?

— Before you set off to buy plants and cram your garden, first take a good look at for example where most sun is, exactly what you want to do with your garden and how much space you have (plants grow considerably once they've been planted, which I sometimes forget). Also get some evergreen plants and shrubs, so you've a green environment all year round. Make a plan and hit the road.

— Choose plants common to where you live rather than exotic ones, as these not only might need more sun, but more water too.

— Do you enjoy food? Then think about the bees! Because their pollination's necessary for almost everything that grows and blooms, from coffee beans to cucumbers. They eat nectar and pollen from plants and flowers. But because cities are increasingly concrete, there's also less food for bees. Make sure flowers bloom in your garden or on your balcony. Go organic, so they don't have to eat poison, and choose native plants, they flourish best. You can also get a bee hotel. Organisations such as Save Bees and SOS Bees provide information and tips about what's best for the bee.

— Whatever you do, try to attract as many animals to your garden as you can. The more hiding places and undergrowth for hedgehogs and birds the better. They're natural enemies of snails and lice. Make a path of wood chips or cocoa pods rather than paving, so water can easily enter the soil – and it's more welcoming for animals too.

— Aim to water plants in the evening, the water will reach the roots before evaporating in the sun. Spraying? Then rather larger drops than finer ones, otherwise everything blows away. And preferably lots less often than a little, more often – this'll make the roots longer and plants will be more able to retrieve water from the soil.

— Make a compost heap to collect all your biodegradable and plant waste – you can use it to fertilise your garden the following year. This can also be done on a balcony, for example with a worm tray. Sounds more hassle than it is, and you transform waste into food.

— Also see the previous chapter about growing vegetables and fruit in your garden or on your balcony. Fun and tasty.

— If you're at a garden centre, look for the organically-grown range. But also try a local plant market, often cheaper. And of course you can swap and share cuttings, you'll find lots about this online.

— Don't forget your roof. A roof terrace or green roof can do a lot for the insulation of your house, and provides more nature in the city.

— Furniture, patios and entire garden sheds are often offered second-hand for practically nothing. We've found pretty much everything in our garden like this, even down to a free rotary-dryer.

— These were just a couple small tips, there are many books and sites brimming with information about natural gardening, animal-friendly gardening, growing your own fruit and veg, and so on (for instance Garden Organic, Eco Warrior Princess or Grow Organic (with how-to videos, and a shop), to name but a few).

477 kilos of waste per person is what council disposal services collected on average in 2015 in the European Union.

No Such Thing as Waste

The Dutch government has just announced that the country should be completely circular by 2050. This means the economy must run entirely on recycled resources, and all waste processed into usable materials. So waste will no longer exist, it's the basis for something new. By 2030, the use of finite raw materials such as oil, gas, minerals and metals must already be halved. Smartphones need to be completely recycled, and the crisp packet – not recyclable because of the aluminium inside – must be 'phased out'. As a result, we will be emitting much less CO_2, so that's good. Manufacturers of mattresses, disposable nappies and clothes will be responsible for collecting and processing their used products. It remains to be seen, but I think it's a great plan. Just like the differentiation rate system, where separated waste is collected from your home, but you must dispose of your general waste yourself and pay for it per quantity. In councils that have already started this, the general waste is spectacularly less, about 50 to 190 kilos per person. There's a lot you can do to reduce waste.

— It goes without saying: separate as much as possible. Hand in paper, glass and, if possible, plastic. You know what to do.

— Say no to the receipt when you shop (and definitely don't want to return it) or ask for it to be e-mailed, and don't take one when getting money from the ATM.

— Do you have another use for all that paper? I write (illegible) shopping lists on the back of teabags and to-do lists on calendar sheets.

— Make it small before you put it in the bin or recycling container: causes less transport.

— Try to also separate green waste: get a compost or worm bin or take it to the council refuse depot.

— Don't stuff cans with other waste, as tin is extracted before incineration to recycle, and this makes it more difficult.

— Watch out for layers on the inside, for example in milk cartons or peanut packets. Because of this aluminium or plastic coating, it often can't be recycled and therefore doesn't belong in the old paper or plastic.

— Put your medicines, low-energy light bulbs (contains some mercury) and batteries in those special disposal containers.

— Recyclebank has lots of tips about recycling, what's better (plastic bags or aluminium foil to wrap your sandwiches, for example; even though a lunch box is of course the real answer) – and you can earn points and exchange them for discounts or donations.

— Obviously you'll have less waste if you borrow, share, rent, don't buy more than you use, go for quality over quantity, mend your stuff when broken and give away or sell what's leftover.

— About a quarter of general waste is packaging. Try to reduce that and not buy unnecessarily packaged things. If you order something from a brand that uses RePack, you can return the packaging in a letterbox. They use them twenty times – and you get a discount at affiliated labels (like Filippa K or Globe Hope).

— Do you have spare stuff that someone else can still use? Put it out on the street and hopefully somebody will take it. You can also set up a cute cupboard in front of your house with unwanted books, shoes and appliances. Nice gift for passers-by.

— Out walking? Pick up any litter you encounter. Mr Eyskoot and I did this for some 10 minutes along a stretch of road, and we came back with handfuls of plastic bottles, sweet packets and other junk. Clearing litter is quite fun to do too, and in any case made us feel good.

— Send back advertising addressed to you as 'return to sender' (and put a 'No Junk Mail' sticker on your letterbox to stop exactly that).

>> In the US, the PaperKarma app helps eliminate junk mail.

— Request for (phone, electricity, etc.) bills to be sent by e-mail.

— Be mindful of the amount of plastic you buy. Goodness me. Since we've been separating it in the Eyskoot household, it's been so noticeable. We've been talking about the plastic soup in the oceans in just about every chapter: the rubbish dump floating somewhere between Hawaii and San Francisco in the Pacific Ocean. The Ocean Cleanup by Boyan Slat is trying to do something about this, just like the Plastic Soup Foundation – there are tips on their website.

INTERVIEW

NAOMI RACHÈL TIMAN

Naomi Rachèl Timan (1991) has her own brand of bags made for example of old sofas, is designer and the picture editor of this book.

What have you done for this guide?
'I put together the image bank and with you and the designers, collected the best pictures. The great thing about this was that I was allowed – indeed had to – read every chapter as soon as it was finished, to request photographs.'

You've also got your own bag label?
'Naomi Rachèl Timan is a sustainable bag and accessory brand. I make every product by hand, from recycled leather. There's a label on every item saying what it was first, for instance: I WAS A SOFA. I find really beautiful leather discarded at the side of the road in the rubbish, and more and more people know how to find me when getting rid of a sofa or jacket. With my bags I want to make people happy and spread the message that not everything has to be waste. It all must be mass-made, as cheap as possible and fast and as a result, lots is discarded. I go against the crowds and overproduction by using this "waste" in a new way.'

DAVID VAN DARTEL

Do you have a motto?
'Make the most of everything, in whatever way you can! Nothing will just come to you and if you really want something: just do it! If it doesn't work, try to learn from it for your next goals.'

Naomi's top tip
The Goodwill Store in State College, Pennsylvania 'I always score the most amazing vintage items there.'

Lots of waste only decomposes slowly. Chewing gum on the pavement takes 20 years. A cigarette butt 2 years. A plastic bottle won't disappear for hundreds of years. Journalist Bahram Sadeghi did an experiment: for three years, he kept all the plastic he used. This resulted in 41 bin bags full.

Loving our Pets .

It somehow always seems a bit strange to 'keep' animals. But at the same time, we feel better, less lonely, we move and cuddle more and can maybe give a sweet animal a lovely life. Preferably then, as sustainable as possible too.

— Help a refuge animal find a new home. There's bound to be a shelter near you (although you might bring back twelve cats instead of one).

— You can also adopt an animal without taking one in. For example, you can support specific monkeys, bears or cats at International Animal Rescue.

— It goes for animals too: eating meat is incredibly harmful to the environment (see the previous chapter). Plant-based food a few days a week doesn't hurt?

— Choose organic food, or as natural as possible – for example, from the brand Yarrah.

— Use second-hand, recycled or environmentally-friendly toys, baskets and accessories and get natural, compostable and/or biodegradable cat (or hamster) litter.

— Don't keep an exotic animal as pet.

INTERVIEW

JONATHAN VAN ALTEREN

Jonathan van Alteren (1978) renovated his house as sustainably as possible. To help others do the same he started a natural renovation and energy-saving consultancy.

How did you approach it?
'My search began for a house with a flat roof. Then we had to find a contractor who not only dared to take on a major renovation but was also prepared to work with all kinds of green building materials. We wanted to step away from using gas for heating and hot water, and went for a heat pump in combination with PVT solar and warm-water panels on the roof, and a high-efficiency wood-burning stove. We store hot water in a buffer tank. Next to that, we insulated the facades with hemp and wood fibre, and the floor with ecologically-responsible foam. To top that off: heat recovery from the shower drain and air ventilation, and wall heating with mud plaster.'

What should we really be doing?
'Start at the beginning by clearly establishing your main framework. You don't know in advance what'll come your way, so this will help you make the right choices. Don't just settle for information you get. Be critical, ask and do your own research. I've found a lot online.'

Do you have a hero?
'Coincidentally, I'm just reading a book about scientist and explorer Alexander von Humboldt. I find him very inspiring, just like Viktor Schauberger, a brilliant Austrian inventor with a special connection with nature.'

Jonathan's top tip
'Stop getting a new mobile phone every one or two years. Switching to sim-only saves you hundreds of euros a year and saves nature a mountain of junk and rare resources.'

Living Differently

How a house is built has substantial impact on the environment. So sustainable (re)building is very important, if you buy a house or rent (pay attention to the energy label if possible). You can also do it yourself, if you're a bit handy and above all have some perseverance. Jonathan van Alteren did it, on the left he shares his experiences and tips. You can also take a different road, and for example start living small.

Tiny House Movement

This movement from America keeps getting bigger and more international. More and more people want to eliminate all their stuff, mortgages and obligations. Getting rid of as many possessions as possible, they move into very small, self-sufficient and movable houses. Dee Williams went to live in 8 m² and described her experiences in a book, *The Big Tiny*. Through her website, everyone worldwide could follow her life in a mini-house, and her book became a bestseller. The Tiny House Movement was born. Now, about 10,000 people live in such a small house in the United States. Most live in slightly bigger ones, between 15 and 20 m², designed incredibly ingeniously. The ecological footprint is low because the houses are built sustainably (and are mini). Living costs are too, meaning you can work less if you want to. Also living closer to nature, the flexibility and the minimalistic, more simple life is viewed by many as being very attractive. You can find out more through documentaries such as *TINY (a story about living small)* and *Small is Beautiful*. Wikkelhouse in Amsterdam makes tiny houses from cardboard in (wrapped) layers. They're constructed from reusable modules you can combine to make your dream house. Sustainably designed, water-tight, movable and beautiful – what are we waiting for?

Share Yourself Rich

Sharing is the new having, is what we keep hearing. And although all these 'this is the new that' expressions sometimes sound a bit lame, there is something to this. Because why should we have all those things for ourselves if we don't use them all the time? It saves money, space and footprint. Sharing a telephone may not be so handy, but a drill, spare room or car? Why not? How often are these things standing or lying around doing nothing? You can even earn money from them if you want too. Initiatives are springing up like mushrooms, here are a few of them.

Everything

According to Peerby, we don't use 80% of our possessions more than once a month. So why would you buy them? You'd be better off borrowing. It takes two to tango, so via the Peerby app (or website) you can ask people in your neighbourhood if they happen to have a party tent, high-pressure cleaner or circular saw. Free and sustainable, because less waste, emissions and trash. You also receive requests, so can give something back. And get to know your neighbours! Streetbank offers this too, and according to *The Times* is one of 50 websites you can't live without. The initiative is from the UK, but active in over 80 countries. Konnektid works similarly, but then with expertise: people with a skill (computer, Italian,

music reading, etc.) offer themselves, and if you use their services you 'pay back' with your own specialism. Everyone knows or can do something – a fun and free way to learn more.

Car

Your car's also doing nothing for a large part of the time. Such a waste! Of money (the fixed costs continue), the environment, the space. Why do we have so many? There are lots of different car-sharing initiatives. Via Snappcar (in Denmark, Germany, Sweden and the Netherlands, but growing quickly) and Getaround (America), you can rent cars from each other, insured and cheaper than from rental companies. The Toogethr app allows you to travel with someone, either to work or somewhere else, just like BlaBlaCar, Carpool-World or LiftShare. Green Motion rents out more environmentally-friendly cars.

Cars stand still about 95% of the time.

FAIRPHONE

Clothes, food and home

We have way more clothes than we wear, and some we only need for special occasions anyway. So long live fashion libraries like Kleiderei and Rent the Runway (see p. 063), where you can borrow outfits from an endless walk-in wardrobe. There are also websites and apps enabling you to share food with the neighbourhood, such as Josephine, Meal Sharing or Olio. Delicious! In the next chapter about leisure you'll find more about sharing your home.

Money for Good

We can't do without, and it also determines a large part of our life and the choices we have and make. Most of us need to work hard for it. Making it important that our hard-earned pennies are invested in something good, and not used to finance exploitation, the arms trade, environmental pollution (oil, coal, nuclear energy) or child labour. This is how you can organise your money matters sustainably:

_____

Take a look at the Fair Finance Guide International (Belgium, Brazil, Germany, France, Indonesia, Japan, the Netherlands, Norway and Sweden, but more and more countries are being added), to see how your bank performs in areas such as climate change, human rights, weapons, animal welfare, mining and corruption.

_____

» Transfer to a bank that does it better, it's really easy. In the interview with ASN Bank (overleaf) you'll find a few tips or look at the Fair Finance Guide or BankTrack.
» Get a green credit card, and put your savings with an ethical bank.
» Want your money to yield a bit more? There are increasingly more possibilities to invest sustainably, and in general these funds achieve good returns. It can also get you tax benefits, so worth exploring.
» You can also invest in innovative, environmentally friendly and/or social businesses. Some banks have special funds for this.
» The other way around's also possible: become shareholder of Shell and try to make them as green as possible from the inside out. Follow This organises this collective activist shareholding.
» Allow your money to support an entrepreneur in a developing country via microcredit. It's often hard to get a loan to set up their own business, while they can give themselves and their families a much better life. You can for example look at Kiva, Global Giving or Lendahand.
» Through crowdfunding you can directly facilitate the development of innovative, creative and sustainable start-ups and products. You'll find many on for example Onepercentclub or Oneplanetcrowd, and Kickstarter also often features sustainable projects. Your deposit's not guaranteed if things go wrong and returns can vary, so investigate thoroughly before investing.
» Simply do something kind for someone who urgently needs money? Via peer-to-peer platforms such as Lending Club, Upstart or Funding Circle, you can, against fixed conditions.
» Buying a house? See if you can get a green mortgage, that's for instance cheaper if you make your house more sustainable.
» Building up a pension? Why not ask your employer whether social and green investments are considered when selecting funds.
» Where does your money go when you die (and something's left)? You can donate your assets to charities such as Amnesty International, Women on Waves or She Decides. Gifts are often exempt from inheritance tax.

Want to know more about the role of banks in the world? BankTrack is the international campaign organisation that examines banks and their activities. They promote fundamental changes in the way banks work, so they become transparent and accountable and contribute to the wellbeing of planet and people. Check out their information about specific banks (worldwide), reports and campaigns.

ASN BANK

Milou Posthumus (1989) is community manager at Dutch sustainable bank ASN Bank.

How's the ASN Bank different from other banks?

'The ASN Bank is a sustainable bank. This means that in all choices we make, we consider people, climate and nature. Every business we invest in therefore undergoes a strict selection by our Sustainable Policy and Research department. We don't for example invest in fossil energy or businesses linked to child labour or the arms industry. Companies must also comply with treaties related to labour rights and with our rules regarding animal welfare. In addition, we try to contribute through other activities. We have a platform for people with smart ideas for a better world where you'll find inspiring blogs, and we organise events, for example the annual ASN Bank World Prize, through which we give people with ideas that (help) solve social problems a flying start. They receive intensive guidance and a shot at a large sum of money. Previous winners include Fairphone and Yoni.'

What are the benefits for customers?

'You get the same service as customers at other banks but can be sure that your money contributes to a better world. For example, we invest in sustainable housing, renewable energy and healthcare. We also support many social partners through the themes of fair trade, (stopping) child labour, sustainable energy, (tackling) the arms industry, and healthcare & well-being. We also manage sustainable funds you can invest in, the returns of which are often very good.'

Tips for sustainable banks

Sweden

Ecobanken: 'Invests money so it has a positive effect on society, and creates more ecological, social, cultural and economic sustainability.'

YONI

JAK Medlems: 'Cooperative bank that considers it unethical to lend money with interest, they run an interest-free savings and loan system.'

Norway

Cultura Bank: 'Transparent bank, with social and environmental criteria for loans and investments.'

Germany

GLS Bank: 'Germany's first anthroposophical bank, operating according to an ethical philosophy.'

America

New Resource Bank: 'Uses the investing and loaning of money for a better world.'

First Green Bank: 'Traditional community bank that stimulates environmental and social responsibility.'

Australia

Bank Australia: '100% customer-owned ethical and sustainable bank, that's been carbon neutral since 2011.'

UK

Charity Bank: '"A bank for good", that loans money to charities and social enterprises.'

Ethical Electronics

Where would we be without our phone or laptop? Wow, we spend so much time on electronic devices (more about that in the next chapter). Their manufacture causes exploitation and environmental pollution. The production of a laptop for example generates huge impact on the planet – especially the extraction of raw materials by mining. But also the people who dig these up suffer immensely. Working in the mines is incredibly hard, poorly paid and very unhealthy: human rights and environmental violations are common. Fortunately, you can do something to make it a little better.

Your smartphone is filled with dozens of materials from all over the world. Unfortunately, all that tin, gold and tungsten often comes from conflict areas, where conditions are on par with diamond and gemstone mining (see chapter 1). Your mobile's also designed to be difficult to repair, and so only lasts a short time. Fairphone wants to do something about this: making a conflict-free, fair and sustainable phone that lasts longer. You can read all about it on page 198. The Finnish PuzzlePhone is trying to make a more sustainable and modular smartphone, consisting of replaceable elements. And then of course there's always John's Phone, which you can only call with. Not necessarily made sustainably, but doesn't have to be replaced so fast because there's no large screen for example and the battery's more durable.

> Consider second-hand if you need a phone or laptop. Saves on resources, footprint and waste. I try to do this, and you'll be surprised by the amount of good devices offered online (be careful though that the offer's not *too* good to be true).

> With a smartphone too, the impact's much more in the production than use. Aim to make it work for as long as possible, for instance by not running the battery completely empty (preferably not below 20%). This'll keep it in good shape for longer and you'll not need a new one as quickly – it can make a difference of up to a year. Turn down your screen brightness too, and don't leave in the charger if already full. Get it repaired if the screen's broken or it doesn't charge properly: cheaper than replacing and the rest can often last for years.

> A laptop's more sustainable than a desktop, as it's smaller (a tablet's therefore even better). Try to extend its life by buying a new battery or hard drive. Switch off or to sleep mode (a screen saver uses a lot of energy) when you're not using it and the brightness below max.

> New TV or monitor? Does it really have to be that big? Costs a lot more energy to make and use (a pair of glasses a lot less, for example...).

> And do you actually have to own it? More and more brands and companies now rent out laptops, televisions and washing machines.

> Or maybe you're handy and can mend it yourself? On the websites iFixit and Instructables you'll find instructions for repairing many brands of smartphones, tablets, game consoles and even cars. On the forum, tips are exchanged and you can ask for help.

> Want to know more about the sustainable policy of an electronics brand? The GoodElectronics network, an international alliance of trade unions, NGOs, activists and researchers working for a fairer and more sustainable electronics industry, has all kinds of information. Greenpeace campaigns against chemicals in clothes and electronics and publishes an Electronics Ranking List on their website that shows how green producers of smartphones and laptops are.

FAIRPHONE

Douwe Schmidt (1981) is community manager at Fairphone.

What is Fairphone?

'Fairphone is a Dutch social enterprise that makes a telephone to discover and improve malpractices in the technology sector. We work with mines in the Congo to ensure the proceeds from mining aren't used for buying weapons and thus contribute to conflict in the region. We also work with a mine in Peru that's certified and supplies Fairtrade gold. At the factory in China we cooperate with employees and owners on good working conditions. The Fairphone 2 is designed to be long-lasting and reduce the need to buy another phone. It can take a knock, is easy to repair and can be enhanced with more memory and better parts. With the purchase of a Fairphone you contribute to our lifecycle programme, where we buy old broken phones and have them recycled in a responsible manner. It's also designed in such a way that it's easier to recycle.'

What's wrong with our phones?

'The main problem in the electronics industry is lack of transparency. We don't know where our phones come from, how they work and where they go when they're bust. There are more mobile phones in the world than people. All these phones are made, used and then thrown away. Ordinary telephones are not made for recycling, repair or reuse. The average lifetime of a mobile phone is twelve to eighteen months. To manufacture a telephone in China, people work on average 10 hours a day, 6 days a week.'

What can people do if they want to be more sustainable with their phone (use)?

'Use your telephone for as long as possible. If it breaks, try to repair it. 90% of the energy and resources needed to use a telephone are in the production. So the longer you can delay buying a new one, the smaller the impact on the planet and the people who live on it.'

What other electronic brands do you admire?

'There are a few other companies, such as Waka-Waka, NagerIT, Little Sun, Ecosia, Nextcloud, that deal with technology in a responsible manner. We don't recommend other companies because we're not able to fully understand their processes and be sure of their good intentions.'

What's your favourite tip for a sustainable lifestyle?

'Look around you in the supermarket and try to consider which of all the pre-packaged products you could actually easily make yourself.'

The organisers of the 2020 Olympic Games in Tokyo want to make medals from old smartphones and other electronic devices. Japan has few metals in the ground, but lots of electronic waste filled with it: about 2.3% of the world's stock of gold is in Japanese e-waste, which they'll collect for this.

WORK

Socially Responsible is Modern

Just about everything relating to living also applies to your workplace. It can be more energy efficient, smarter and less wasteful (and so more fun and cheaper). But there are also a few topics that specifically have to do with working life. Corporate social responsibility has become increasingly important in recent years, and companies are progressively recognising their own, significant role. This applies both to what you make or do, and to the way how: people, planet and profit need to be in balance. Modern, forward-thinking companies see this as logical, and make sure their activities have a positive impact on the community and the environment – and make a profit. Stubbornly clinging to a system that exploits people and nature to squeeze out as much margin as possible is really old-fashioned. New brands are transparent, see the advantage of sharing and working together, investing in better, more efficient methods and being open to criticism. Because ultimately this will yield more: more knowledge, more progress, more profit. This only works if corporate social responsibility is an integral part of policy, specific goals and actions are linked to it and there's public reporting about it (for example in the annual report). Only when everyone can read how it's produced, what the money is spent on and what steps the company still wants or has to take, is it credible. And smart, because you open yourself up to suggestions and improvement. You're truly clever as a company if your sustainability is part of internal targets, skills you're looking for in new colleagues and terms of employment you offer. And if you're not just about the environment: taking good care of your people is equally essential. Reward fairly, allow employees to come into their own, welcome people back to the workforce, don't age discriminate, prevent overtime, and so on. Being social is an enormously important part of sustainable working. Don't be afraid to be a pioneer. But it'll only succeed if everyone feels, understands, wants and embraces it. So make sure the whole company is on board. It delivers savings, a better world and proud, committed colleagues. What's not to like?

>> *The European Coalition for Corporate Justice has lots of information about green and fair enterprise.*

Commuting and Other Transport

More than three-quarters of all kilometres covered by Dutch people are done in the car. Then the train (8%) and the bicycle (7%). They jump into the car for half of all short distances (less than 7.5 kilometres). Half! I don't think I need to explain much about the impact of travel and transport on the environment. But at the same time, travel also gives us a lot. It gets us to work or where we need to be – and it expands our world and possibilities. Preferably, we go faster, further, frequently. But what sustainable choices can you make to also safeguard this world full of discoveries?

Walking
It's best. For the environment (zero emissions), for your health, to experience your surroundings. Wonderful!

Cycling
Not many people have the luxury of walking to work (but perhaps going to the shops, friends or the café is possible?). Do grab a bike if you can. So many benefits. No traffic jams. Cheap. Healthy. Streamlined bum and leg muscles. Wind in your hair. Burning calories. In big cities you arrive much faster than by car (over 10%).
— Need a new bike? There's quite a few in the world, in the Netherlands nearly 23 million (so more than inhabitants). Do go for a second-hand one if you can.
— You can also choose a sustainable bike made from second-hand frames, local wood, recycled skateboards, bamboo and cork – for example from Roetz-Bikes or Bough Bikes.
— Would you like to travel long distances, but

without a car or moped? Then an electric bike may be a good idea – still 50 times less harmful than a car. Roetz-Bikes also has one, for example. Still prefer a moped? Then get an electric one, which saves a lot of emissions.

— Don't want to arrive at work all sweaty? Ask your employer for a shower and changing room – and in any case of course, a beneficial bike lease-plan. There should be some benefits to your good behaviour!

— The app Burn Fat Not Fuel stimulates bike use for commuting (and can be used by employers for extra rewards).

Public transport

According to the European Environmental Agency, the train is the most energy-efficient method of passenger transport. The tram, train and metro are also better than the bus (because they're electric). And although trains may not always be on time, at least you're not stuck in traffic jams. And there's plenty you can do during the journey: type emails, prepare meetings, listen to a thrilling audio book, have breakfast or apply your mascara – much easier than in the car.

Car

I don't drive, but do of course need a car now and again, and am then pleased they're there. But goodness me, the pressure our car use puts on the world. The less you drive, the better. Luckily they're become more efficient and cleaner, and because of the tax advantages for more economical cars, we're not doing too badly here. But

---

In Europe, transport is responsible for over a quarter of CO_2 emissions. If you travel by train you cause about 75% less CO_2 than the (average) car.

The number of cars on the road will practically double around the year 2040, reaching 2 billion.

still. Norway is banning all cars with a fuel engine from 2025, they'll only allow cars run on sustainable energy. We can do much more. Three quarters of our commuting is done by car. This offers opportunities.

Collectively
Sharing a car has many advantages, such as reduced costs and fewer cars on the road. In the Netherlands, more than 90% of cars driving to a work destination contain only one person. Page 194 gives options for shared cars, rentals and borrowing. Carpooling may sound a bit dorky (does 'luxury lifts' sound better?), but is of course very modern and fun. Via Toogethr for example, you can online find a splendid car-date.

Efficient and electric
— A small car is more economical than a bigger one. It's also much easier to park and quicker to clean. Need a larger one sometimes? Hire or borrow one, smarter than constantly driving around in a 'limo'.
— In any case, use a car with the best energy label. Also costs less in fuel and add-ons – there's your profit.
— Second-hand is a good idea of course. But technology is advancing quickly, so older cars are more detrimental for the environment. Preferably, don't buy a car from before 2001.
— An electric car is cleaner and doesn't cause noise and exhaust-fumes nuisance. The average radius is 170 kilometres, and this keeps growing. The amount of charge points is also rising, and if you charge with wind or solar energy then emission-savings are even more attractive. The number of brands with an electric model is increasing – the Nissan LEAF, the Tesla Model S and 3, all new Smart models, the Volkswagen e-Golf and the list goes on. This can also provide lots of lease benefits. The purchase price is higher, but fuel costs lower.

— Still concerned about the distance? Then maybe look at a hybrid, that has less emissions than a normal petrol-run car. Use the battery as often as possible.
— You can also go for a car that runs on alternative fuel. Natural gas is cleaner than petrol but's also a fossil fuel that's running out. Green gas or biogas is better, if it's made of cast-off biomass like fertiliser, waste and sludge. But if the bioethanol or biodiesel comes from natural resources like rapeseed, palm oil, soya or corn, it'll compete with food production and take land away from farming – reducing the advantages.
— With the European Commission's Green Driving Tool you can calculate your CO_2 emissions, cut down fuel costs and find the most suitable car for your needs.

2016 was a record year for the sale of electric cars worldwide: 37% more than the year before, in total more than 750,000.

Smart
There all kinds of ways to drive smarter, benefitting both you and the environment considerably. About 85% of the environmental impact of a car is due to use. By consistently running your car economically, you save about 10% on fuel costs.
— Keep your tyres correctly inflated. This can save up to 20% on emissions and your tyres wear less.
— Drive as smoothly as possible, for example using cruise control. Excessive acceleration and braking costs lots of extra fuel.
— Come to a halt? Turn off your engine. And while we're talking turning off: the less aircon and rear windscreen heating, the better.　　　　→

We often take the car for distances we could cycle or even walk. In America, 28% of all journeys are shorter than 1.5 kilometres. Lots of acceleration and braking causes above-average fuel consumption. Not only expensive, but extra damaging to the environment and air quality, and causes extra wear (and therefore maintenance) by driving with a cold engine.

— Move up a gear sooner: 50 in fourth or 80 in fifth is fine.

On websites of organisations such as Energy Saving Trust and Your Energy Savings you'll find more information about efficient driving, buying a car (or fleet), winter driving etc.

At home
I work from home regularly, as do an increasing number of people. We now have the technological possibilities to work at home more (or in that great café or lovely hotel around the corner). Perhaps it's possible in your line of work too (or for your

employees)? It makes you more flexible (for example, enabling you to be with your kids when they come out of school and work in the evenings, or start at the crack of dawn and then go the gym) and saves on lots of transport emissions. Make sure though you don't go overboard: your boss or colleagues mustn't start expecting you to always be available to work.

>> *Taking a taxi? Use an electric one! There are increasingly more sustainable options, for example run on green gas. Do ask for it.*
>> *Hiring a van? Get an electric one!*
>> *Need a courier? Book a bike courier! Need to go further? Go for electric.*

Greenify your Office

Whether you're working from home, flexible, self-employed, have a small office or a gigantic workplace – the greener, the better.

> First of all, literally: plants provide freshness, can purify the air and have a calming effect.

> Heating and light cost a lot of energy in offices. Can it be turned down a few degrees (at the end of the day, turned off completely), are there LED lamps and do you turn off the lights if there's no one there or you've all gone home?

> Bit stuffy? Open the window rather than turning on the aircon or investigate ventilation grills.

> Do you (or the cleaning company) use environmentally-friendly cleaning products for the office and toilet (and is there a stop button for flushing)?

> Do you limit your trash and separate paper, glass, plastic and green waste?

COYUCHI

> How much can you save by recycling or choosing second-hand? Good options can be found online for office supplies or equipment such as printers.

> Does the office challenge you to take the stairs, work standing up and move regularly?

> Can you get out? Is there space for a patio, a balcony or maybe even a green roof garden? In any case, try and leave the building at lunchtime or during breaks, fresh air helps relaxation and productivity.

> Do you wear company clothes? They would look even better if they were made ethically and sustainably. Quite a few workwear companies are affiliated with Fair Wear Foundation for better conditions in the garment industry. You'll find some options in the guide.

> Do you get promotional items or business gifts made? Then see if you can make them more sustainable, by not choosing disposable items for instance, or going for a green brand. Fair Wear Foundation also has members providing promotional products.

> Want to know where savings can be made in your office? Calculate your footprint, for example at the World Wildlife Fund.

> No guts, no glory. Ask for more sustainable coffee and tea, less printing or recycled paper. Maybe nobody's thinking about it, and suppliers are going to offer it if they know there's demand.

HEAR HEAR

> The Sustainable Business Toolkit website has information about a more sustainable office. The EU Energy Star label certifies office equipment (the website also features an energy calculator).

'We see roofs as the lungs of the city. Currently, they're black and tarred. We're giving cities their healthy lungs back, and transform unused roofs into spaces for nature development, recreation and water storage. Vegetated roofs provide more green in the city. They've lots of benefits, such as a longer lifetime for the roof and cooling of the floor below. A green roof catches rainwater, which prevents flooding on the streets and indoors. They also contribute to biodiversity in the city, and to the conservation or restoration of endangered species such as birds, butterflies and bees. Green also has a therapeutic effect on people and helps to reduce stress or depression. Almost every roof can become green, so explore your options. One of my favourite green roofs is Klunkerkranich in Berlin, a fantastic place on top of a parking lot.'

Friso Klapwijk, director of green roof innovators De Dakdokters

**Employees who eat fruit and vegetables
at least four times a week are on average
20% more productive.**

Conscious Catering

The impact of more sustainable food on the world is considerable, and by eating healthily you simply feel a lot better.

— Organic and fair-trade coffee and tea is the least they can do, and nice and easy. Set large pots if you can, instead of per cup.

— Also make sure everyone gets their own mug (which they wash at the end of the day or put in the full dishwasher), or you use disposable cups that are collected separately and recycled.

— Taking lunch to work? It stays tastier and is more sustainable in a box or container you can reuse, particularly if you keep the box for a long time and wash it sustainably.

— Lunch provided? Make sure healthy is the easiest choice (or the cheapest). Offering salad or soup immediately cranks up vegetable intake too.

— We should be eating less meat anyway, so also at the office. Maybe a vegetarian-day two/three times a week (or at least meat-free Monday)?

— Tasty vegetables and fruit, nuts or popcorn (instead of sweets or cake), other healthy snacks and enough water with mint and lemon on-hand to tackle the four o'clock dip?

— The fewer small pre-packaged containers of for instance butter, jam, meat and cheese in plastic, the better.

— Get lunch delivered? Consider local, organic and in season.

TWENTYTEN FOR ZTRDG

From Paper to Digital

Although it appears that the digital era's in full swing, you'll be surprised how much paper's still being used. Over a third of felled wood in the world is for paper, and compared to 40 years ago, we're using 400% more paper (Americans, for example, 340 kilos each a year). A paper-free office would be top-notch, but reducing's a great start.

Paper

» Print as little as possible. No mails, preferably no agenda or one copy for everybody and definitely double-sided. Save used pieces of paper and use the back as note paper.

» The Ecofont typeface is designed to use 20% less ink. Black and white instead of colour really saves, squeeze as much as possible onto one page and put the settings of the printer to 'draft'.

» If you've got lots of empty cartridges and toners, you can donate them to charity. There's also a growing number of places you can have them refilled.

» Buy FSC, recycled or tree-free paper. And don't forget the toilet paper (you can find recycled in most supermarkets). Paper towels in the toilet are wasteful, rather go for cloth ones (or none).

» Print work can also be ordered sustainably, on FSC and/or recycled paper, with plant-based ink, reusable and energy neutral. It really doesn't have to be expensive.

Digital

» Buy IT equipment with certification or that scores better with GoodElectronics.

» See if your screen can be dimmed a little. A screen saver costs lots of energy, so it's better to turn your computer off if you're taking a longer break or leaving.

» Turning all your devices off and pulling the plugs out of the sockets helps, including printers, chargers, projectors, TVs and so on. A stand-by killer is also effective, or get one of these sockets with an on/off switch.

» Replacing the computers? Give them away to an organisation like Close the Gap or World Loop, who want to bridge the digital divide and ensure that good IT equipment ends up in social, medical, educational projects or start-ups in developing countries.

» Google is probably your friend, but there are alternatives. Search engine Ecosia uses advertising revenue to plant trees, and Blackle saves energy because the search screen's black instead of white.

KANTOORKARAVAAN

Tom van de Beek (1977) is one of the founders of Dutch wild office KantoorKaravaan.

What is KantoorKaravaan?
'Doing your daily work and thoroughly enjoying nature at the same time. Technological innovations such as mobile Wi-Fi and solar energy, in combination with the upcycling of vintage caravans, provide the ideal workplace. Landowners and conservationists make their land available for our temporary outdoor office, naturally without compromising nature. In this 24-hour economy, we as busy city dwellers occasionally long for the peace, quiet and space of nature. You can of course go on holiday, but what if you can make that holiday feeling permanent? This was our starting point.'

How should our current working culture change?
'A lot of work is no longer necessarily dependent on location. We can go online anywhere. Not always desirable of course, but it also creates opportunities. Moving your desk to the forest, for instance. I'm a big supporter of spending more time in nature. It has a proven beneficial effect on our creativity and is stress-reducing. It makes us healthier and happier and therefore also more productive.'

Can you give some suggestions?
'Brainstorm sessions, meetings and team meetings are not only more fun, but also more effective with a change of scenery. Alternate brain work with movement (a walk through the forest) and action (for example chopping wood) and you'll see it has a positive effect on results. In Japan, special therapy trails have already been set up for managers to prevent imminent burn-outs. This positive effect is very logical, when you consider we've spent 99.9% of our time in natural environments during our evolution to modern humans. When we synchronise our rhythm of life with nature, we experience a sense of comfort, a sense of belonging.'

What makes you happy?
'All over the world initiatives in the field of permaculture and food forests are sprouting up. The challenge now is to connect them and demonstrate that a healthy system can exist without even larger-scale monoculture farms and the use of artificial fertilisers, pesticides and GMOs.'

Tom's top tip
'If you're going to Portugal and enjoy "glamping", then don't forget to visit the amazing eco-campsite Into The Wild Algarve.'

Tom's motto

'What if you can make that holiday feeling permanent?'

Work Your Way to Happiness

We don't live to work. And yet we all do it, lots and hard. Making long days, being busy and earning more money is often the norm. Becoming rich and influential raises status. Surely we could do better? So we have more time to live, to discover, to spend with our family and friends? In Sweden, they're experimenting with a six-hour working day. It appears to be extremely successful: participants are healthier, happier and just as productive. We want this too! We could also arrange things differently and for instance only work say three nine or ten-hour days, and then until you're seventy or

It's clear from many studies that most people need about eight hours of sleep per night to be as productive as possible. Employees of an American insurance company can therefore earn up to 300 dollars extra a year if they achieve seven hours or more. It's up to you whether you take part: 17,000 of the 48,600 employees do. They register their sleeping hours (the boss doesn't check). Sleeping yourself wealthy!

older if you prefer. Working less would in any case lead to less unemployment, and more opportunities to better distribute the balance between work and private life. A basic income of, for example, 1,000 euros per month is another variant that's being considered, in Switzerland among other places. This means that people have to work less and can spend more time on care, parenting and volunteering. Whatever happens, working smarter would be welcome. We spend so much of our lives working that it better be a bit of fun too. Here some suggestions.

— Working longer doesn't automatically mean you get more done. Make the agreement with yourself to work six hours instead of eight, then your head will focus on that limitation. You work faster, are more focused and less distracted.
— Focus is vital if you want to work shorter hours. Turn off your notifications, don't look at social media and check your mail less frequently. Do take some time for lunch: your brain (or hands) need fuel, and after a longer interruption you can sometimes look at something you're stuck on with fresh perspective.

— Able to organise your own time? Then work when you're most productive or when it suits you best. Start early if you're a morning person, or take the afternoon off when the sun's shining and work in the evening instead.

The Forest app helps you work with focus. If you don't look at your phone for an agreed time, a tree grows. With the reward you receive, you can get a real tree planted. Win-win!

— Create a pleasant working environment – light and not too hot. And preferably with other people who are getting on with it: it's contagious.
— If you can, choose work that gives you satisfaction, makes you proud, where you can take responsibility and use your talents. This isn't always easy, but worthwhile if possible. To matter makes you happier than money.

CELEBRATING AT WORK

Want to give something to colleagues or a business relation? Make it an even bigger gift by going for a sustainable brand. Corporate gift? Go for inspiring, innovative labels, or choose locally produced. There are an increasing number of companies and brands offering sustainable Christmas hampers. Or opt for a voucher – at least it won't end up in the bin if it doesn't suit someone. (No ideas? How about the book you're holding? Great gift, and fits perfectly into a Christmas hamper too... *insert smiley*). Company trip? Find something that's not too wasteful or polluting, and choose, for instance, an organic restaurant. There are of course also sustainable activities out there. You could even volunteer together: good for the world and for team building.

GREEN KIDS by Laura de Jong

Used Baby Items
Many children grow up in poverty. Various foundations collect new and used baby items, such as clothing, bedding and care products. They distribute this to expectant parents. Do you have anything spare? Head for Baby2Baby, Donation-Town, Oxfam or GiveNow.

Good Night
Co-sleeping can be a solution for broken nights. But: then it is important you sleep together safely, for example without cushions and cuddly toys. James McKenna researched this and has prepared guidelines. And if you're going to sleep together, a special or extra-large bed is welcome. For the first months for example, a Bednest co-sleeper. The American brand Ace has an extra-large bed for up to four people.

Sleeping Outside
Children who take their nap outside sleep longer and deeper. Too cold? They disagree in Scandinavia. Only at -10°C or if your child is ill do they recommend sleeping inside. Be aware of animals, from insects to cats or dogs.

NOESER

GUIDE

STORES

There are many shops all over the world with household, interior, cleaning, office, kitchen supplies and so on, and organisations engaged in energy, transport or the sharing economy. Here's a start to inspire you.

Afro Art
Stockholm, Gothenburg + webshop (Swe)
Interior accessories, textiles and gifts from African, Asian and Latin American artisans.
afroart.se

Buy Me Once
webshop (UK/US)
Indestructible brands, such as Dr. Martens 'For Life' collection and the '30-year sweatshirt'. Ships to UK and US, but international site is being worked on.
buymeonce.com

Eco at Home
webshop (Aus)
Bed, bath, kitchen, energy, lighting, interior, paint, cleaning, garden, health, stationary and much more.
ecoathome.com.au

ethical.market
webshop (UK)
Large market place for home accessories (furnishing, kitchenware, tech, animals etc.), stationary, care products, clothes (m/f), diverse kids' products, gifts and blog. The products are sent by the brands themselves, also internationally.
ethical.market

Ethical Superstore
webshop (UK)
Groceries, food, household products, interior, garden, electronics, care products, kids, clothing and gifts. You can search on certified organic, vegan, fair trade, FSC, recycled. Ships to UK and Ireland.
ethicalsuperstore.com

Green Elephant
webshop (NZ)
Extensive collection of home and garden, household, pets, outdoor and so on, but also health and beauty, food, kids, fashion and more.
greenelephant.co.nz

Green Home
webshop (US)
Bathroom, kitchen, cleaning, interior, solar energy, garden, pets, jobs, travel, office, recycling etc.
greenhome.com

Grüne Erde
stores + webshop (Ger/Austria)
Wide range of beds, mattresses, interior textiles, furniture, home accessories, care products, clothes, and so on. 14 stores in Germany and Austria.
grueneerde.com

Norrgavel
stores + webshop (Swe)
Swedish more sustainable interior chain, with sofas, tables, cupboards (from FSC wood, natural latex, etc.) and furnishings such as bedding, bathroom supplies and rugs.
norrgavel.se

Oxfam
stores
In several countries, NGO Oxfam has charity shops, where you can buy (and hand-in) second-hand clothing, books, furniture and much more, and they sell Fairtrade certified foods. Including: oxfam.org.uk (650 shops, also webshop) / oxfamireland.org / oxfam.de / oxfam.org.au (see also vinnies.org.au)

>> *In countries such as Australia, UK and Ireland there are lots of charity shops, run by organisations such as the British Heart Foundation, Cancer Research and Red Cross, where you can find great second-hand goods, and your money is used for help.*

Ruohonjuuri
stores + webshop (Fin)
Extensive stores with food, supplements, household products, kitchen equipment, care products etc.
ruohonjuuri.fi

Trade Aid
many locations and stores + webshop (NZ)

Large collection of fair-trade made homeware (crockery, textiles, etc.), foodstuffs, stationary, accessories and gifts.
tradeaid.org.nz

>> *In many countries you'll find world shops or fair-trade stores, where your money can do good.*

Violey
webshop (Ger)
Household, cleaning, baby and child products, care, food, and much more. Ships to many countries.
violey.com

AND ALSO
abchome.com (homestore, US) / biome.com.au (zero waste and eco-living, Aus) / eartheasy.com (garden, home and energy, US) / ecochic.com.au (furniture and furnishings, Aus) / ecolateralshop. com.au (home, care, clothes, Aus) / ecostore.co.nz (home, dishes, skin cleansing, NZ) / greenheartshop.org (interior and accessories, US) / groninterior.se (bed, bath and lifestyle, Swe) / manufactum.com (everything-store for high-quality goods, Ger/int) / memolife.de (interior, building, garden, paper, furniture, care products etc., Ger) / naturalcollection. com (home, garden, electronics, household etc., UK) / realgoods.com (off-grid living, US) / shop-generalstore. com (local interior and care products and accessories, US) / shop.original-unverpackt.de (unpackaged products, Ger) / theperishtrust.com (well-curated kitchen, interior and care products, US) / thegreenstore.com.au (home, body, garden, Aus) / uncommongoods. com (products with a story, US) / vivaterra.com (interior, furniture, sleeping, bath, also own brand, US) / wholefoodsmarket.com (everything, Can/UK/US)

Second-Hand
blocket.se / craigslist.org/about/sites (many countries) / ebay.com (many countries) / gumtree.com (Aus/UK/US/ZA) / tradera.com

DIY and Renovation
ecobau-markt.de / ecohomecentre. co.uk / eco-logisch.de / enviroshop. com.au / greenbuildingcentre.net.au / greenchoices.org / greendepot.com

Office Supplies
buyecogreen.com.au / ecooffice.com.au / goinggreensolutions.com.au / greenhome.com / memo.de / paperkarma.com / thegreenoffice.co.uk / thegreenoffice.com

---

BRANDS AND INFORMATION

Energy

Sustainable energy
energysavingtrust.org.uk (renewable energy, home insulation and energy effiency, travel) / energy.gov / ethicalconsumer.org / greenelectricityguide.org.au / homepower.com / renewableenergyhub.us / renewableenergyworld.com / solarcalculator.com.au / yourhome.gov.au

Energy consumption
energyusecalculator.com / footprint.wwf.org.uk / shrinkthatfootprint.com / topten.eu / yourenergysavings.gov.au

Energy labels
energyrating.gov.au / energystar.gov / eu-energystar.org / newenergylabel.com

WakaWaka
Social enterprise that makes lamps and chargers on solar energy. The small version only charges your phone, but the bigger ones are more powerful and real lifesavers for people without access to power. For each item sold, a family without electricity in a disaster area or crisis situation will receive a WakaWaka lamp.
waka-waka.com

Home and Furnishing

Auro
Natural paints, floor wax, varnish and maintenance products based on plant-based raw materials and pigments.
auro.de

AND ALSO
aglaia.de / biofapaint.co.uk / earthbornpaints.co.uk / eco-paints.nl / naturalpaintsonline.co.uk

Blom & Blom
The brothers Blom retrieve lamps and home accessories from old, deserted factories and renovate them.
blomandblom.com – see also p. 184

Carpet of Life
Rugs made in Morocco from your own discarded clothes, towels and bedding (or those of your grandmother or friends). You can also buy ready-made rugs.
carpetoflife.com

AND ALSO
bymolle.com / ecobalanza.com / foreverinteriors.com / industrialdesignnz.co.nz / myakka.co.uk / nordic-ecolabel.org / offecct.com / palais.com / recycledinteriors.org / rescued.nl / revivalfurniture.co.nz / stemgoods.com / urbantreesalvage.ca / westelm.com / woodloops.com / yardfurniture.com.au

EKOBO HOME / DESIGN BY BOO LOUIS

Pans and tableware
by-ekobo.com / greenpan.com / lecreuset.com / riess.at / zuperzozial.com

Cleaning

Ecover / method
Dishwashing, washing and cleaning products based on natural raw materials, produced in a more environmentally-friendly factory. The packaging is made of vegetable and recycled plastic, and the brand launches initiatives to clean up plastic. Together with natural and stylish detergent brand method, they form one company (both B Corps), their more sustainable factory is in Chicago (you can tour).
ecover.com / methodhome.com

AND ALSO
cleanhappens.com / ecoforce.co.uk / faithinnature.co.uk / greenscents.co.uk / mirjamdebruijn.com/twenty.html / mrsmeyers.com / seepje.com –

see also p. 186 / sonett.eu / thegentlelabel.com / thesimplyco.com

Sleeping

COCO-MAT
Beds, bedding and accessories made by Greek brand of materials such as natural rubber, coconut fibre, organic wool and/or hemp (also for children). You can stay overnight in one of the partner hotels too.
coco-mat.com

Coyuchi
American brand with bedding, duvet covers, blankets, towels, table linen and pyjamas. Largely certified organic, and you can also rent bed and bath linen and return after use, so they can process the textiles and ensure it's not thrown away.
coyuchi.com

AND ALSO
bedino.se / bhumi.com.au / ecolinen.com.au / hessnatur.com / lifekind.com / looporganic.com / naturalbedcompany.co.uk / naturalbedding.com.au / thecleanbedroom.com / underthecanopy.com – bedbathandbeyond.ca / bedbathandbeyond.com / bedbathandbeyond.co.nz also sell some sustainable brands/products

Scented Products

Good Candle Brooklyn
Handmade scented candles from American soya wax, cotton wicks and essential oils. Poured in New York, in great fragrances.
goodcandlebk.com

P.F. Candle Co.
Collection of hand-poured (yet affordable) well-scented candles from local soya wax, with cotton wicks. They're made in LA – you can visit the factory. Also diffusers, sprays, incense and unisex eau de parfum.
pfcandleco.com

AND ALSO
doterra.com / haeckels.co.uk / juniperridge.com / paddywax.com / primaveralife.com / purenature.co.nz / seoc.com.au / thedirtcreative.com / wemakelocht.nl

Green and Animals

De Dakdokters
Transform roofs into green hotspots: places for relaxation, nature development, water storage, allotments and animals.
dakdokters.nl (for inspiration; do explore local options, like greenroofers.co.uk for instance)

KantoorKaravaan
Self-sufficient, reused caravans on solar energy in nature, for rent to work in.
kantoorkaravaan.nl – see also p. 206 (for inspiration; maybe there's an equivalent in your neighbourhood, or head for a beach bar, a café in the woods or another place you enjoy)

AND ALSO
Green
botanoadopt.org / ecoorganicgarden.com.au / forestapp.cc / gardenorganic.org.uk / groworganic.com / planetnatural.com

Animals
hsi.org / internationalanimalrescue.org / peta.org / savebees.org / sos-bees.org / wildlifewitness.net / worldanimalprotection.org / yarrah.com

Money and Knowledge

ASN Bank
Paying, saving and investing with respect for people, environment and climate. With your money, this Dutch bank invests in projects and companies that make the world better.
asnbank.nl – see also p. 196

BankTrack
International campaign organisation that examines banks and their activities. Have information about specific banks (from all over the world), reports and campaigns you can join.
banktrack.org

Fair Finance Guide
Initiative of NGOs such as Amnesty International, Oxfam and Friends of the Earth to compare the main providers of bank accounts on environmental issues and human rights.
fairfinanceguide.org

Crowd funding, borrowing and microfinancing
follow-this.org / fundingcircle.com / globalgiving.org / kickstarter.com / lendingclub.com / onepercentclub.com / oneplanetcrowd.com / startsomegood.com / upstart.com

Electronics and Transport

Fairphone
An ethical as possible phone, long-lasting and consisting of replaceable modules. The Dutch brand wants to change the electronics world and show the entire production chain, including what everything costs.
fairphone.com – see also p. 198

GoodElectronics
Lobby organisation that fights for fairer and more sustainable consumer electronics.
goodelectronics.org

Repair Café
Free meetings worldwide where you learn to repair electronics, furniture, toys and clothes. Expertise and tools are offered.
repaircafe.org

Roetz-Bikes
Bikes made to last, from as much reused parts as possible. For the rest, sustainable solutions are developed, such as handles made of cork and mudguards of old wood.
roetz-bikes.com

AND ALSO
boughbikes.nl / burnfatnotfuel.nl / greenpeace.org (Guide to Greener Electronics) / johnsphones.com / puzzlephone.com

Sharing and hiring cars
blablacar.co.uk / carpoolworld.com / commutewise.com / getaround.com (US) / greenmotion.com / liftshare.com (UK) / snappcar.nl (Den/Ger/NL/Swe) / toogethr.com / wego.nu

Driving economically and electric
consumerreports.org / ecotest.eu / electricvehicles.govt.nz / green-driving.jrc.ec.europa.eu / nextgreencar.com / tesla.com

Search engines
blackle.com / ecosia.org

Sharing, Recycling and Repairing

Peerby / Streetbank
Borrow your things form people in the neighbourhood – good and fun.
peerby.com / streetbank.com

>> *konnektid.com is similar, but then with expertise*

AND ALSO
– freecycle.org / ifixit.com / instructables.com / recyclebank.com – josephine.com / mealsharing.com / neighbourfood.org / olioex.com

Recycling, plastic and electronics
close-the-gap.org / originalrepack.com / plasticsoupfoundation.org / recyclesmart.com / recycleapp.co.uk / theoceancleanup.com / worldloop.org

Workwear and CSR
bluelooporiginals.eu / continentalclothing.com / corporatejustice.org / fairwear.org / littleyellowbird.co.nz / schijvens.nl / stanleystella.com / sustainablebusinesstoolkit.com / vptex.com

GREEN KIDS

Oeuf NYC
Furniture, children's clothing and bedding. This American children's brand makes it all, safe and of natural materials.
oeufnyc.com

Fabelab
Danish brand with special 3D properties. The bedding can be folded into a bag, so that your child feels at home during a sleepover.
fabelab.dk

Teehee
This Spanish brand makes combinable furniture you can therefore use longer. You can keep adding extra components.
teehee.eu

AND ALSO
acesize.com / baby2baby.org / bednest.com / cosleeping.nd.edu / donationtown.org / givenow.com.au / oxfam.org.uk

INTRODUCTION

5625

billion goes around in the worldwide travel and tourism industry; 1 in 11 jobs is connected to it

1.2

billion tourists travel to another country for at least one night every year

40

minutes more free time British men have daily than women (in total 6 hours and 9 minutes)

The more free time, the better – right? Just like travelling, if you ask me. I've been lucky enough to see quite a lot of the world. For my job with the Clean Clothes Campaign I visited countries such as Thailand, Bangladesh, America, Turkey, Poland, Romania and pretty much all of Europe. In recent years I've travelled to Australia (honeymoon with Mr Eyskoot), Iceland, New York, London, Paris… The more, the merrier. I can't wait to discover and experience as much as possible. But I can already hear you thinking: nice and sustainable, girlfriend. No! Of course not. I too struggle with this, I'll readily admit. I try to travel as sustainably as possible, and hardly ever fly within Europe for example – I enjoy travelling by train the most. But most definitely, it has an impact on the earth, especially the flying. Yet, I wouldn't have been able to do my work in the fashion industry without travelling, and I'd have met less people and brands to together increase our impact. My encounters with nature and different cultures have taught me about the richness of the world and other ways of living. Travelling can open your eyes, show you how beautiful and vulnerable the planet is and inspire you to take good care of it.

I love all kinds of travel. Airbnb, hotels, weekends away, long journeys, faraway places, around the corner, tropical, ice cold, cities, nature… There's so much to see, so much to be surprised by – and I enjoy all that's different from the everyday. According to my parents I'm a born camper, something we did often when I was small. I still find the sound of rain on canvas enchanting; and what's better than zipping open your tent and immediately being surrounded by the wonderful world of nature? We never went far – the Netherlands, sometimes Germany or France – but we didn't have to. There are enough fun things to do close by. Some of the most beautiful sights are often just around the corner, but for one reason or another we tend to visit them less in our own country.

Leisure is about more than just holidays of course. Sport, playing or listening to music, attending festivals, doing volunteer work, going out, to the cinema or museum, hiking, exploring – where does the time go? I wish there was more of it, the days seem to fly by. But we can try to spend the time we do have as well and as positively as possible (and have as little negative impact as we can). And what about festivities, celebrating and giving (or receiving) gifts? Having a birthday, getting married, anniversaries, remembrances: there's so much to be grateful for, and that all provides opportunities to make a difference. The same goes for births, kids' parties, toys – you want to do it right for your children even more. And celebrating sustainably is definitely double the fun. Enjoy!

My goal is to build
a life I don't need
vacation from

TRAVELLING AND HOLIDAYS

True Tourism

Travelling, holidaying and exploring is inspiring, and ideally really relaxing. You've probably worked hard and deserve to leave everything behind and just enjoy yourself. Even better if it's at as little expense as possible to the climate or others. Travelling burdens the environment, whether you go by train, bus, bike or plane. Which is why it's usually not referred to as sustainable, but responsible travel. You do often use less energy and gadgets on holiday, and you can also try to have positive impact, for example by helping the local economy and nature. People can earn much needed income from tourism, which is one way your holiday can contribute. For many countries it's a major source of income; Aruba for instance is 90% dependant on it. Because the impact on nature is substantial, a growing number of eco-trips or green holidays are now on offer. A good sign, but be a bit careful with the jargon. It's fine for example if the flight is carbon compensated, but if the rest of the trip is packed with wasteful buffets, airconditioned rooms and luxury taxi rides, then something's not quite right. See how you can cause as little environmental damage as possible, and support the people.

» Avoid mass tourism if you can and try to make sure the money you spend goes to the local community. Treat people with respect, hire a local guide and don't be tempted by well-known chains, instead going for small family restaurants or artisan souvenir shops.

» Respect local traditions and customs, and try not to make any blunders, like climbing the sacred mountain you're not actually allowed to be on.

» Ask for permission when taking photos of people or children. Learn a few words of the language or use your hands and feet.

» Don't always barter as low as you can go – try to pay a fair price.

7.5

times a year is how often Finns on average take a trip, Americans 6.7 times and Swedes 6 times

YONI

» Preferably stay away from all-inclusive packages: little of the income actually finds its way to local businesses (but it does to large hotels or international corporations), and lots of the buffet that comes with it is often thrown away.

» Care about the animals too. Don't ride on an elephant, give money to dancing bears, bet on fighting dogs or hens or attend a bull fight. Also don't buy souvenirs made from animals.

» And in any case, go for lightweight gifts (saves CO_2), whose proceeds go to locals, and your friends really want to have.

» The lighter you travel, the less energy it costs. Can you make less clothes work? Buy small bottles to fill with your own beauty products. When we went travelling across Australia I started reading books on my smartphone. Now I can't do without – always a book on me if I have to wait somewhere.

» Bring a refillable bottle for water on the go, so you don't have to buy any plastic.

» Can you travel outside of high season? Great, then the pressure on nature, people and animals is also better distributed. And you'll face less crowds in all those beautiful places.

» Try and choose small groups if making tours or nature trips – for the same reasons. Booking with a travel organisation? Have a look at their sustainability credentials, and preferably choose a conscious operator such as Baobab, Intrepid or Responsible Travel.

» Walk or cycle through a city if you can, it's wonderful and you really get to see more. Longer distances? Opt for public transport or shared cars/vans/buses, instead of taking a taxi, moped or hiring your own car.

» Going into nature or water? Know what you're doing, find out where you're allowed and make sure you don't cause any damage.

» Swimming, snorkelling, walking or mountain biking are better than safaris, jet skiing, off-roading or other motorised activities that impact or damage the environment (do keep to the paths).

Golf courses cost lots of space and water and can cause pollution.

» Avoid using plastic straws and/or disposable cutlery, plates, chopsticks or cups. Bring your own or choose another restaurant (and become a waste-busting hero).

» Don't leave behind any litter or mess. Perhaps you've something you no longer need, that people who have less could really make use of? Book finished, extra toys? Make sure it gets to someone – for example with a nice note for the cleaners or the people that have cooked all that delicious food for you.

» Can you spare some money? Then of course you can leave behind or give it away, most people in the service industry don't earn very much.

Do you want the local population to be involved and well paid, and that attention is given to nature conservation and animal rights? Then there are many alternatives to standard travel organisations. Here are just a few of the possibilities, you can find more online.

— GreenHoliday provides tips for natural holiday addresses in nearly thirty European countries. Green Key certifies holiday accommodations.

— Fair Trade Tourism certifies holidays to Africa, with a code of conduct based on fair pay, sustainability, respect for human rights, culture and nature, transparency and whether everyone involved in the activity can participate in decision making.

— In many large cities, so-called 'alternative tours' are offered, showing you hidden gems, instead of the major tourist attractions. They've often got a theme, such as 'eco hotspots', 'street art', 'unknown history' or 'green in the city'.

— Want to experience a European city as if you lived there? Then book a tour or activity with a local via Global Greeter Network. From photo tours and art connoisseurs to experiencing sport together or cooking – these people know the best tourist-free places (Airbnb features such a function now too). A City Made By People is a network for exchanging stories and lifestyles: in cities ⟶

My Personal Travel Trips

INTERNATIONAL

01 / London
69b Stylish boutique of fashion expert Merryn Leslie, who selects the very best sustainable fashion and lifestyle brands.
Southbank Centre Excellent arts centre; every time and again something surprises or stays with me.
Charity shops Why aren't there more everywhere? Head for the richer neighbourhoods for the good stuff: Kensington's my favourite.

02 / Reykjavik
Heilsuhúsið Great health-food store, also offering a wide array of skincare, such as the special Icelandic brand Sóley.
Hot springs The volcanic ground in Iceland as force of nature and endless source of energy – stepping into a pond that turns out to be warm is something you should do at least once in your life. The Fontana sauna is built on a hot spring and gets its heat from it (including sulphur smell).

03 / New York
Bhoomki en Kaight Cool, sustainable fashion stores in Brooklyn. Annie's Blue Ribbon General Store also has great brands.
Gospel I'll never forget the performance by the Abyssinian Baptist Church gospel choir. Nor the cable car to Roosevelt Island, and heightened park The High Line of course.

04 / Paris
BIS Boutique Solidaire Lovely second-hand boutique, supporting people who need help in various ways. There are also lots of Emmaus charity stores in Paris!
L'Oasis d'Aboukir A fully-overgrown corner façade with seventy different plants: a gigantic green wall in the open air. If you like green, then make sure you also visit Le Comptoir Général, a café annex vintage store annex curiosity cabinet with indoor jungle.

L'Habibliothèque The fashionable clothes library, with young designers and sustainable brands. Centre Commercial also has a number of nice sustainable labels.

05 / Sydney
Royal Botanic Garden If there's a botanical garden in a city we always head there, and this one is truly beautiful, right next to the Opera House. The shop's also excellent.
The beaches The Manly Scenic Walk and the Bondi Beach & Coogee Walk are some of the most stunning walks we've ever done, as is the one through The Royal National Park, an hour outside Sydney.

AMSTERDAM

01 / Sustainable gems
Visit the amazing sustainable concept stores, salons and cafés: the Pijp for example offers studio JUX, SLA, O My Bag, Charlie + Mary and Venkel, the Haarlemmerstraat Nukuhiva, Sukha and Vinnies, in West you'll find LENA, C. Cosmetics, Berry, Sugarless, the Dutch Weed Burger Joint and Koffie ende Koeck, in the East, Het Faire Oosten, Beter & Leuk, Hartje Oost, Instock and Mr. & Mrs. Watson, and in the centre for instance MHOOM, Verse, Gartine, Bocca Coffee and Lavinia. Say hi from me!

02 / Ferry to NDSM island
Take the free ferry for a joyous trip over the water, one of my favourite activities in the city. Once across, you can visit conscious city-beach café PLLEK, the Noorderlicht café and the creative free-space NDSM.

03 / Mezrab
Story-telling café with theme evenings (true story, comedy, improvisation etc.) and original music. I absolutely love stories, and in this unique place, master storyteller Sahand Sahebdivani maintains the (Iranian) tradition. You'll always hear something unusual, and Sahand's parents make the best soup.

such as Berlin, Copenhagen, Los Angeles, Melbourne, Oslo and Vancouver you can request a meeting with a 'likeminded' local, who also tailors a map of the city for you.

— The websites Ethical Traveler, Go Green Travel Green, Green Travel Guides (videos), Green Traveller, Leave No Trace, The International Eco Tourism Society and Sustainable Travel International have information about more sustainable travel. On social media and blogs like Eco Traveller Guide or Green Global Travel you can also find all sorts, especially if you're looking for hotspots or local tips. Don't forget Instagram's location function (really handy for cities), search online for your destination in combination with vegetarian, sustainable or eco, and of course ask your friends for suggestions.

From A to B, Responsibly

How you get somewhere makes a big difference to how much you burden the environment. As does how often you go, and where. We've already discussed transport in the previous chapter – whether you're going to work or on holiday doesn't matter much for how sustainable you can be. Here a few extra travel-specific tips. Going by train or coach is best (unless you're going to walk or cycle). If you want sun, then choose the destination closest to you. Whatever you do, don't forget to offset your emissions, for example by investing in renewable-energy projects, through your travel agent, airline or do it yourself online (more about this later).

Walking and cycling
It's best. Emission free, you only use your own energy, and there's so much you get to see. Sound a bit meh? It's not – camping is really now, and for example more and more people are two-wheeling it from festival to festival. You'll come home from your holiday tanned, toned and fit, instead of bursting at the seams. Online all kinds of walking and cycling holidays can be found. The EuroVelo, IBike, Modern Hiker, Responsible Travel (travel guides) websites have lots of routes, tips and information; more in the guide.

Train or bus
I love to travel by train – you can admire the views,

time slows down so you really have the feeling of going somewhere, and in general it's pretty stress-free. I've seen many a European-capital station, but in Australia for example, Mr Eyskoot and I also travelled a lot by rail. We spotted our first kangaroos out of a train window. It seems to take a lot longer than for instance flying, and for very long distances, it does. But for a destination that's an hour's flight away, that you need to be at the airport for a few hours in advance, check in, wait for your luggage and travel from the terminal to the city-centre, I doubt whether flying would actually beat the train. You don't have to park or navigate, arrive in the heart of the city, have free wireless internet increasingly often – fab. With an Interrail ticket, you can discover thirty European countries by train. The Man in Seat 61 is a website by a train fan and expert, full of tips about international train travel. You'll find more websites in the guide.

Travelling by (not too old) coaches is also a good idea, and can be cheaper than by train.

Campers and caravans stand still an average of 48 weeks per year. So why don't we share them? On Goboony, private owners offer their vehicle, so you can hit the road more sustainably.

Car

I may not have a driving licence, but a road trip is still the ultimate in romance in my book. I'd love to tour America, or for example Scotland, Ireland or all around Iceland. Should anyone fancy taking the wheel – I'm a great planner, reasonable map reader, bake tasty cakes and sing my heart out. Fortunately, fitting as many people into a car as possible is one of the ways to make driving a bit more sustainable. Not travelling too far helps too.

Renting bicycles instead of taking them with you saves fuel. Just like packing as little as you can and keeping the car as light and aerodynamic as possible (so preferably without a box on top). Renting a car once you're there? Then go for small and electric. And check the sharing websites from the previous chapter to see if you can catch a ride – saves money and emissions.

Flying

It's very simple, and oh so annoying. Flying is extremely bad for the planet. Someone, somewhere really needs to think of something. More and more people are doing it, while we should actually be doing it less... By burning kerosene, aeroplanes emit CO_2 and contribute to the greenhouse effect. A trip by air harms the environment seven to eleven times more than the same journey by train. The difference is largest with short distances, of less than 700 kilometres. Ouch! There are things you can do to make it better, but not a lot. Travel on as full a plane as possible, then the damage per person is lowest. So these are often charter flights and budget airlines. Do choose an airline with an environmental policy (and modern machines), like for example Air France-KLM or

---

RECONSIDERED

Jessica Marati Radparvar (1986) is social impact strategist and avid traveller. With her consultancy Reconsidered, she helps organisations build social-responsibility strategies and communications. She's worked for amongst others EILEEN FISHER, West Elm and Fashion for Good. These are her international recommendations.

New York

Maiyet Collective – 'Ethical luxury brand Maiyet has gathered brands like VOZ, Raven + Lily and ARTICLE 22 under one roof.'
ABC Carpet & Home – 'A grand bazaar of delightful furniture, homeware and gifts, with a delicious farm-to-table restaurant.'

Warby Parker SoHo – 'Wonderful spot to browse glasses and sunglasses with a one-for-one model.'
Elsa & Me – 'Made-to-measure women's fashion, born in Sweden, designed in New York and made in Nairobi.'
Peet Rivko – 'A line of all-natural plant-based skincare products.'

Nicaragua & Cambodia

Buena Vista Surf Club – 'Gorgeous, sustainably-designed eco-lodge that offers surf, yoga and meditation retreats.'
Roots & Soul – 'A Dutch-designed brand of handbags, shoes and lifestyle items made by Nicaraguan artisans.'
Romdeng – 'Inventive Cambodian fusion restaurant with farm-to-table food and skills-training programmes for vulnerable child populations.'

---

easyJet. Try and book direct flights, as taking off and landing cost extra energy. And compensate your CO_2 emissions – through for instance Atmosfair, ClimateCare, Greenfleet, GreenSeat or Native Energy (more in the guide, and see p. 266 for the dos and don'ts of offsetting).

Ace Accommodation

Getting away from it all, including your own bed (so you start missing it terribly as a result). How do you make your stay away from home more sustainable? To start with, by pulling out all the plugs at home, switching off the heating and cancelling the newspaper. Look forward to your holiday by eating your way through your fridge, so it can also be turned off. But what else?

In the tourism industry too, there are certifications you can look out for. Green Key is an international, independent certification for hotels, holiday villages, campsites and B&Bs, but also restaurants, spas and beach pavilions. It has three levels: bronze, silver or gold. The more environmental measures (around water, waste, recycling, food or energy) implemented, the higher the level. The European Commission's EU Ecolabel also covers tourist attractions. Green Tourism is the International Centre for Responsible Tourism's certification in the UK (distinguishing gold, silver and bronze). Green Globe is an international certification (American, environmental and social aspects, particularly the business market), just like Travelife (Dutch, also environmental and social aspects, and distinguishes gold, silver and bronze), Ecotourism Australia (certification and information, including a green travel-guide) and Earth Check (Australian, certification and consultancy). Website BookDifferent provides a clear overview. Great of course that more attention's being paid to sustainability, but always keep a critical eye on what the accommodations actually do.

KARTENT

Hotel or holiday home

> Choose one with a certification, from Green Key, EU Ecolabel, Travelife or Golden Globe for example, but above all take a good look at the actual providers and ask questions if you want to be sure they serve organic food, recycle waste or treat their employees well.

> Don't throw your towels on the floor, so they won't be replaced every day. You don't do this at home either (I reckon?). Indicate that your room doesn't have to be 'done' (for example hang the DO NOT DISTURB card on your door), then your bedding won't be cleaned as well.

> Don't shower more often than normal (or maybe even less, you're on holiday after all).

> Leave the miniatures and disposables be (after all, you've got your own refillable bottles with organic products, right?).

> In a warm country? Turn off the aircon and open the window or buy a fan. Ask for a sheet if they've only got duvets, it might help you sleep better too.

ECOMAMA HOTEL

> Going on a cruise may sound like heaven, but unfortunately isn't very sustainable. The enormous ships cost huge amounts of energy, as does the luxury onboard – which also contributes to waste. The crew often have to work hard for little money.

About 15% of the total environmental damage from tourism is caused by accommodation, the largest portion (75% to 95%) is due to transport.

> Worldwide, there are various pioneers in the field of sustainable and modern overnight stays. Dutch initiative Conscious Hotels (see the next page) is one of the first chains with socially and environmentally-friendly hotels. Zoku Amsterdam (see p. 225) is a long-stay hotel that designs space as smartly as possible. Good Hotel London (and Amsterdam) focuses on doing business locally and socially. Almodóvar in Berlin is an organic, vegan/vegetarian four-star hotel, QO Amsterdam combines luxury and experience with aiming to be the most circular and sustainable hotel. BIO HOTELS has more than 100 eco-friendly hotels in seven European countries – and this is just the tip of the iceberg. Also take a look at Hotel 1 in Brooklyn, Hi Hotel France, I Love Eco Hotels or search online for eco-hotels and resorts… Hopefully this will increasingly become standard, also in lower price categories.

> Booking website BookDifferent wants to increase the number of sustainable travellers and shows you how green hotels and accommodations are, so you can take this into consideration when making a choice. With every booking, a donation is made to a charity of your choice. They feature over a million hotels and have a lowest-price guarantee.

INTERVIEW

CONSCIOUS HOTELS

Marco Lemmers (1971) is co-founder and CEO of Conscious Hotels.

What's a Conscious Hotel?
'They're eco design-hotels, where sustainability is integrated throughout. A 100% electric buil-ding, cradle-to-cradle beds and organic food and drink. With every decision, we look at the com-plete life-cycle. We want to save the planet and believe people are also part of this. With us, this translates into working with people distanced from the labour market, investing in employees such as sponsoring training and education, and above all having fun and making guests happy.'

Which hotels do you recommend?
'CitizenM is a modern and contemporary hotel concept. Zoku due to the innovation and cross-over between hotel and long stay.'

PAMKATPHOTOGRAPHY

Marco's tip
'Sustainable is more expensive. Phew, that's off my chest. Besides the climate-change-deniers, there are also sustainable-is-not-more-expensive fanatics. It's better not to deny it and actually talk about the better quality.'

Stockholm Tips from Green Kids Expert Laura

'I lived in Stockholm for six months and it's my favourite city. Should we ever emigrate... If I had one day there now, I'd visit my favourite places.

01. Lunch at Rosendals Trädgård, a beautiful gar-den with views over the city.

02. Filippa K's second-hand store is perfect for scoring timeless basics.
03. You've never seen as big a vegetarian buffet as the one at Hermans. Eating here, you also look out over the city.
04. An evening stroll at Vinterviken, a stunning natu-re reserve just outside the city. In the summer, you can swim there. My husband proposed to me here in the winter, when there was a thick layer of snow.'

843 billion euros were spent worldwide in 2016 on business trips.

Sleepover

More and more travellers sleep at local people's homes, and rightly so – it's great. They can give the best tips, it's fun and provides the opportunity to earn some extra cash. But then it does have to work this way, of course. There's increasing criticism of the most well-known provider, Airbnb. Started in America as a way to stayover on airbeds, it's now grown into an international multi-million company. Rent your house or room to a tourist: you earn money, they pay less than in a hotel and get to sleep at a local's. Sounds good, and at face value is – but there's a downside. In neighbourhoods where lots is rented via Airbnb, house prices are rising because they generate money. This makes these areas more inaccessible for the less wealthy. It's often the people that already have money and thus spare buildings or space that get the benefits, anyway. So the gap between poor and rich grows. Landlords continuously rent out complete inner-city houses on Airbnb (even though it's not allowed), which causes major nuisance. And because no tourist tax's paid, a city experiences the burden (more people and more waste), but no income to compensate for this. There's more to earn from tourists than regular rental, so the danger is that they displace those really in need of housing. These negative aspects are a product of its large size, and it can still be really fun to stay the night at a great couple's place. Personally, my experiences with Airbnb have only been very positive, but we do always choose to sleep at a native's home – because we indeed want the contact, the local experience and the secret hotspots. You can also opt for an alternative, less well-known site, such as Wimdu. If you don't mind someone else sleeping in your house, then you can swap via Home Exchange or Home for Exchange. Via Couchsurfing you sleep in someone's house – and indeed, sometimes on the sofa.

ZOKU / EWOUT HUIBERS

>> *Would you love to see more of the world? The Wanderbrief platform offers remote jobs and provides the freedom to travel the world working, as a 'digital nomad'. This way, they want to create better understanding between different cultures, and of course offer an amazing experience.*

ZOKU

Veerle Donders (1989) is responsible for community and guest experience at Zoku – which means she primarily ensures people are having a good time. I wrote big parts of this book in Zoku's 'living room'.

EWOUT HUIBERS

What is Zoku?

'Zoku is Japanese for family, tribe or clan. It's a new category in the hotel industry: a home-office hybrid also suitable for longer stays, with the services of a hotel and the social ambiance of a friendly neighbourhood. Zoku facilitates the new global living and working, and is a place you can call your second home. Regular hotels focus primarily on people sleeping. Zoku wants to extend this into a place where you feel comfortable and where it's easy to meet other people, for example through community events.'

Zoku has a Green Key Gold label – what do you do in terms of sustainability?

'We've used as many sustainable materials as possible, like bamboo and energy-saving bulbs. We're in a former office building, the entire structure of which we've made more sustainable. We make the city a little greener with our roof garden, and use Fairtrade and organic towels and bedding. We also offer bikes, electric cars and taxis, including charging station. And we focus on long stay – this produces less emissions than short business trips. We approach the term sustainable more broadly than the normal definition. UNICEF states that in 2050, about 70% of the world population will live in urban areas. This means significant space shortage, so we focus on smart, multifunctional and hybrid use. Office buildings are used on average for only about 2,000 of the 8,700 hours. Many people aren't at home during the day and not at the office in the evening and at weekends. Everything's empty! We offer space where you can both live and work.'

Who's your hero?

'Elon Musk. I have huge respect for how he sees innovation (and sustainability) on a global scale and completely reinvents different industries. The car industry with Tesla, the online-payment industry with PayPal, the solar-energy industry with SolarCity, living on the moon with SpaceX.'

Veerle's recommendations

Conscious Hotels – 'Super-likable hotel chain which, without compromising on comfort, makes its guests happy and the planet a little bit greener.'

Hotel Tierra Patagonia – 'The design of this eco-friendly hotel blends with the hillside it nestles on and the wooden walls and smart lighting save lots of energy.'

Cuyana – 'Fashion brand from the lean-closet movement: the idea that you're happier with less clothes, as long as they're timeless, beautiful, good-quality items.'

Eco-leaders – 'Consider sustainability when booking a hotel. Look for example at the Eco-leaders of TripAdvisor.'

Camping

The most sustainable you can do. Fun, romantic and cheap.

— Going on a camping-cycling holiday is often even more sustainable than staying put, because at home you usually use more energy. And you're even more of a star if you do it without electricity: your mobile will be just fine with a solar charger. Choose local, seasonal food (and being on holiday's no excuse not to separate waste).

— Eco Camping collects more sustainable campsites in Austria, Croatia, Germany, Italy, Slovenia and Switzerland. If you want to be as close to nature as possible, then look at Huttopia for forest villages or natural campsites in France. Rural campsites and holiday villages in the UK can be found on Countryside Discovery.

— Camping in the US? Hipcamp aims to help people get outside and connect with nature, as it's essential to a happy, healthy life. They've gathered nearly 300,000 unique camping sites, from public parks to private land: ranches, nature reserves, farms, tents, treehouses, cabins, yurts, airstreams, tiny houses, car-places and much more.

— Gamping makes it possible to rent a pitch on someone's private ground (or to rent out some ground yourself to earn a bit of extra money). More than 10,000 original spots in over 50 countries – coastal, in the mountains or under the stars…

— Camping on a roof, in the rainforest, the desert or another unusual place? Campspace views the world as one big campsite, and brings providers together with adventurers.

— There are more and more sustainable tents, like those for example made by MEC (and brands such as Klättermusen have good sleeping bags, see the guide for more). KarTent is a cardboard tent that can be put out for recycling after use. Ideal for festivals where lots of cheap tents are simply left behind after being used once and end up in the trash. In general, it's best to get a tent that'll last for as long as possible. And do you actually have to own one yourself? I always borrow my friend Rachel's (thanks, Rach!); I think we've probably used it more often than she has.

COLIN MCCARTHY

DOING THINGS

Let's Go Outside

What do we do with our free time? Stare at screens lots – I do, anyway, more than I'd like to. Because it would be much better to just get up and go outside. Into the big wide world and nature, inhaling fresh air. The interview with Hall Newbegin (see p. 113) features the many advantages. But actually, we already know. It does something to you – most people feel fitter, freer, calmer, clearer in the great outdoors. Even half an hour a day in nature is said to reduce the chance of depression. Which I believe! Enjoying it more often may also help to protect it better.

— There's lots of wildlife in the city too. Birds, mice, fish, squirrels, grass snakes, sycamores, elms, dandelions, butterflies, bats, everything lives around us. Amsterdam has about 10,000 animals and plant species, the whole of the Netherlands 40,000 (and that's a miniscule country!). Why not go on a city safari, organised yourself or by an ecologist, and discover what's out there.

— *How to be an Explorer of the World* and other books by the amazing Keri Smith help you go on adventures in your neighbourhood (for children and parents) and see the world differently.

— Enjoy walking with your head in the clouds? I'm member of the Cloud Appreciation Society, an organisation that doesn't want us to just adore a blue sky. How much more exciting, interesting and imposing is a wild cloud cover? And how boring is a clear sky? Of course, I love it when the sun's shining – but I can also be delighted by a threatening cumulonimbus or dreamy cirrostratus...

— We've got such stunning nature reserves worldwide. Cycling, hiking, walking the dog, jogging, wonderful (okay, the jogging not so much for me). Don't forget all the lovely areas close to home! Do you like cycling and prefer the city? Take a look at Cycle Chic, which aims to inspire everyone to cycle more (on the Copenhagen website you'll find the links to other cities).

— I don't visit the forest often enough. I realise this every time I'm there. The smell in particular is beyond compare, but also the colours, leaves, looking for delicious tame chestnuts ... Go out exploring yourself or find a woodland organisation with activities and paths, and if you want to stay longer you can even camp in some.

— The beach is also magical. Image editor Naomi lives right next to it, and her workshop looks out onto the sea (wow!). The home of green-kid expert Laura is also not far from the beach. We do need to take good care of it: there's a huge amount of junk being washed ashore (especially plastic). Ocean Conservancy and many others fight for a healthy ocean and aquatic life. Find out if there are initiatives in your neighbourhood to clean up the beach – and/or go to a sustainable beach café with organic food, solar energy, recycling etc. Blue Flag has information about more sustainable beaches, marinas and boats in 45 countries.

— At a café or restaurant, ask for sustainable options on the menu and avoid/decline plastic straws (also when travelling).

— You can also of course simply hang out in the park, your garden, on your balcony or roof terrace. You don't always have to get out and about to be outside. Or put a chair on the pavement – we do this sometimes in the evening when the sun's out. A great opportunity to have a chat with your neighbours.

Ethical Exercise

I love moving and exercising. It empowers the body (hello Michelle Obama-arms) and empties my mind. I've played volleyball since the age of four (because my mum did) and I was really fortunate to also be allowed to do ballet and tennis. Later, I started ballroom dancing with Mr Eyskoot (told you I was lucky). I also like intense fitness classes and squash, and wear an activity tracker.

If you're into exercise too, here some suggestions.

» Need sport shoes, a hockey stick, skis or skates? Take a look at second-hand, there are plenty of people who try a sport, but don't enjoy it, or for some other reason don't use their equipment. I actually buy all my sport shoes on sites such as eBay.

» Jogging, cycling, yoga, working out in the park; everything you don't need a lot of electricity or equipment for is a gain.

» Increasingly more sport brands use recycled materials, for instance plastic bottles or fishing nets. Especially in the field of outdoor sports, a lot's already available. Patagonia (see p. 230) is a pioneer, they go beyond recycling and also work on labour rights, nature conservation and animal rights. Vaude is also active in the areas of working conditions and environment, through membership of Fair Wear Foundation among other things. In the guide you'll find more brands, including Houdini, MEC, Klättermusen, Paramo, Rapanui, Röhnisch and United by Blue. Girlfriend Collective is a cool yoga and leisurewear label made of recycled materials, that celebrates diversity and real shapes. O'Neill is collaborating with Pharrell's Bionic Yarn on swimwear made of plastic waste. It's still only a fraction of the collection but will hopefully become more. In the surf world more and more's happening to protect the sea and beach. Icon Kelly Slater has started his own conscious brand and increasing numbers of boards and wetsuits are becoming more sustainable. Female-run brand Swish Suits makes eco-wetsuits (for women) – see p. 233 for more. There's also a growing number of swimwear brands made from recycled materials, such as AURIA, Mara Hoffman (stylish fashion too), Shapes in the Sand, Summerlove, Woodlike Ocean and so on.

» Does your sport club have a canteen? Maybe you can help them transition to organic snacks or local ingredients? Is lots of paper used or waste not yet separated? They might not really have thought about it, and doing things differently may save money.

» Switching to green electricity is a step in the right direction, and perhaps savings are possible? Do the lights stay on when nobody's on court? Do they have LED lighting, good insulation or maybe a roof that's perfect for solar panels? Dutch indoor ski-centre SnowWorld for example has mounted eight-thousand solar panels to their locations. Try asking around at the club – who knows, there may be experts among the members, or people who work at sustainable companies, and they can help. Sustainable Clubs is focused on the UK, but online you'll find general information (and an energy calculator for your club). Green Sports Alliance aims to make sport more sustainable.

» A growing number of sport and yoga clubs are trying to be more aware of sustainable issues. Ask about it if you want to become a member and look around online – if clubs realise that they can differentiate themselves and attract more clients, it'll only trigger more improvement.

» Your club can also have a profound social impact. Maybe those on a minimum income can join for nothing, refugees are welcome, or sick children be given an unforgettable day? Benefit tournaments for a charity or participating in a sustainable activity are fun, increase the sense of community and help the world.

» Check whether balls or equipment, that schools or refugee centres would be able to make use of, are thrown away at your club. Do you have to or want to stop playing your sport? Give away your clothes and accessories, sell them or donate them to a thrift store.

RÖHNISCH

'Realise that the adventure starts as soon as you step out the front door. You don't always have to go far to have wonderful experiences. If you don't see it here, you won't see it on the other side of the world either. The only thing you'll bring home, is the story that you've been. Discover your own back garden. Don't fill up your weekend, but use the time between 5 in the evening and 9 in the morning. Choose another route and another mode of transport to get from home to work. Stimulate your mind. Be open for new things and take your time. Embrace the slow lifestyle and discover how small things can be grand and compelling.'

Natasha Bloemhard, editor in chief *Salt Magazine*

MIKEY SCHAEFER

PATAGONIA

Ryan Gellert (1972) is General Manager Europe, Middle East & Africa of pioneer outdoor brand Patagonia. He's also on the board of The Access Fund, that protects climbing areas in the US, and of Protect Our Winters, an organisation for positive climate action.

What's Patagonia's mission?

'Patagonia has been making clothing and equipment for climbers, skiers, snowboarders, fly fishers, surfers and trail runners since 1973. Our mission is to make the best products, cause no unnecessary damage and to use trade to inspire solutions for the environmental crisis – and to implement them.'

How is Patagonia sustainable?

'When we'd just started, research confirmed the pollution, global warming, acid rain and disappearance of wild animals and rainforests that we saw on our travels. We decided to donate to grassroots, committed groups that can really save our nature. Currently, as standard, we reserve 1% of our sales or 10% of our profit (whichever is more) for these types of organisations. Annually we organise an educational campaign about an environmental topic, and we hold conferences to teach activists skills, for example publicity-related. Naturally, we must also look at our own role as corporate polluter. We started to reduce our energy consumption and use solar energy early on. New stores are undergoing environmentally-friendly renovations, and since 1996 all our cotton clothes are organic. A living wage for the workers is an important goal for us. Fair trade is a step in that direction. Consequently, since 2014 over 7,000 workers have received more than 360,000 euros in extra income. We now have more than 200 kinds of clothes sewn in 6 certified factories, and since 2017 our entire collection of swimsuits for men, women and children is being made in fair-trade facilities.'

What are your most significant material innovations?

'Early on, we already made fleece from recycled plastic bottles. Now for example, we have a renewable, vegetable substitute for neoprene, the oil substance used for surfing suits. It's made of FSC-certified rubber from the Hevea tree from Guatemala. The raw latex is tapped from the trees and processed into natural rubber. This process costs far less energy and CO_2 emissions than making neoprene in a factory.'

One of Patagonia's most famous campaigns was 'Don't buy this jacket'. Why did you urge people not to buy your clothes?

'We wanted people to think about the protection of the planet by reducing over-consumption. And although Patagonia has grown strongly since this campaign, we still link ourselves to our underlying desire to extend the lifecycle of your things, and we encourage our customers to think about whether they really need something before they buy it. We teach people simple restoration tricks and have repair centres over the whole world. We also work with platforms organising the sale of used clothes, and experiment with offering second-hand Patagonia clothes in our stores.'

Ryan's favourites

'My favourite destinations are the Utah desert (but also the winter snow in the far corners of the state), the limestone towers in South-East Asia, the Alps and Hokkaido in Japan.'

Have you always wanted to surf, ski, kite, rock climb or paraglide? Then download the Shakabookings app, that directly links you, Airbnb style, to a professional instructor. The way to learn from an insider.

Volunteer work can be an excellent way to spend your free time. You do something positive for the world, feel useful and meet new people. Go for it! It's increasingly organised by employers, also as teambuilding for example. Nothing wrong with that, although it's of course paramount to make sure you have your own business in order first. Building a school somewhere or donating to a charity makes no sense if you harm the environment and violate human rights in your supply chain. I sometimes call it 'the new wrong' if a company proudly boasts about the wells dug with their money, while their own production causes water shortages and pollution. You can't pay off behaviour this way. Individually, you may want to do more, and for example go abroad to help. This can be great, but be careful not to fall into the 'white saviour syndrome'. We don't necessarily know better here, and we can't just determine what people need there. They're perfectly capable of doing this themselves. A country can earn quite a bit of money by bringing in volunteer work, which is tempting – while getting the school built by locals instead of international students would have been better for employment opportunities. In short: absolutely, you can contribute a great deal, but go about it smartly. Make sure you properly research what you want to do, with whom and where. A week's not always worth it (barring exceptions of course, for example when helping during a disaster); if you can free up a month or longer, you've a better chance to matter. Make sure you go with a well-respected group that works closely with the local population. In Volunteer Correct's Transparency Index, you can see how they score on issues such as mission, partners, finances and so on. Check out Fidesco, Local Dreamers, VSO or WWOOF for inspiration and information.

Your food tastes even better outside, especially if you're barbecuing. With these tips you'll be doing it a little bit sustainably too:

» Choose organic meat and vegetables, preferably local and in season.
» Normal charcoal isn't so sustainable – it costs forest. 8 to 10 kilos of wood are required for 1 kilo of charcoal. Get charcoal with FSC certification or give coconut a try: BAST briquettes are made of coconut shells, a coconut-industry waste product. There are also producers of better charcoal, like BioRegional Homegrown.
» Those white firelighters contain paraffin (you probably smell it). K-Lumet blocks are made of recycled wood and old candle wax. They're produced by people handicapped by an accident or illness. You can also use them to light an open fire or bonfire. Household-product brands like If You Care also offer more sustainable options.
» The smoke from a barbecue (or bonfire) contains harmful substances and can affect people with lung conditions. Try to limit the nuisance by looking at the wind direction. A gas or electric barbecue doesn't have this disadvantage, and you can turn it off when taking a break.
» Don't buy a gigantic barbecue if you'll only be grilling for a few friends, and borrow one from your neighbours if you don't do it regularly. Rather no disposable plates and cups, of course (dishes for those who don't cook).

LIKE SAILING?

Be careful with polluting diesel, engines emitting nasty substances, emptying your toilet, or lubricating oil that ends up in the water. Get as small and economical a boat as possible and investigate environmentally-friendly options. Many boats aren't used for most of the year, so why not share? On the Barqo platform you can rent thousands of insured yachts and boats from local owners worldwide. A savvy way to sail in unique places.

Out and About

Going out for a lovely day or evening is wonderful – and why do we often do it abroad, but less at home? Here some tips.

> On the Green Key website you'll find more sustainable restaurants, swimming pools, theme parks, museums, theatres etc. Some are bronze, others silver or gold – not perfect, but at least they're doing something.

> Cinema? Projecting of course costs quite a bit of energy, and the snacks available aren't often very sustainable (and expensive, phew). Leave those be, I'd say, and try looking out for climate neutral or solar theatres.

> I always find zoos a bit difficult. Great for children (and us) to learn about animals, and how important they are for the world. But certainly in older zoos where there's less space, the captivity quickly feels uncomfortable. So above all try to go to zoos where the animals have as much freedom as possible, and preferably with Green Key Gold.

>> *Fancy dining out? In chapter 3 you'll find tips for ethical eating (p. 154), and in the guide, addresses of conscious restaurants.*

INTERVIEW

FRANK REEF

came with similar initiatives. Westkustvin technicians have put fin templates online for free, so that everyone can (3D) print and improve them.'

Frank Reef (1975) is a sustainable surf-entrepreneur.

What are your best sustainable tips?
'Surfers should be the ambassadors of the sea. We spend so much time in it, if the water's polluted, we're the first to get ill. If we keep our beaches clean, take our rubbish with us, don't toss any cigarette butts (including on the street, as that's just a longer way to the sea), it would be terrific. The money it costs the government to clean the streets and beaches would be better spent on other things. Surfers travel a lot, always in search of the waves, and the favourite Volkswagen camper is certainly not the cleanest. I prefer to surf with a few friends and we carpool increasingly often. It's more fun and easily saves a tank of petrol a month.'

Frank's favourites
'The downside of the sport is that it's a major global industry. Boards, wetsuits, fins – basically everything you need is made of plastic and almost never recyclable. Fortunately, more and more's happening. Patagonia introduced a natural, FSC-certified rubber wetsuit, without neoprene (made from petroleum). Brands such as Picture and VISSLA

233

On average a festival-goer produces about 2 kilos of rubbish per day (twice as much as normal).

Future-Proof Festivals

Festivals are fabulous! Listening to music, dancing, discovering new things, the great outdoors, seeing amazing performances... They cost a lot of energy to set up, of course, cause a lot of waste (including disposable cups and abandoned tents), mobile toilets use chemicals, the food's usually not very environmentally friendly, the noise a disaster for the animals and so on. But this is changing. Festivals celebrate life, and a growing number of organisations believe that with this goes responsibility. And so waste is recycled, and sometimes countered by reusable return cups. Water's being dealt with increasingly better, with water points to fill your bottle, and toilets flushing used instead of drinking water. Catering's becoming more sustainable, with options for vegetarians and vegans, and electricity's becoming greener. There's more respect for nature, animals and people (working at a festival is demanding, and not all employees and volunteers are always treated fairly). Organisation A Greener Festival aims to make festivals worldwide more sustainable; Glastonbury Festival, Mysteryland and Welcome to The Future are frontrunners.

GERRARD STREET

>> Like listening to music on headphones? According to founder of rentable headphones Gerrard Street (only in the Netherlands for now), 15 million kilos of headphones are thrown away worldwide every year – not a bad idea then to have a go at trying to change this. Thinksound makes them from more sustainable wood and PVC free, and you can return them to be recycled. Woodbuds is a group of friends that wants to make as little impact as possible: their earplugs feature more sustainable wood and recycled packaging; they plant trees for every hundred pieces sold. LSTN wants to change lives through the power of music: their proceeds go to hearing aids for people in need. They also work a lot with wood (for headphones, speakers and accessories), which is degradable and sounds better. Speakers also need to improve: produced more sustainably, and easier to repair. The Swedish Transparent Speakers wants to cause that revolution.

FLORIAN WOLFF

Florian Wolff (1985) is singer-songwriter. He's been dubbed most sustainable musician of the Netherlands.

How do you connect sustainability and music?

'It started with a CD cover made of recycled paper, printed with environmentally-friendly ink. After that, I made band shirts from organic cotton and my website's hosted by a green company. Eventually I developed the Green Tour where my former band and I performed on a stage powered by solar, wind and human energy. Nowadays I perform with a stripped-down version of that stage, the Green Machine. This is a bicycle installation that, when the public cycles on it, generates enough electricity for all the equipment that I use in my performance. I also standardly request vegetarian and preferably organic meals, and travel as much as possible with public transport.'

What are the dos and the don'ts of green clubbing?

'Every time you pay, you vote. Whether in a club, on a pop stage or festival: consciously choose the organic specialty beer instead of the standard one from the main sponsor. You'll increase the demand for that product. Get your festival grub at the vegan food-truck with local ingredients instead of at the hotdog stand that imports all its meat. Your money has more effect than you think.'

Are there more sustainable artists?

'As surf pro, Jack Johnson has a close relationship with the sea and is committed to nature conservation. At his worldwide concerts, sustainable alternatives were sought throughout the entire production. He even reports on the impact of each tour on his website. I think highly of Ben Harper because he raises social themes and goes his own way musically. Bob Geldof is special too: with Live Aid he used the power of music so perfectly to globally expose a social theme. Michael Jackson is of course everyone's hero, both for his oeuvre and his loving message.'

Suggestions for those wanting to live more sustainably?

'Don't let that voice that says you're only one individual and can change little stop you. A small step can cause huge progress, especially if we do it en-masse. Discuss the things you do or don't do to live more sustainably. We're in this together and can learn a lot from each other.'

Florian's motto

'Be aware of all the beauty and goodness that's around and within you. You can plan and reflect all you want, but in the end you're always in the here and now. The art of living, I believe, is to feel okay at every moment and place.'

CELEBRATING

Hack the Holidays

I celebrate everything left, right and centre, and preferably multiple times. The more festive, the better. I also love traditions and enjoy creating new ones. Holidays are absolutely my thing. Christmas, Easter – I'm not religious, but I do connect with the pagan background of honouring the harvest, giving thanks for what the earth provides us with, celebrating the light and the seasons. Whatever we celebrate, it must of course be for everyone and be positive. Let's make celebrating sustainable.

» Why not create your own traditions? Certainly in the time of feasting and remembering they can easily centre around the world and our fellow human beings, right? On the day after Boxing Day, we always organise 'Leftmas', and invite friends to bring all their Christmas leftovers with them. The excess, we can eat for days! Assembled, it always results in the most extraordinary and tasty menus (in combinations you never imagined), and a warm, relaxed evening. Instead of an Advent calendar you can make an Adventist box, adding an item daily you no longer need (food, clothing, things), to give to a homeless person or shelter at Christmas time. Give free Easter hugs – anything goes, you can't go wrong.

» Don't cook ridiculous amounts of food. Or do, and eat it all with a large group of friends or hand it out.
» Go for ethical and sustainable gifts. Buy fair trade and/or organic Christmas cookies, presents from sustainable brands or stores, quality over quantity and preferably no knickknacks, gimmicks or other junk that nobody really wants.
» I love having a Christmas tree, and always start looking forward to it again in October already. We get one with roots and try and plant it in the garden: you've got most chance of success if you water it enough whilst in the house (also spray the branches) and plant immediately afterwards in fertile soil. Keep watering it, even in the winter, and fingers crossed. A good alternative are trees you can chop down yourself in some places to sustain the forest, which is fun to do. Or adopt/rent one! You can collect an (organic) Christmas tree and return it, then they're replanted and wait for you for a year. You can even bring your 'own' tree back home. Find an artificial tree easier? Make sure you use it for a long time (otherwise it's no more sustainable than a real tree) or buy one second-hand. Cheaper too! The same goes for Christmas decorations, you really don't have to buy them new: you can find all kinds online or in thrift stores. Or DIY your own of course, from pine cones for example – ours adorn the tree for years

Americans buy about 27.5 million real Christmas trees a year, Brits 7 million. Annually, Denmark exports 10 to 12 million Christmas trees, only a little less than frontrunner America.

Every year, we shoot about 1.7 billion euros worth of fireworks into the sky.

now. Do you need new lights? Think LED: more environmentally-friendly and cheaper to use.

» Dressing up as Father Christmas or Rudolph? Rent or borrow a suit (an appeal on social media works wonders).

» Every year at Christmas we send a digital, home-made video, song, spoken wish or something else. Great fun to do – and better than sending lots of cards. Although I'm very much in favour of the paper card and probably post more than most, so this isn't necessarily for me to say... Through organisations such as Cards for Causes or Giving-Cards you can have a card printed and directly donate to a charity. Via FairMail cards you support young people in developing countries: they learn photography, and receive half of the money raised for their education. You can also find more and more cards made of FSC paper or from special materials like stone and growing paper.

» I'm a sucker for celebrating, but think fireworks are nonsense. I'm sorry, but I just don't get it, so much money fired into the air for a bang or flash? Millions are starving... What could we do with all those billions? And there's also the pollution: all that fine dust and heavy metals (for the colours) in the air, and the huge mess on the ground. All needs to be cleaned again. And then the animals! The poor pets and city animals, who really suffer for days. It's not my thing at all, but if we really must, why not have a short, professional display, organised by the council instead of each to their own. Much more sociable too.

Celebrate Good Times (Come On)

I even celebrate my half-yearly birthday, so have quite a bit of experience with this. Here are some ways to happily give parties, that impact the environment (and hopefully yourself) less. Have your cake and eat it too!

> Make it easy for yourself. Ask people to bring some food or snacks (preferably organic/fair trade/local/homemade) and a pretty candle or homely plant – even instead of a gift, and you're immediately free from a lot of stress in terms of cooking and decorations.

> Try not to go for disposable tableware. Don't fancy washing up? Request everyone brings their

own plate, cup and cutlery. I often organise a picnic for my birthday, where this works really well.

> Food left over? Give it to your guests as they leave, put it in the fridge for the coming days or freeze for later.

> You can of course also get your party catered, particularly if it's a bit bigger. Choose organic and/or local (and preferably vegetarian) catering, there's more and more out there.

Americans spend on average 1,033 euros during the holiday shopping season.

> If you're having a bigger party at home, then rental is a good option. Try to find a company that has sustainability high on their list, and for example uses green energy and efficient equipment. Or try to borrow a party tent or bar tables via an app like Streetbank from someone local. Maybe you'd prefer to buy (because you often give parties, of course)? Pay attention to whether the crockery/cutlery/furniture will last, is produced sustainably, and if you have to go for disposable anyway – that it's made of recycled resources (and can be re-used), and never from polystyrene.

> Getting everything delivered is less sustainable if you're giving a big party, considering the transport and emissions. If you're hiring a location, ask about the food, energy consumption, cleaning, waste separation, Green Key certification and such, and choose somewhere central that everyone can reach easily by public transport. $\longrightarrow$

> Sending invitations? Create a cool digital design, or use recycled, FSC certified, plantable or edible and preferably not very thick material. Every little helps. You can also use old maps, scraps of wallpaper, music scores or other leftover paper. Go wild!

> Decorating is great fun. Balloons really aren't though (and they only last for such a short time too). They cause pollution, birds mistake old balloon scraps for food or get tangled in them. The same goes for paper wish-balloons (which can also cause fires on thatched roofs). Helium is a non-renewable gas, and experts predict that it'll be exhausted in 25 to 30 years (problematic, as MRI scans for example need helium). According to experts, helium balloons are far too cheap for the valuable material they're filled with, and should cost closer to 100 euros. Try to use balloons made of natural, fair trade or FSC rubber, or go for foldable pompoms that can be used for years. Glitter appears extremely festive, but it's plastic snippets that behave exactly like microbeads – and so end up everywhere, in your hair and bed for weeks, but also in the air, sea, birds and fish. Still want to shine? Then go for biodegradable alternatives like BioGlitz or BioGlitter. You can use saved glass jars to make welcoming candle holders, or fill them with scraps of wool, twigs, fir cones or whatever takes your fancy. Garlands are great fun to make yourself, from used print-paper for instance, or other leftover materials – there are all kinds of examples online. Love flowers? More in the section on gifts (p. 241) about the ins and outs of cut flowers.

Giving and Getting

What's not to like about presents? Giving or getting – I love them both! In any case, my goal is to give more away in life. Minimum effort, maximum pleasure. I dare say I'm pretty good at thinking up gifts. Sometimes though it's challenging, because what do you get people that have it all already?

— My top tip for everyone: make a wish list. Really, it's the best thing. You just have to get over that initial feeling of it being greedy. It's not, it's handy. When it's my birthday, Mr Eyskoot is always sweet enough to manage my list and prevent any doubles, but you can do it online too (or ask if you can make one at your favourite conscious shop). And it's sustainable, because waste-preventing. How awkward is it having to gracefully accept a gift that you don't like at all? Such a joy to only receive what you really want or can use. During the year, keep a list of things you come across – for birthdays, celebrations and to simply wave in front of your partner now and again.

— By any means gift what you've got spare. It's such a waste to buy new things, while we often own lots that would make someone else happier.

— Preferably give or ask for sustainable, local products from independent or progressive brands (hopefully you've already found a few favourites whilst reading). Shops can for instance help women to economic autonomy, brands can stimulate exciting innovation; all labels and stores in this book improve the world.

— It doesn't always have to be things. Why not give yourself away: as babysitter, film date, DIY help, masseur, dinner companion... You're valuable! Organise a nice walk (or treasure trail) or give someone all compliments you can think of on a note. A big present can be an experience, such as a weekend away, visit to the theatre, a nature activity or another welcome outing.

— Something homemade always hits the spot. Sachets of dried lavender, or fruit and veg from your own garden (or balcony). Homemade biscuits, jam or pickles. A specially put-together collection of music, a scarf you knitted, I'm sure there's something that you can, and I want.

— A subscription to remarkable chocolate (from Cocoa Runners, for example), a goat for a family in a developing country, or school books for a disadvantaged child (from Oxfam, for instance) are wonderful gifts for people who don't want or know anything. Just like gift certificates, for dance, film, books or sustainable shops and brands.

— Receiving a card is lovely and always a surprise. Makes sending around some paper worth it, if you ask me. Or put a tea bag or gift voucher in an envelope, for a birthday or birth, or just because. Digital post's also a possibility of course. Send an e-card, make a video, record a message or sing a song. ⟶

Make a list
of things
that make
you happy.
Make a list
of what
you do
every day.
Compare
the lists.
Adjust
accordingly.

SAYING YES?

Congratulations! Your wedding will probably be one of the biggest parties you'll ever throw – which can also become pretty costly. Let's make it smarter, greener and cheaper.

» Choose a wedding outfit you can also wear after the special day, have your parent's ensemble altered or go for a second-hand dress or suit.

» You can also donate your outfit afterwards: my mother gave hers to the nuns, they collected them so people in Africa who wouldn't otherwise be able to afford it could wear them to get married. Hopefully it made lots of women happy. If you're handy, you could maybe turn your wedding outfit into something else or save it for your kids.

» Let your face and hair glow with natural make-up and beauty products.

» You can make decorations and invitations yourself if you want to/have the time: fun to do with friends, it saves money and if you reuse materials, it's more sustainable. Prefer to get in a stylist? Choose one who makes getting married naturally and sustainably cool.

» Go for sustainable catering, with local, organic products; often tastier too.

» Why not travel to the wedding by tram or other public transport? There are also an increasing number of cool electric cars for hire, even classic ones.

» Get your wedding rings made from Fairtrade and 'green' gold or recycle your, or your family's jewellery.

» An average wedding emits about 14.5 tonnes of CO_2; hopefully this book helps you reduce this.

INTERVIEW   .

JACOMIEN ROOBOL

Jacomien Roobol (1989) has been working as a model for years, and travels the world.

What did you notice during your time abroad?

'In Northern Europe we prefer a natural, clean style, but in Los Angeles you see more people that clearly have been under the knife. The perfect image is prevalent there. In Cuba, there's a completely different self-image altogether. Fat, thin, tall, short – it doesn't matter. Women in general are very self-confident there and convey this too. They're not concerned at all with getting the "perfect" body or elusive six-pack. They just consider themselves beautiful the way they are.'

Jacomien's Spanish hotspots

'I live in Barcelona for a few months a year and there, the tap water's not drinkable. The locals usually buy bottled water. So much plastic waste! I opt for a filter on the tap or a BRITA jug that purifies the water and gives it a mild taste.'

01. Flax & Kale – 'My favourite restaurant – organic/local/flexitarian food.'

02. Veritas – '*The* eco supermarket in the city.'

03. Home on Earth – 'Lovely, sustainable interior goods.'

04. Palo Alto Market – 'Vintage/street-food market with local products.'

05. The Farmacia in the basement of the El Corte Inglés on Plaza Catalunya – 'Wonderful, natural beauty brands, like Korres and Apivita.'

06. Natura – 'For great fair fashion, home products and accessories.'

— Only have larger wishes, such as a solar panel, a trip or that beautiful, sustainable winter coat? Great – a joint present or asking for money makes life even easier for your friends.

— Received a gift? Save the paper and use it to wrap other presents. Or make the most of old magazines, newspapers, fabric scraps, paper bags – whatever you've got.

— Do you like giving flowers? They often come from afar, are usually grown using loads of chemicals and water, cut for single use and the working conditions in the flower industry can be difficult and sub-standard (the Fairtrade organisations have information about this). Not very festive, unfortunately. Go for organic and/or Fairtrade-certified flowers (more and more chains like Marks & Spencer sell them, and hopefully your neighbourhood shops too), local flowers in season, pick them from your own garden or choose a pretty plant that'll at least last a long time.

— Somebody doesn't have to have a birthday, be a newlywed or a brand-new father to receive a present. Give more (often), it's brilliant.

— Book finished? Give it to someone you think will love it or leave it behind in a café. Via BookCrossing you can label and register them and become part of a worldwide book-sharing movement. In more and more places, bookcases appear on the street where you can take one for free. Do you enjoy giving books (or buying them)? Better World Books for instance sells (second-hand) copies worldwide, donates books and supports literacy

AURÉLIE CHADAINE / LAURA BONNEFOUS

projects. A magazine is such a nice mini-gift if you find one in a train or get one from a friend. Do you have lots? Then you can also donate them to a refugee shelter or give them to a hospital (or turn them into a stool by bundling them together).

— Really can't think of anything for your list? Ask your friends to donate to a charity, for example via Just Giving. Charities such as Care, Oxfam and Women for Women offer life-changing gifts, such as school fees, clean water and education. Major players like Amazon and eBay have special sites through which you donate directly to charities when you buy (see the guide), and via iGive you can activate something similar at over 1,800 stores.

Recommendations from The Green House – the designers of this book

---

Babylonstoren 'Here sustainability and aesthetics meet. A beautiful vegetable garden in South Africa with a greenhouse, restaurant, hotel and spa. All ingredients directly from the garden to your plate.'

Daluma 'An inspiring café in Berlin with a minimalist interior full of plants. The best food for your body, delicious and sustainable.'

Honest 'Artisan chocolate from Cape Town: organic and raw bars, packed by hand in a wrapper designed by illustrators.'

WENDELINE WIJKSTRA

Wendeline Wijkstra (1989) is dancer with the Dutch National Ballet, one of the best companies in the world.

Does sustainability play a role for you as dancer?

'It's an important part of my life. I think this is also a result of dancing. The resurrection of century-old choreographies and scores is something I really value. I believe that nowadays, in a time in which everything is produced quickly to earn as much money as possible, there's more need than ever before to preserve art and crafts. This is why I select everything I buy consciously. It's no longer acceptable to close your eyes to the fact that lots of large companies don't take any responsibility, and we're being played the fool by misleading marketing. I live in an environment where we try to create ultimate beauty. For me this is a major aspect of sustainability. Attention for what you choose to buy and how you take care of yourself.'

Is sustainability also part of your future?

'Through dancing I've been able to travel extensively which has opened my eyes to how people in different cultures live and deal in other ways with what the earth has to offer. I really want to dedicate myself to people and animals that need help. I don't use palm oil, for example, because the production is so destructive, and I want to create more awareness about this.'

What concerns you?

'My big sister is mentally handicapped, and I still learn lots from her. She is caring and loving, social and uninhibited. Through her I've also learnt that you shouldn't be prejudiced. You can't form an opinion about something or someone if you don't know anything about them. Assumptions, in my eyes, are very destructive.'

BAS ANDRIES

What tips do you have as top sportswoman for fellow sporters?

'Our schedules are often so intensive that we have little recovery time, and so much of our energy comes from what we eat. I therefore choose everything I consume with care. It helps me stay fit and I like knowing where everything comes from. This is why I'd strongly advise people to eat organic, taking good care of both yourself and our world.'

GREEN KIDS by Laura de Jong

Baby Gifts

Looking for a gift for a new baby? Maybe consider something practical, like a homemade fresh meal for the parents or cleaning help. Another nice idea is the TimeCapsule from Make History. You can save your memories in it, from first shoes to favourite cuddly toy.

Don't Fly

We travel as much as possible by public transport with our kids. Relaxed, because you can look outside together, play a game or picnic in the train. For holidays, we also choose consciously not to fly. Why would you? By public transport too, there are all kinds of wonderful things to discover.

Experience

Celebrating a birthday is not about an expensive present or big party. The unwrapping alone is often already extremely exciting. A party hat or decorations are a must. Singing and having breakfast together is the perfect start to a day of celebrations. Particularly with candles in your toast.

All Those Toys...

Having lots of toys unfortunately doesn't ensure that children will play better. On the contrary: they're less inventive and develop less solutions themselves. So choose a few things and store the rest. After a while, you can swap some. Do this in particular after a birthday or festivities, when there's suddenly lots of new things on offer. Up to 24 months, the amount of 'necessary' toys is minimal. Divide the age in months by 3: two toys are therefore enough for a 6-month-old baby.

Rituals

Not only birthdays are festivities. There are so many moments to celebrate. The transition to a new season, for example. Anthroposophy has beautiful rituals linked to nature, you'll find a lot of inspiration there.

PINCH TOYS

GUIDE

TRAVELLING

Travel organisations
baobabtravel.com / bouteco.co /
ecocompanion.com / entdeck-die-welt.
de / feelingresponsible.org /
intrepidtravel.com / responsibletravel.
com / shoestring.com /
worldexpeditions.com

With locals
acitymadebypeople.com / airbnb.com /
globalgreeternetwork.info

Information and inspiration
ecotourdirectory.com / ecotourism.
org / ecotravellerguide.com /
ethicaltraveler.org / gogreentravelgreen.
com / greenglobaltravel.com /
greenholiday.info / greentravelguides.
tv / greentraveller.co.uk / lnt.org.au /
sustainabletravel.org /
travelsocialgood.org

Certification
earthcheck.org /
ec.europa.eu/environment/ecolabel /
ecotourism.org.au / fairtrade.travel /
greenglobe.com / greenkey.global /
green-tourism.com / travelife.org

Bike/train/hike
americanhiking.org /
bushwalkingaustralia.org / cycletours.
com / eurovelo.com /
hollandcyclingroutes.com / ibike.org /
internationalrail.com / loco2.com /
modernhiker.com / nsinternational.
nl/en / parktours.com.au / raileurope.
com / seat61.com / thegreattrail.ca

Sharing
barqo.nl (boat) / goboony.com
(camper)

Hotels
1hotels.com/brooklyn-bridge /
almodovarhotel.de / biohotels.info /
bookdifferent.com / conscioushotels.
com – see also p. 223 /
ecomamahotel.com /
goodhotelamsterdam.com /
goodhotellondon.com /
iloveecohotels.com / livezoku.com –

see also p. 225 / qo-amsterdam.com /
tripadvisor.com/GreenLeaders /
uniqhotels.com/hi-hotel

House swap
airbnb.com / couchsurfing.com /
homeexchange.com /
homeforexchange.com / wimdu.com

Camping
campspace.com /
countryside-discovery.co.uk /
ecocamping.net / gamping.com /
greenholiday.info / greenkey.global /
hipcamp.com / huttopia.com /
kartent.com / klattermusen.com /
mec.ca

HIPCAMP / STEPFANIE A

Worldwide working
wanderbrief.com / teleport.org

Offsetting
atmosfair.de / climatecare.org /
ekos.org.nz / greenfleet.com.au /
greenseat.nl / nativeenergy.com /
sustainabletravel.org

DOING THINGS

Beach and forest
blueflag.global / campingintheforest.
co.uk / oceanconservancy.org / tcv.
org.uk/greengym / trumpforest.com

Barbecue and bonfires
bast-bbq.nl / bioregionalhomegrown.
com / ifyoucare.com / k-lumet.de

Volunteer work
fidesco-international.org /
localdreamers.org / volunteercorrect.

org / vsointernational.org / wwoof.net

Pleasure
bookcrossing.com /
cloudappreciationsociety.org /
copenhagencyclechic.com /
florianwolff.com – see also p. 235 /
mediamatic.net / mezrab.nl /
shakabookings.com

International Recommendations

GreenMe Berlin
Blog and podcast about the eco
scene in Berlin, with guide books,
green map, shops, brands, cafés and
destinations, tours etc.
greenmeberlin.com

AND ALSO
buenavistasurfclub.com (eco surf
lodge in Nicaragua) / greenglasses.cz
(Prague) / greeninitiatives.cn (China) /
littlegreendot.com (Singapore) /
loylyhelsinki.fi (sustainable spa in
Helsinki) / organicexplorer.co.nz
(New Zealand)

BRANDS

Information
detox-outdoor.org /
greenoutdoorgear.wordpress.com /
veganoutdooradventures.com

Outdoor Clothes and Accessories

Girlfriend Collective
American label for yoga and leisure
wear made of recycled materials,
that's transparent about production
and shows the beauty of diversity
and real women in a cool way.
girflriend.com

Houdini
Swedish outdoor brand with an
extensive collection, that produces as
sustainably as possible and recycles
and repairs clothing. Own stores, e.g.
in Gothenburg, Oslo and Stockholm.
houdinisportswear.com

MEC
Canadian collective for hike, camping,
travel, bike and snow gear. To be able

to purchase, you become a member and support the community. Works with more sustainable and recycled materials and fair-trade factories. mec.ca

Patagonia

American pioneer in sustainable outdoor wear (offering a complete range of clothes and gear), from material development to using the brand to achieve social change. Sued President Trump, for example, for shrinking protected nature reserves. patagonia.com – see also p. 230

AND ALSO

ecogear-products.com – Eco-friendly backpacks, travel and messenger bags from America.
fjallraven.com – Swedish brand with a large collection of bags, coats and equipment. Are implementing environmental improvements, for example fake fur and responsible down.
hanwag.de – Handmade walking shoes from Germany, produced to last. Part of the collection is made of CO_2-neutral leather, and some models of eco leather from cows from certified farms.
healthyseas.org – This Dutch initiative retrieves abandoned fishing nets from the sea to make the material Econyl, which is for instance used to make socks and swimwear.
howies.co.uk – British leisure, outdoor and sportswear and accessories made of more sustainable materials.
klattermusen.com – Swedish outdoor label (clothes, gear) from a group of friends that never wanted to become a brand; use organic and recycled fabrics and provide repair tips on their website.
nau.com – American outdoor clothing and accessories made of more sustainable materials such as recycled down and Tencel. Part of money raised goes to change organisations.
outerknown.com – Outdoor brand for men, that amongst other things uses Bluesign material and was founded by American surf icon Kelly Slater.
paramo-clothing.com – British label that works with fair-trade factories, is committed to long-term wear and takes clothes back to recycle.
rapanuiclothing.com – GOTS-certified British brand that wants to change the fashion industry. Develops own techniques, lets you

customise your clothes and takes back their items.
rohnisch.com – Swedish active and workout brand for women, from more sustainable fabrics. Contributes to initiatives for female entrepreneurship in India.
sealandgear.eu – South African brand with bags and accessories made of recycled advertising, sails and truck tarpaulin.
unitedbyblue.com – Want to show that a successful brand can contribute to conservation. For every product sold they retrieve one pound of waste from the ocean or river. American B Corp with more sustainable materials, lifetime guarantee and own stores in Philadelphia and New York.
vaude.com – German outdoor brand affiliated to Fair Wear Foundation for improvement of working conditions, makes more sustainable products (look out for 'Green Shape') and reports transparently.
wearpact.com – American Pact offers leisurewear and underwear made of organic cotton, from fair-trade certified factories.

SWISH SUITS

Sustainable surf

abysseofficial.com (US brand: wetsuits, bikinis and activewear made of eco-friendly rubber and recycled material) / patagonia.com (wetsuits of natural FSC-certified rubber) / surfinggreen.com.au (Australian webshop for surf/skateboards and accessories) / sustainablesurf.org (American NGO that wants to make the surf world more sustainable) / swishsuits.com (American eco-wetsuits for and by women) / thegreenwave.co.uk

(UK webshop: boards, clothing and accessories) / westkustsurf.nl (opensource surf-design)

Swimwear

auraiswimwear.com / auria-london.com / koruswimwear.com / liarthelabel.com.au / manakaiswimwear.com / marahoffman.com / mimeswim.com / shapesinthesand.com.au / summerloveswimwear.com / woodlikeocean.com

Sports

greensportsalliance.org / sustainableclubs.co.uk

Gadgets

bioliteenergy.com (cool American off-the-grid brand for cooking, energy and lighting, makes the products also available in poorer parts of the world) / voltaicsystems.com (portable power company from Brooklyn, with solar kits and bags) / wasteboards.com (Dutch skateboards made of recycled bottle caps)

Sound

jambooheadphones.com / konohazuk.com / lstnsound.co / thinksound.com / transparentspeaker.com / woodbuds.com

Natural bug-repellent

badgerbalm.com (also skin, sun and fragrance) / bubbleandbee.com (also soap, deo, face etc.) / remixbygisellewasfie.com (also body/essential oils, fragrance, candles)

CELEBRATING

Cards

amnesty.org / cardsforcauses.com / fairmail.info / giving.cards / stone-paper.nl

Gifts

betterworldbooks.com / ecobookstore.de / gifts.care.org / gifts.womenforwomen.org / givingworks.ebay.com / globalgoodpartners.org / goodsearch.com / igive.com / justgiving.com / smile.amazon.com (and of course all the brands and stores mentioned in this book)

Party
biofutura.com / bio-glitter.com /
bioglitz.co / disposables.bio /
juriannematter.nl /
repurposecompostables.com (also
blog) / thenaturalweddingcompany.
co.uk

Flowers and trees
fairtrade.net/products/flowers.html /
forever-green-christmas.co.uk /
livingchristmas.com /
loveachristmastree.co.uk /
oneworldflowers.org / slowflowers.com

GREEN KIDS

Flatout Frankie
A house full of toys, but they'd rather
play with a cardboard box. Familiar?
This New Zealand brand has respon-
ded with a racing car or kitchen made
of cardboard. You can paint the
boxes and they're sent folded (so
more environmentally-friendly).
flatoutfrankie.com

WEE GALLERY

Grimms
Wooden toys in rainbow colours.
Stimulate creativity through irregular
shapes, so you can use them to make
anything. The German brand also
offers a small collection in black and
white, originally intended for children
with a visual impairment, but also very
suitable for a minimalistic interior.
grimms.eu

Ostheimer
Ostheimer's wooden animals are not
cheap, but beautiful and of very good

quality. Handmade and painted in
Germany.
ostheimer.de

Pinch Toys
Minimalist toys from Croatia, made
of natural materials like cotton, wood
and felt, decorated with natural paint.
pinchtoys.com

Wee Gallery
Who says that black and white's
not fun for children? For the first six
weeks, your baby sees nothing else.
These American art cards, blankets,
pillows and crockery are brimming with animals, allowing you to
create all kinds of stories. Siddu, the
owners' son, also draws along.
weegallery.com

Wishbone Bike
Designed in New Zealand, this
wooden balance-bike has three
heights and grows with your child.
You use it first as trike with three
wheels, then as a regular balance
bike. Because you can turn the frame
around, it lasts up to five years.
wishbonedesign.com

AND ALSO
make-history.com

06

KNOWLEDGE

INTRODUCTION

7.6

**hours we spend
worldwide per day
on media such as
(mobile) internet, TV
or newspapers**

The previous chapters revolved mostly around doing and buying, but *knowing* is of course also part of a sustainable lifestyle. Thoughts, beliefs, opinions – and above all, learning more. Being open to other traditions and possibilities. Going in search of new insights that will perhaps replace your old ones. Feeling surprised, looking at something from a fresh perspective or hearing something you've never heard before is great, right? As is discovering new restaurants, beauty products or destinations. Welcome to the wonderful world of sustainability.

Such a world's not possible without transparency: we have to know the story behind what we eat or rub into our skin, who's responsible and what we can do ourselves. (Social) media is powerful and can play a crucial role. Just like pioneers, innovators or contrary thinkers, for example. That's why I sometimes ask the people I interview for their heroes. A few words from someone special can turn your life upside down or show you the light. I'm really honoured that some of my role models are part of this book. No positive, modern lifestyle without frontrunners.

8

**men currently together have
the same amount of money
as the poorest half of the
world population combined**

Equal rights for everyone are also essential for a sustainable society. Each individual, regardless of background, colour, (chosen) gender, sexual orientation or belief has the right to be here, belongs and has equal worth. I'm glad that street harassment is finally getting more attention; it's unacceptable to be addressed by complete strangers in a threatening or sexually intimidating way. Inclusive, not exclusive – and 'no' to sexism, racism and homophobia. Full stop. We need the powerful know-how, wisdom and contributions of *all* (sub) cultures, backgrounds and ages to make this planet a better place.

32%

**is how far women are
behind men when it comes
to equality in economics,
politics, education and
health, according to the
Global Gender Gap Index
(Iceland, Norway, Finland
and Sweden are joined
by Rwanda in the top 5 of
smallest gaps)**

What we don't need is greed, selfishness and an incessant drive for profit. Time and time again, it turns out this isn't what life is about. Helping a refugee matters. As does seeing someone who is lonely, sharing what you have with someone who has less. There is so much poverty and suffering, from America to Zambia and everywhere in between. You can call me idealistic or unrealistic, but just ask people nearing the end of their life. Friendship, looking after each other, a feeling of belonging or contributing to something is what counted, not consuming, gaining or achieving. We're more than just customers or targets, and we are able to take on other identities (involved citizen, dear friend, helpful neighbour) – by wanting to know more, being there for each other and working together on this sustainable challenge. So that ultimately you can say you were part of it, belonged and mattered.

Whether you think you can or you think you can't – you're right

KNOWING

ANDREW MORGAN

Andrew Morgan (1986) is an American film maker and opinion leader. Amongst other things, he directed the influential documentary *The True Cost*, about the impact of the fashion industry on people and the environment.

Why did you make *The True Cost*?
'I had never really thought much about where my clothes came from. Growing up, they just seemed to appear in the shops. Later I learned that people in developing countries made them, and that this was great because it meant they had a job. Only when I read in the newspaper that 1,138 people had died because a clothing factory in Bangladesh had collapsed, did I start asking a lot of questions. In the days that followed, I read everything I could get my hands on, and by the end of the week I was convinced this was a film I had to make. The size, scope and scale of the damage caused in the name of fashion surprised me. It's managed to stay under the radar for a long time, but take a good look and you'll see the staggering impacts on the earth and our fellow human beings.'

What can we do?
'Taking the time to understand what story you're buying and what model you're supporting will consistently lead you to better choices. This goes beyond loving clothes, it's about falling back in love with fashion for what it really means. Beauty, but never at the expense of somebody else's story. Fashion can be a driving force for so much good. If we're able to reconnect with the people behind what we wear, I believe that this can resurface

once again. For me, clothing represents a doorway to curiosity and empathy. Something I wear on my body is actually touched by someone half a world away. This is remarkable, and opening my eyes to this has been enriching, because it allows me to align my choices with the future I so desperately want to see unfold.'

What can the press do?
'Tell the real story. Each year, a multi-billion dollar consumer fairy tale's being sold to the world, and must continue finding thoughtful and exciting ways to entice people to a bigger and better story.'

Large companies have lots of powers – how can they use them for good?
'To be honest, I try not to waste too much time thinking about them. They're gigantic and rich, and yet fundamentally stand on the wrong side

of history. Stop buying into business models you don't believe in. This may sound small, but for me it's a very important step towards reclaiming power and saying: I'm not supporting this any longer. Focus your energy instead on companies that do beautiful work. Support them, become an evangelist for brands you love. This often makes a real difference, as the biggest challenge they face is often marketing.'

Who is your hero?
'Several of the trade union leaders that I've met around the world. They work to improve human and working rights, and are among the boldest, bravest individuals.'

What are your favourite tips for becoming more sustainable?
'See it as a journey and have fun. Don't feel guilty or embarrassed about what you didn't know before, and just do your best with what you know today. Life is full of seasons and change, and there's so much to discover when we pursue playing a part in something bigger than ourselves. As for brands, I'd like to reach out to Industry of All Nations, Reformation and Behno.'

We're online 2 hours and 20 minutes a day, 70% of which on a mobile device. We use traditional media such as newspapers, magazines and radio for 5 hours and 15 minutes – nearly 3 hours of this is television.

Media Muscle

The media plays a massive role in the way we see ourselves and the world. The moment a certain leather jacket is proclaimed a must-have, things go crazy. Buyers start frantically searching for a factory that can make thousands as quickly as possible – preferably this week. And they always find one, even when painfully clear it's not possible within that timeframe (and budget). The manufacturers are dependent on the brands and desperately want the work. We know what the consequences of this pressure is on people and the environment. Fortunately, the media can also be crucial in other ways. Journalists report undercover from factories and critical research makes the news(papers). As a result, the media can pose a risk to major brands. The more injustices they expose, the greater the pressure and the more important it is to have your business in order.

Glossies have an special position, because they're made for a particular target group and paid for by advertising. They also exist to appeal to us as consumers. If a magazine says that buying something will make you happy, the advertisers are happy too. Lots of people enjoy reading them. And don't let me stop you – as long as you're aware of this. They can influence how we think, meaning they also have a fantastic opportunity to mainstream ethical fashion. Luckily, the realisation that sustainable lifestyle is not just a fleeting trend is growing in magazine land. Australian *Vogue* appointed a sustainability editor-at-large, titles such as *Harper's Bazaar* and *Marie Claire* publish special eco-issues, and magazines such as *Conscious, Eluxe, IMPRINT* and *Peppermint* are entirely dedicated to it.

Much can improve in the film and television world, although attention is slowly growing. Production (light, catering, energy, transport, clothing etc.) costs huge amounts of energy. This can definitely be done more efficiently, using LED lighting and solar energy, sustainable catering, the stylists for films/programmes, celebrities and photoshoots can choose ethical fashion and make-up labels – and hopefully this'll happen increasingly often. There are also of course many documentaries about a better world. In the guide I've included some impressive productions about sustainable issues. And the potential of social media – wow. The more ethical brands, adverts and videos are shared, the better (if we did this as often as we shared cute cat videos, we'd change the world in the blink of an eye). The reach, the power and might are unparalleled. There are a growing number of great blogs about sustainable lifestyle, such as Eco Warrior Princess, EcoCult and Viertel\Vor – I've listed several in the guide.

INTERVIEW

BLOOMERS

Margot Guilbert (1989) is founder of Bloomers, an online destination for sustainable fashion and lifestyle. The blog aims to spread the work of conscious brands, and strive for a fair and circular economy. Margot is French, has lived in Switzerland and is currently based in Lisbon – these are her top tips.

Fashion 'My favourite is the French website Dressing Responsable, which supports local brands and ethically-made goods.'
Beauty 'Find organic products online at NUOO, or at Handmade Beauty in Madrid.'
Food 'I truly love the zero waste and delicious restaurant Silo in Brighton, or the vegetarian/vegan-friendly restaurant Sama Sama in Lisbon.'

Travel
Portugal
'Shop at fashion boutique Burel for beautiful woollen garments and accessories. Do your groceries at zero-waste store Maria Granel. Go to Organii for natural cosmetics and baby goods.'

Switzerland
'I love XaaNuu natural mascara, a Swiss brand with Mexican influence. You can buy it online but also at natural and zero-waste shop Nature en Vrac in Geneva. Find vegan cheese at Crémerie Végane, and get a haircut at Les Petits Peignes, they use organic haircare.'

Bali
'Shop sustainable fashion and goods at Love Stories Market in Ubud. I love FeelGood ethical pyjamas and S A Y A Designs eco hair-sticks. Eat healthy at raw/vegan restaurant Alchemy in Ubud, where you can also find mindful lifestyle-products. Bali Buda in Ubud and Canggu offer natural beauty and lifestyle items and fresh, organic and bulk groceries.'

'We've become good multi-taskers. But this doesn't please your mind. It's also about living in the here and now. When you're on your bike for example, be aware that you're cycling and don't think about your destination or what you'll have for dinner. These things will happen anyway.'

Nina Pierson, Dutch conscious entrepreneur and co-founder of SLA salad bars

Role Models and Innovators

Individuals can make the difference. *What* you say matters, but also *who* says it. Celebrities can use their status to give a stage to issues they find important – and more and more are actually doing this. Incredible innovators and inventors are pushing the world forward. Like this, for example.
» Michelle Obama wears vintage and African brands, and created an organic vegetable-patch at the White House to promote healthy eating. While being (the first African-American) First Lady, she promoted same-sex marriage and LGBTQ rights. Although both her and Barack received quite some criticism (for not supporting equal rights for people of colour enough, for instance) – how much do we miss their dignity, sanity and kindness (and fun!) now? Singer and producer will.i.am promotes recycling and works with Beats by Dr. Dre, Levi's and adidas to make products from old bottles and cans. Singer Neil Young has been involved in environmental activism since the sixties. He only wants organic band merchandise, and sings about political activism and protecting the earth. And there are so many more (Beyoncé, Annie Lennox, Alicia Garza, Angelina Jolie)... (see below).
» There are heaps of innovators doing extremely inspiring work. Too many to mention. Blond & Bieber dye fabric with microalgae, which means the colour is alive and changes. Carmen Hijosa makes textiles from pineapple leaves. Tesla's (and SpaceX and SolarCity's) Elon Musk is the hero of many, as is Daan Roosegaarde: he creates astonishing design to improve the world, for example to tackle smog, or illuminate cycle paths with solar energy. Pauline van Dongen combines fashion with science and creates wearable solar-panels and luminous sportswear. Brit Helen Storey, with Catalytic Clothing develops a product you can apply to clothes to capture harmful substances in the air, such as particles in exhaust fumes. If you move, you purify the air for the person behind you. Afterwards, you wash the dirt out of your clothes.

Superheroes Don't Always Wear Capes

I asked various people I spoke to for this book who their heroes are. This resulted in a colourful collection of pioneers, inventors and entrepreneurs. I've also got some myself of course! Quite a fair few in fact. The interviewees themselves, for example, and the other frontrunners who appear in this guide. Here I'll single out a few; I wish I had enough space to honour everyone doing great things...

Livia Firth

Livia, wife of actor Colin Firth, is one of the leading innovators in high-end sustainable fashion (also see p. 021). She walks countless red carpets, and wants to wear ethical fashion as much as possible. As a result, for the past few years she's been motivating designers with her Green Carpet Challenge, to make a sustainable outfit for her and other actors and celebrities. Armani, Stella McCartney and Gucci have for instance taken part. She's also very vocal (and visible) when it comes to wearing items in public more than once – something just not-done in the fashion world. Her husband also gets in on the act: he just keeps putting on the same organic wool Tom Ford tuxedo. Livia had her own more sustainable line for Marks & Spencer, and also collaborates with jewellery brand Chopard to improve the industry. Her consultancy agency Eco-Age helps luxury brands to produce better, and she's not afraid to confront big chains about issues such as overproduction and wage.

Katharine Hamnett

Katharine Hamnett dares, in a way I'd also like to. In the mid-eighties she became famous for her white T-shirts featuring boldly printed slogans (that she still makes), such as:

———

CHOOSE LIFE /
SAVE THE WORLD /
NO MORE FASHION VICTIMS

———

This last statement testifies to the significant importance Katharine Hamnett has for the ethical fashion movement. Since she at the end of the eighties discovers the extent of the malpractice, she lobbies tirelessly for reform. It's a huge honour to have been able to interview her for this book.

KATHARINE HAMNETT

Katharine Hamnett (1947) is one of the most important pioneers in ethical fashion. From a self-proclaimed 'bitch with blood on her hands, who invented stone washing, used to design fur coats, and owes the world a huge debt', she developed into a dedicated and world-changing champion of organic cotton. Hamnett personally made slogan T-shirts fashionable (remember Wham!?), with statements such as USE A CONDOM, DON'T SHOOT and WORLDWIDE NUCLEAR BAN NOW. The outspoken political activist won the first ever British Fashion Award and has been royally awarded for her services to the fashion industry.

How can we really make fashion sustainable?
'Consumers will buy sustainable in preference to non-sustainable if it's the same price. But how can you compete when you're paying a European wage, to people working in slave-labour conditions? The only way we can change this, is through legislation. Laws which only allow clothes into our economic system made with the same environmental standards we have, for which a living wage was paid, from certified and inspected factories. Only clothes that have ticked all the boxes should be allowed into the EU. This is the only way we can do it. Otherwise we'll continue to lose out to cheaper clothes, which people will of course buy. So, we need to make ask for it. We should put pressure on our elected representatives, and tell them we won't vote for them next time, unless they stand for our views. This is their weak spot, they're scared they won't get re-elected. We have to press that button.'

Can the industry exist without pesticides?
'There are so many horrible issues connected to pesticides. Farmers are in debt because of it – over the last five years in certain areas of India alone, 250,000 farmers have committed suicide. In Mali, they are starving, and farmers' wives are losing babies at the breast because they don't make enough milk. Farmers are forced to sign a contract for pesticides before they can get a contract for cotton. We can have a world without pesticides, before the Second World War they didn't even exist, as they were developed from the poison we

used in that. We don't need them, and moreover: without them there will be more jobs for farmers. This is why for instance the Better Cotton initiative is greenwashing: all pesticides are bad, also a little bit. So we shouldn't go for less, we need to push for none at all. Bamboo is greenwashing too, it's just another viscose, and it needs a lot of chemical treatment to make it into fabric.'

What's your advice for the sustainable fashion-movement?
'Don't get stuck in the eco look. It's horrible, it doesn't help. People buy jeans to get laid, they'll do anything to get laid. It needs to be glamorous and sexy, otherwise it's not going to work. Make clothes we want to wear. Young kids are now very keen on sustainable, they have a passion for it. So why the fuck are Burberry coats not made in organic cotton? These brands need to get on board, and they need to recognise the business opportunity. Also, we need to stress the importance of buying less. The Chinese say: think 11 times before you do something. We need to use our consumer power, choose well and spend money on what's right. It's up to all brands to stimulate this.'

What does your ideal fashion industry look like?
'Safe for all involved, certified ethically-made and of sustainable materials such as organic, recycled, chrome and PVC free – all of this protected and reinforced by legislation. Curious, super-informed consumers questioning everything, seeking out ethical brands and buying lasting quality.'

Katharine Hamnett transformed into a designer-campaigner, setting up an alternative supply chain to buy directly from the cotton farmers, weavers and manufacturers. As a result, she nearly goes bankrupt, but perseveres. Now, she's the founder of many developments worldwide. She designed a line for supermarket chain Tesco, for example. Normally offering cheap fast fashion, these pieces are made of organic cotton, long-lasting and packaged in recycled plastic. She forces Tesco into better purchasing practices and settling for less profit. It's a controversial collaboration, but she aims as always to demonstrate it's possible – as she's doing now with an Asos T-shirt line, all proceeds of which going to refugees.

Oprah Winfrey

Where to start? Queen of the talk show. Richest self-made woman in America. Ranked as most influential woman in the world. Against all odds, and in a field dominated by white males, she became the most beloved television-host of all time, and a media mogul. She has used her leverage for good ever since. Her show had huge impact, even though it was criticised for promoting consumption too, and put many topics on the map, such as self-help, diversity and reading. It's also credited with making the LGBTQ community more visible and mainstream. In the episode of *Ellen* in which Ellen DeGeneres comes out, Oprah plays the therapist she tells she's a lesbian (Oprah is a respected actress – in the film *Beloved*, she portrayed the protagonist, a former slave, and she was Oscar nominated for her role in *The Color Purple*). Her wealth increasing, she became a significant philanthropist, and started Oprah's Angel Network, giving generously to charities worldwide (like the big student demonstration for gun control in the US). She's a Democrat, and fervently supported Barack Obama's run for office. Her acceptance speech at the 2018 Golden Globes ceremony focused on women's rights and the Time's Up/#MeToo movement, and was widely seen as one of presidential calibre…

Stella McCartney

Stella McCartney brought environmentally-aware high fashion to the catwalks. Thanks to her it's now accepted and even cool to make luxurious, more sustainable accessories and clothes. The daughter of Paul McCartney is a vegetarian and animal-rights activist, and reportedly refused to use leather and fur when she worked for Chloe and Gucci. Gucci subsequently supported her in setting up her own label, the first to include bags and shoes made of fake leather. In the luxury-fashion industry, these materials are extremely important, and until recently it was not-done to use fake. That McCartney nevertheless stood up for her ideals and proclaims them too, is therefore pretty courageous and unique. It helps that she's got influential friends like Madonna, Kate Moss and Gwyneth Paltrow – hopefully her beliefs will rub off on the entire A-list. She calls herself a vegetarian brand that wants to be ethical and modern. She launched a sunglasses range made of bioplastic and a sustainable skincare brand, and uses wind energy and occasionally organic cotton. Her clothes are not perfect, she admits, with quite a few non-sustainable materials. But when animal-friendly high fashion finally becomes normal, it'll be largely because of her.

Leonardo DiCaprio

The committed actor and director makes films and series about environmental issues (*The 11th Hour, Before the Flood*) and blood diamonds, and treats us to one impressive speech after another about our endangered ecosystem. He founded the Leonardo DiCaprio Foundation to further environmental awareness and is a UN representative for climate change. He's on the board of NGOs and has been recognised by many organisations for his promotion of the movement. In 2016 he addressed world leaders prior to the signing of the Climate Agreement in Paris. In that year he won an Oscar for *The Revenant* and used his acceptance speech to highlight environmental challenges. He regularly donates money to charities, for example organisations that improve the image of LGBTQ people in the media.

Vivienne Westwood

Designer Vivienne Westwood grabs the clothing industry by the throat, and us too. According to her, we all wear disposable junk. We all look the same and have never dressed so badly. We should revolt and buy something better. 'Buy less, choose well and make it last', is her famous statement. Fashion exists to make you look amazing, but in her view, such clothes are now hardly available – it's all synthetic, cheap and boring. We should want to look extraordinary and special, but nobody dares anything anymore. It doesn't have to be expensive, as long as it's high quality, suits you and nothing or nobody has suffered for it.

Mark Ruffalo

Calls himself 'husband, father, actor, director, and a climate-change advocate with an eye on a better, brighter, cleaner, more hopeful future for all of us.' The actor is co-founder of The Solution Project, that wants to accelerate the transition to 100% renewable energy. Besides this, he actively promotes different movements, such as pro-choice or the Standing Rock Indian Reservation, that was threatened by the construction of an oil pipeline. He's extremely engaged (and admired) on social media and was one of the first to take a stand in the #MeToo discussion. Ruffalo supported Bernie Sanders and Jeremy Corbyn as political candidates and tweets almost daily about social and environmental issues (from refugees or free birth-control to internet freedom or palm oil).

Emma Watson

I think Emma Watson is amazing. Secretly, I want to be her. Besides being unforgettable as Hermione in the *Harry Potter* films of course, she's an activist for fair trade and women's rights. In 2010 she designed her own line with People Tree, raising lots of attention for ethical fashion. She also works with Livia Firth, Net-a-Porter and Zady to make sustainability in the fashion industry cool. During the press tour for *Beauty and the Beast* she only wore sustainable fashion and make-up brands and opened a special Instagram account to advertise this. Emma's also Women Goodwill Ambassador for the United Nations, and campaigns for gender equality. She's figurehead for the HeForShe campaign, in which she invites men to also be a feminist. Her work has given feminism a major boost.

Worldwide, women earn 43% less than men, and this gap is widening. Around a third of all companies have no women in senior management at all, and women occupy only 22% of seats in national parliaments.

THEKLA REUTEN

Thekla Reuten (1975) is one of the Netherlands' most acclaimed actresses. She's starred in films and television programmes including *Red Sparrow*, *The American* and *Stan Lee's Lucky Man* and is ambassador for children's rights NGO Terre des Hommes. She's been nominated for an *ELLE* Style Award, and aims to support making sustainable fashion and lifestyle mainstream.

Why do you use your fame for a better planet?
'Because I want to contribute to the change I'd like to see in the world. My portrait is part of a Terre des Hommes campaign against child labour, and it's the first time I've put my face where my mouth is. It's quite scary, but also a natural step. I'm very reserved in the media and avoided social media for a long time. It can be so crude, whilst I always look for purity – also in my roles. I make very conscious choices, and really want to stand behind them. It can sometimes prove difficult to take the right steps. I'm glad you convey it doesn't have to be perfect, because that can really get in your way. You can earn lots of money for a regular shampoo advert, but I can't do it any longer. I only want to support brands that ring true or are consciously working to change direction.'

What brands and initiatives do you support?
'Esse Probiotic Skincare, because the effects are scientifically supported and go deeper than the surface. And Stella McCartney, because she's the only one doing it at high-fashion level. Although I do sometimes question with her why it must be so expensive. But that also goes for leather bags. Guys, don't splurge 4,000 euros on a Chanel handbag, do something else with that money. Terre des Hommes is committed to tackling child exploitation in all areas, from child trafficking, prostitution, webcam sex, household slavery, everything. On my birth announcement, it said: "Thekla has enough clothes and toys, if you want to give something anyway, then please donate to Terre des Hommes." When they asked me, it felt right immediately. I realised how much I admired what my parents had done.'

What else do you do in your life to make a difference? And what don't you do?
'Particularly in the world I work in, you can get carried away by all the gorgeous clothes and bags you're offered, fake hair, beauty clinics – everything. I want to look good too of course, and I understand that turning such things down isn't easy. But for me, change in the world matters far more than a free bag or coat. I think it's important people realise that all those beautiful magazines are sponsored by the brands they feature. That we're being directed by the brands with the most budget. If a label wants to give me something, I'll always ask questions about sustainability. Fortunately, there are now plenty of ethical brands you can feel just as happy with. I also try to do as much as possible at home. We have solar panels on our new house, I compensate for long flights. Sometimes I don't do things right either. I'll all of a sudden toss glass in the bin and think: why?'

Who's your style icon?
'Charlotte Rampling is so avant-garde cool. And Katharine Hepburn was literally wearing the trousers, of course. So feisty.'

Do you have a life motto?
'There's a crack in everything, that's how the light comes in. I'm quite a perfectionist, but the moment you let go, things nearly always improve. This is from a beautiful song by Leonard Cohen.'

What are your best sustainable tips?
'Watch the film *Tomorrow* (Demain), because it's so positive and gets you in the right mood. Check out those amazing sustainable brands, try everything on and explore, for sure there'll a few that could be your new go-to labels. And we don't have to keep looking like we did when we were twenty. Wrinkles are chic and part of life, they're there

because you laugh so often throughout the day. Try not to keep yourself young artificially. Compare it with nature, seasons have a reason. They're all gorgeous. The unbelievable beauty of glorious summer or vibrant autumn is wonderful, right? Billboards and magazines practically push you into shops. Sustainable fashion and lifestyle needs to be just as visible, but then via another way.'

GOOD GUYS / BEN PIER

Women in the Netherlands have about the same amount of free time as men – on average about 40 hours a week that don't have to be used for work, care, eating or sleeping. But whether or not they have children, they experience that free time as much less relaxing than men. They continue to check whether everyone's okay, feel responsible for chores and continually 'on call', and therefore suffer more regularly from agitation and stress.

(Girls Just Want to Have) Equal Rights

I am a feminist. Women are equal to men, everyone should earn the same amount for the same work and have just as much access to top functions. Inequality is one of the causes of social and economic injustices and stands in the way of sustainable development. The #MeToo movement is one of the most important of recent times. If women, or people from the LGBTQ community, or of colour or a non-dominant religion, are oppressed, treated inferiorly or disadvantaged, they can't

contribute to society. This is at the expense of our development – not to mention the fact that it's of course immoral and unfair. I wish we didn't have to talk about this anymore, because let's face it, it's of course nonsense that your gender, orientation or colour should determine what you can and do. I just can't believe that homosexuals are still being verbally abused or beaten up. I'm deeply ashamed about this. So frustrating, I can't wait for this to be behind us. I'll do what I can to contribute to that. Fortunately, the subject is on the agenda, more and more men are daring to call themselves a feminist (and to act accordingly) and worldwide the equal-rights movement is growing.

> The speech Emma Watson gave at the launch of the HeForShe campaign is amazing. As is the TEDtalk 'We should all be feminists' by Chimamanda Ngozi Adichie and the work of Naomi Wolf (her book *The Beauty Myth* is a must). And brilliant author (*How to Be a Woman*) and comedian Caitlin Moran, who put her three rules for feminism on a tea towel (you can buy it!):

———

01 / Women are equal to men
02 / Don't be a dick
03 / That's all

———

> Stop Street Harassment is an American NGO, that identifies and aims to end gender-based street harassment worldwide. On their website you'll find lots of information, a telephone hotline and calls to action. The Everyday Sexism Project collects global examples of sexism as experienced on a day to day basis. International group Hollaback! wants to tackle discrimination and aggression against women and LGBTQ'ers, both in real life and online. Everyday Feminism is a platform for personal liberation, that aims to help people escape oppression, daily violence, discrimination and marginalisation (covering topics such as class, privilege and body).

> The movement Gurls Talk was founded by model Adwoa Aboah to empower girls and provide a safe place to share experiences – offering interviews with experts, special videos and cool motivation.

> In 2016, for the first time more Dutch women competed at the Olympic Games than men. Women also won more medals. The fact that girls do better at school has been known for a long time and that more women go to university than men – all the more reason then why it's wrong that less women are in high positions. Fortunately, Angela Merkel is the most important politician in Europe and Christina Lagarde leads the IMP, but still...

> Male emancipation is of course just as important. The sharing of care, right to parental leave, protection against (sexual) violence or the fight against prejudices regarding masculinity and emotions: it all has just as much to do with gender equality. MenEngage is a coalition of men campaigning for female empowerment, which also creates a better world for themselves. They question role patterns and work to support social justice.

> It's often more expensive to be a woman than a man. In New York, research was done on 800 products – from razor blades to shirts. 42% of the items aimed at women cost more than the equivalent for men. Added up, this can make thousands of euros difference to a woman's life. Shampoo was the worst: on average, 48% more for women than men. According to experts this is because women are more likely to be expected to look good. So they 'have to' buy the products. Luckily women aren't helpless, and we can opt for the cheaper men's razors or bottles. But such 'gender pricing' is just crazy.

Diversity and White Privilege

More and more coloured models grace the covers of magazines and feature in advertisements and campaigns. Finally. The groundbreaking Black Lives Matter movement is having a huge impact. But I'm in no way saying that we are where we need to be (we're nowhere near), and I'm of course not the right person to assess this anyway – I don't personally experience it. At the same time, that doesn't mean I can't say, think or do something about it. I can of course find racism unforgivable, explore where I should change and support my fellow humans in this struggle. But I was born white, and therefore benefit from white privilege in this society. I'm becoming increasingly aware of this, and there's plenty of food for thought. Researcher Peggy McIntosh wrote a groundbreaking essay about it in the late eighties. She lists fifty examples of her privilege: in the media she primarily sees people representing her own race, she doesn't have to teach her children to be aware of systematic racism for self-protection, she can easily buy plasters or powder that matches her skin tone, if she does something that annoys people – like arriving late or smelling – it's not reflected on her race etc. Important thought leaders like Gloria Wekker and Robin DiAngelo speak out on these issues; I'm honoured that presenter and journalist Nicole Terborg wants to talk about her perspective in my book.

NICOLE TERBORG

Nicole Terborg (1976) is a Dutch journalist, television and radio presenter and moderator.

How do diversity and sustainability belong together for you?

'Without diversity there's no future and therefore no sustainability. This applies in all areas: from an ecosystem or society to editorial staff and companies.'

How do you see diversity in the media?

'In media land, my territory for a while now, it strikes me how little diversity there is. There's too little colour, both in front of and behind the camera. There's no proportional representation at all. The Netherlands I see on the street, I don't see reflected onscreen. Which saddens me, because we live in a visual culture. In our complex social society, people derive ideas, norms, values and meanings from that visual culture. But what we now get served up, through adverts, billboards, television, textbooks and internet is disastrous for how we form opinions. Too often, we remain in our own, familiar circle. We only know "the other" from images and stories. If these are one-sided, stereotyped or non-representative, people get a distorted picture. There's a lot of misunderstanding, but in particular, ignorance. As children's book author Mylo Freeman says so well, we need both mirrors and windows. Many children of colour only see the world through windows, while they need mirrors. Other children only see mirrors and need to learn to see the world through windows. Something's immediately very obvious in journalism. Editorial staff in the Netherlands are very homogenous. They're often well-educated, white people from the big cities. But the more diverse the group of programme makers, the more diverse the content. Now you open the news-

paper in the morning and instantly know what topics you'll see in the talk shows that evening. The same guests, spokespersons and perspectives everywhere.'

What needs to change – and what are you doing?

'More employee diversity in television and radio, the shows and content. I often make programmes in which I show or give voice to the other side or the other story. For example, by reporting about black feminism in the Netherlands or the story of three bicultural bloggers who now have a successful fashion label.'

ROB KLUITENBERG

How can we change the predominant story?

'As consumer of news you can demand that other story or information. Fortunately, this is already happening. Traditional journalism must change direction if it wants to survive, because more and more people are getting their information from other sources. Of course, there's also a lot of junk on internet, but the medium does provide more space for that other story. And it's good that makers are no longer solely dependent on broadcasters to share their series or programme.'

Do you feel that everyone can live and speak in freedom in current society?

'No, unfortunately. In the Netherlands there seem to be first and second-class citizens. Those able to say what they want and those that will always remain a "guest" even though they've got Dutch nationality. It's down to the lack of collective memory. The colonial past has left its traces, and influences current power structures and ways of thinking. But many are unaware of this. During history lessons at school we learn for example very little about mass executions in the former Dutch India, or our role in the slave trade. It's unfortunate that we as a country don't look in the mirror and recognise we're not so progressive and tolerant. Ethnicity plays a role in different domains in society, such as my nephew with the highest grades who doesn't belong at a top-tier secondary school according to the teacher. Unfortunately, we live in a society where there's institutional and individual racism. Authoritative institutions such as the Council of Europe confirm this. The racist torrents of abuse on social media make it visible. Certain groups have privileges, Dutch children don't all have the same starting position. Let's start with talking and acknowledging, only then something can change. I'm now focusing on ethnicity, but the fight for equal rights is also about gender, sexual preferences etc.'

How could readers and I help to increase that freedom?

'By looking in your own life at where you can fight for equal rights. By becoming aware of who has certain privileges and who does not. By opening your mouth when you see that someone is being wronged. By being an example for others.'

Nicole recommends:

Black Heritage Tours

'Do the Black Heritage Tours by the American-Dutch Jennifer Tosh, which show the hidden story of Amsterdam, New York or Brussels.'

Dutch New York Histories: Connecting African, Native American and Slavery Heritage

'This eye-opening guide focuses on traces of the Dutch presence in New York city and state.'

Racism without Racists: Color-Blind Racism and the Persistence of Racial Inequality in America

'Eduardo Bonilla-Silva wrote a great book about colour-blind racism, for anyone who wants to know more about the current state of racism and racial structures.'

White Fragility: Why It's So Hard for White People to Talk About Racism

'Author Robin DiAngelo first coined the term "white fragility" in 2011: the defensive moves white people make when challenged racially.'

White Innocence

'Professor Gloria Wekker explores a central paradox of Dutch culture: the passionate denial of racial discrimination and colonial violence coexisting alongside aggressive racism and xenophobia.'

Colour Code

'This Canadian podcast shares honest and real conversations about race issues and racism, and how subtle it can be (for instance in Canada, which prides itself on their multicultural society and progressive prime-minister).'

Get Out

'This film is a comedy/horror story about what it means to be black. The villains aren't neo-Nazi's, but middle-class white liberals.'

Doll/Eyes tests

'Search online for "the original doll test" or "modern doll test" to see racial prejudice in action or explore Jane Elliott's Blue Eyes/Brown Eyes exercise.'

Europe has 468 billionaires, America 576, Australia 60 / 1% of the world population has more than the other 99% / 836 million people worldwide are extremely poor / 795 million people suffer from chronic hunger / 1.2 billion people have no access to electricity

For Richer or Poorer

The rich are getting richer, the poor are getting poorer. Inequality figures are shocking, and a consequence of unfair distribution and selfishness. If we don't want to share, we don't have a sustainable future. I was born in a wealthy part of the world by coincidence, with a good economic situation, an advantageous climate, human and women's rights. I didn't do anything for it, I simply had it handed to me. And so I don't have any more right to it than anybody else. Borders are arbitrary, just like gender constructions. That you flee a country you're not safe in, where there's war, where you're harassed, stalked or oppressed or where you don't have enough to live on, I can definitely imagine. And yet at the same time I can't, because I've the good fortune to have no idea what that's actually like. But we can't just act as if we have the right to benefit from everything more than someone else.

» If people have too little to get by, they'll not easily get around to improving their circumstances or protecting nature. You probably feel you have more (head)space for this, when you have enough to eat, a safe home, can send your children to school and live in dignity. And yet so many heroes do it.

» We can help by making different choices. If for example we're prepared to pay more for things with a good and credible story, and not always choose the easiest path. We vote with our wallets for what we want the world to look like and how our fellow human beings can live. We feel rich if we can afford lots of cheap clothes, when actually they're only making us poorer...

» Government and businesses have just as big a role. Companies should pay taxes in the countries where they produce, not dodge them. Big brands often do everything they can to pay as little as possible and register themselves in countries where tax levies are low, or rules are advantageous (such as the Netherlands). As a result, developing countries, where many of their products are made, are missing out on billions. And that's what's keeping them in poverty too. Unacceptable that it's allowed. As is the possibility to make products elsewhere in a way that would be completely unacceptable in your own environment. Why is it actually tolerated to exploit people and planet to make a profit?

» Companies like Starbucks, Google and Apple use all kinds of constructions to avoid paying taxes. Apple was ordered to pay back 13 billion euros to tax-haven Ireland. The Netherlands is

'A culture change is needed, in which pollution is not-done and sustainable is cool. Then the crowd's shifting. And this is already happening, I think, but sometimes the focus isn't on the right things. If for example you worry all year about packaging, but fly to Barcelona for a few days, then you've cancelled out all your efforts. What's needed apart from knowledge, is a bigger sense of urgency, for example by linking news items more clearly to the environment. Refugee flows, for instance, are often partly due to climate problems, but the media doesn't often make that connection. People also need the possibility to do it better. Offer people fun solutions and they'll happily adopt them. That's also why I think this guide is great.'

Babette Porcelijn, Dutch impact researcher

also known as desirable letterbox country, where companies only have to have an address (and letterbox) to fall under our flexible rules, without actually being established here. Tax Justice Network is an independent network tackling the harmful effects of tax evasion, competition and havens. They aim to trigger reform, especially in poorer countries.

» Client Earth describes itself as 'activist lawyers committed to securing a healthy planet.' They litigate in the areas of clean air, oceans, health, energy, wildlife, etc., and use the law to find practical solutions to essential environmental challenges.

» There's a lot of tax on labour, meaning that companies want to hire as few people as possible. At the same time, resources are taxed less, making them too easy to use. The Ex'tax tries to reverse this. Higher tax encourages smart use of materials, and when labour becomes cheaper, more people can find a job and there's more room for craftsmanship and creativity.

Compensate Great

We can compensate for the emissions we cause. CO_2 production decreases for instance by investing in renewable energy projects (you often see tree-planting programmes, but trees can be logged or burnt, so rather choose something else). It's certainly not a pardon: limiting your emissions has a much greater effect than offsetting them.

That compensating is available is great, but there are some catches. So this is good to know:

» You use energy both directly (by flying for example, or heating your house) and indirectly. It's in everything you use, so your food, clothes, telephone and so on. In terms of the household, indirect emissions are twice the size of direct ones. So keep that in mind if you're going to compensate (which you can of course do for your office or company too).

» Usually only the CO_2 emissions are calculated, but indirectly you also cause other greenhouse gases. Cows for example emit methane gas, so if you eat meat or dairy, this should ideally also be included. Instead of being CO_2 neutral, you're then going for climate neutral. For this you can compensate three or four times what a CO_2 calculator indicates.

» Make sure you calculate and compensate via a reliable organisation that takes environmental, social and local impact into account, and works with the community where the project is carried out. Go for organisations that invest in real, additional reductions (that without the project wouldn't have happened), in permanent projects (energy efficiency or replacing fossil-fuel based energy with wind, or solar) and are independently verified. The Gold Standard was set up by a group of international NGOs such as the World Wildlife Fund and Germanwatch, to ensure that climate-compensation money is well spent.

Colin Beavan became famous as 'No Impact Man'. He tried to live in New York for a year without impacting the environment, by for instance causing little waste, not eating meat and doing good deeds. This was so inspiring to him, that he wanted to share his experiences. An enormously successful book and ditto documentary followed, and a worldwide No Impact Week.

BUFFI DUBERMAN

Buffi Duberman (1968) was born in Brooklyn, but now lives in the Netherlands. She's a writer and English language coach, including at *The Voice* and for singers and actors, and works a lot with refugees.

NOL HAVENS

You use many positive thinking methods in your work – why?

'For me, believing is seeing. I live in gratitude, and that really shapes who I am and how I see the world. If you realise how fortunate you are that you can do what you do, live where you live, love who you love and so on, it's so hard to complain. So I don't. I'm my own best friend and I teach others to really enjoy themselves and love their own company. If you take good care of yourself, you can look after others better. If you love the skin you're in then people tend to gravitate towards you as you radiate joy. Believing in yourself is a magnet for making good things happen in your life. I see the results every day.'

What can we do now to feel better about ourselves?

'Be your own best friend. Look in the mirror and love what you see. Your body has worked so hard to drag you around for so many years – when was the last time you thanked it? Be kind to yourself. If you're not happy with your body, do something about it and stop complaining, or become happy with it. Grab a mirror and wink at yourself. I do this every day. I love the woman looking back at me, I'm so happy to see her every time. This includes the wrinkles. I feel 27 inside and am sometimes shocked by the wrinkles. But I'm so happy to have lived long enough to get them! Now I'm getting older, I put more in my "fuck it-bucket": I'm learning about what truly matters and focus on that. And the next step is to do something for someone else right now. Helping someone takes you out of your bubble and creates gratitude. Why wait?'

How did you get involved with refugees?

'A centre opened near my house, I drove there and offered my help. I began collecting clothes, and then moved on to language lessons. Now I'm helping friends get settled in their new homes and organising their administration etc. It's a pleasure to do. If we change the word "refugee" to "war victim", perhaps people would realise nobody wants to go through what these people have gone through. Take some time and talk to them. You'll learn a lot – I promise.'

Do you have a hero?

'My grandmother, who as single parent got her family out of debt by becoming a bookkeeper, and still danced all night to Sinatra. Jane Goodall, I met her once and burst into tears. David Lynch, for writing a book about meditation that changed me and got me started. Barbra Streisand for not getting the nose job. Amy Poehler, Lena Dunham, Caitlin Moran, Tina Fey – all for being smart and funny and never fitting in. And so many more!'

Buffi's top tips

'My grandmother used to make me kiss food before I threw it away. Think – can I freeze it? Make it into an omelette tomorrow? Throw it into soup? Fling all your clothes onto your bed and get overwhelmed by how many things you have. You don't need it all, and you can make someone else so happy with what you haven't worn for over a year.'

With a Little Help from My Friends

We can't do without each other. No sustainable society without friends and looking after each other. Ultimately, it's not about having, but about being and sharing. What we experience together really matters, and makes life much brighter than any amount of sunglasses we could buy. I try to treat my friendships sustainably, to be loyal, thoughtful and involved. Not always easy in this era of distraction and temptation, and something that can slam the door in your face. That's okay, just carry on. Love is everything. Do something for your fellow human beings, whether you know him or her (well), or not. Minimum effort, maximum pleasure. Surprise your husband, parents, friends, neighbour, acquaintance, fellow passenger, the homeless person on the street. Tell your partner you love him or her – do it now! Tell it to yourself as well – yes, also now!

– Giving to others proves to be a great factor for happiness, time and time again. Give, give, give: things, money, love, care, pleasure, send a card, donate, whatever works for you. We have so, so much.

— Many studies show how important friends are. They come in all shapes and sizes, from the good neighbour you can call on in time of need, to the best friend that's your soul mate, a group of pals or even your family. There's something for everyone, but take good care of them. They're difficult to get, but easy to lose. Forgive, say sorry, do send that message if it's actually been too long. Really, life will be better for it.

— Lots of people have fled their country. Leaving everything behind is without doubt excruciatingly difficult, as is building a life in a new place – after having been through all kinds of things. Maybe there's a way you can support them? By volunteering at a shelter or donating things or money? Look for opportunities close to home, or at organisations like Help Refugees, The International Rescue Committee, the UNHCR, the Red Cross or The White Helmets. Refugees Welcome links refugees looking for a home to people who want to share their house; it's in many countries, including Australia, Canada, Germany and Sweden.

— Loneliness is more common than you might think. Since I've been self-employed, I experience it now and again, while I'm probably not part of a group considered vulnerable. It's still quite taboo to talk about or ask help for. Try to keep an eye out for isolation if you can, don't lose sight of people, invite them around. Life's becoming increasingly self-absorbed. Fortunately, more and more's happening, check out the Campaign to End Loneliness or the Australian Coalition to End Loneliness, a local initiative or international community Sunday Assembly, which organises inspiring meetings to connect people (like a church without the religion).

— The Street Store in South Africa gives clothes to the homeless, but also the dignity of a shopping experience, where they can choose what they want themselves. In the cardboard pop-up stores, people that need them can 'buy' free clothes, complete with staff providing advice. The concept is open source, and there are now Street Stores in Canada, the US, Norway and Argentina among other places. On their website, they show you how to make it happen.

— In New York, homeless women, school kids and prisoners receive free tampons or sanitary towels. The council has unanimously recognised that this is just as necessary as toilet paper. In the UK a similar campaign is running under the name #TheHomelessPeriod.

What happens once you're no longer here? However consciously we live, we're all going to die at some point. Maybe not pleasant, but definitely smart to dwell on sometimes. To subsequently enjoy the here and now more or think about how you'd like things to be. Perhaps a sustainable burial is also part of that? The wood of a normal coffin is often treated with chemicals, that end up in the earth – together with the metals and fabric. Nowadays, there are more and more natural cemeteries, for example in woods or on heathland, where they use biodegradable shrouds and wicker baskets or cardboard coffins. A tree trunk or rock marks your resting place, or an environmentally-friendly urn that decomposes and eventually mixes with the earth. You can also consider local flowers, electric transport, sustainable paper for the cards and compensating the emissions. With a natural burial, the circle of life is complete.

Always be... A little kinder than necessary

'All the stuff that comes from distant countries with a foul-smelling boat really bothers me. The seventeen largest ships in the world emit just as many pollutants as all cars combined, according to the documentary *Sea Blind*. And start-ups from Silicon Valley – parasitic websites that contribute nothing at all themselves and with lots of venture capital enforce a monopoly position by buying new initiatives. Often they start under the title of sharing economy, but the opposite is true. Social media's not social, but a tacky advertising platform. Google focuses primarily on collecting information, and then bombarding you with ads for useless products. Airbnb, which started off great, is now more valuable on paper than General Motors, with campaigns to above all get you out of your house on weekends. It's the new cash cow for the greedy landlord: twenty Airbnb guests per month is better than one student. This has nothing to do whatsoever with the sharing economy. There are alternatives, such as the Camarilla app instead of Facebook. It's the smallest social network, you can be friends with up to fifteen people. Less exhibitionistic, but be honest: fifteen good friends are plenty, right?'

Guido A. Keff, one of my Dutch publishers

Power to Change

We are so much more than consumers. It's a role we're often forced into – every time we see, hear or are unconsciously influenced by an advert. But we are people, citizens, human beings of flesh and blood. And our choices have real, profound impact on others and the world. We're not only here to achieve, to score, to succeed. This too is a very limited interpretation of being human, that can hold us back.

» More and more people have had enough of all the buying. The restlessness, the greed and the regret of your latest purchase(s). So why do we keep doing it? Probably because we're programmed to gather, to grab everything we see in case it's no longer there later. Journalist Asha ten Broeke did an experiment: she bought nothing for six months, to break the cycle. She noticed that she did lots of (online) shopping out of habit, and that at the start she kept longing for things. What she didn't buy, but did want, she put on a wish list. Only when she really committed to the project for a longer time she improved, put less and less on the list, and was able to resist the calls of her primal

brain. The (now closed) Free Fashion Challenge, in which you bought no new clothes for a year, addressed this – online you'll find other interesting projects, for shorter and longer periods, individuals or groups, focussing for instance on decluttering or the need to fill inner emptiness.
» A longer period probably indeed works better, because behavioural change needs time to become engrained. We're steered by automatisms and often prefer short-term above long-term reward. In addition, specific goals are better than abstract ones, so rather 'eat less meat' than 'improve the environment'. You'll have to stick at practicing desired behaviour, in my case showering shorter, for a while should you want to turn it into a new habit. Difficult, but possible. We're sensitive to rewards and compliments, and peer pressure also works well: if we see others doing something we know we should be doing, we also change faster.
» The School of Life teaches you all kinds of things about friendship, creativity, having conversations, a calm mind, arguing or making choices. There are also of course lots of blogs with interesting information related to self-help and development, such as mindbodygreen, Tim Ferriss, Becoming Minimalist and Gretchen Rubin.

'In fashion everybody wants to get rich and famous and it's easy to get rich and famous by being a bad person. But the challenge is to achieve your goals – whatever they are – while staying a decent human being.' Katharine Hamnett to Ecouterre

Know More? Do More?

The sky's the limit! There's so much more than what's in this book. You can look up, follow, read, watch, pursue, like and learn all kinds of things. Lots of sites, films, books and organisations in the guide, and here a few pointers.

Ask for it

Ask for ethical products when shopping. Talk to staff about where and how their products are made. They may not know the answer, but if they get such questions often enough, they'll have to start asking their boss for some answers. And this is how the ball starts rolling…You can do it on your own, but also with a group of friends. Try taking turns visiting a shop for a week and inquiring how sustainable their products are – everyone would only have to do it once for them to be asked every day. Make it known that you'd buy more if you were certain that the brand or store is sustainable. It really does help. This by the way also applies to services you can't avoid, such as hospitals, insurers or pension funds. Huge changes still need to happen here. Imagine how much water and energy a hospital uses, or how much waste it creates. Steps are certainly being taken to make the care sector better, but what if you could select where you are treated or insured in the future, based on that criterium? The client is king, the more people that let them know it's important (and would base their choices on it), the better.

E-mail or send a letter

Why not send your favourite brand's customer service, director or CSR person an e-mail to let them know what you want? Find their addresses on the website or fill in the response form; a paper letter's of course great too.

Use social media

Ask your question on Facebook, Twitter or Instagram, then it's public and everyone can see what answer they (don't) provide. This steps up the pressure even more. News spreads rapidly on social media. Share the brands and stores that you do support too – they can really use it.   ⟶

ECO WARRIOR PRINCESS

GOOD QUESTIONS

To ask a shop or brand: Are they sure this product is made ethically? How many hours did the people have to work for it? Did they receive a wage they could live from? Can they choose to join a union? In what factory/factories is it produced? Are their materials (certified) sustainable, how do they ensure as little energy consumption, waste and CO_2 emissions as possible? Do they use recycled resources? Do they take their products back for reuse? Do they have a code of conduct and who independently verifies their compliance? Why isn't this kind of information available on their website, actually? The power of individuals as consumers can truly transform the world. We have made it what it is, so we can also change it. Who else?

Get informed (and be smart)

Search online, read books (borrowing them from friends or the library is very sustainable), compare reviews, look around, keep your eyes and ears open, talk to friends (multiplying your impact if you inspire them to take steps too), watch documentaries, keep questioning. There's so much to know and learn. But be aware of these things:

» Companies are desperate to make you believe they're green and ethical – particularly now there's increasing demand. Don't be played for a fool. Explore if there's evidence for the claim, if the certification is independent or not, if statements are vague or specific, or whether the claim even matters or is meaningful. Some things are simply required legally, and salt for instance is *always* natural. Those kinds of things. In chapter 1 (p. 027) you'll find more about greenwash busting.

» Websites like Google, Facebook and AOL follow you online. Via trackers on other sites (like for example Huffington Post) they see what you visit and look at. Your interests and 'likes' are collected and very valuable, and can be used to influence you. For instance to show you products you may want to buy, or politically-preferable information to steer your vote. Find out how you can protect yourself digitally –

the American Electronic Frontier Foundation gives tips and tools, or you can check out the book *Fake It! Your Guide to Digital Self-Defense*.

Become a volunteer

Organisations often have too little budget to do what they'd actually want to or are capable of. Volunteers are hugely important. Also great for you too – you learn lots and meet new people. I definitely did at Amnesty International, the Amsterdam Medical Centre and radio station AmsterdamFM, for example. It can, but doesn't have to cost a lot of time. You can also use your skills for a specific project. Are you for instance a good writer, designer, translator, film maker or do you know all there is to know about the law or bookkeeping? This can all be incredibly useful to an organisation. Just shoot them a message.

Do something small

Put your signature on a petition to improve the world, via Change or Avaaz for example. Sign up for SMS or emergency activities with Amnesty International and support them with a single click. Register for newsletters from NGOs you find important and let your (digital) voice be heard.

And, perhaps every now and then some of this:

Laugh
A smile spreads joy and happiness and can really make someone feel a lot better. Smile at passers-by, during conversations, at people in the train. The simplest bringer of happiness (also for your-self – try giving it a go… see!).

Help
Hold a door open, carry shopping upstairs, pick up what fell, help someone cross the road, turn off a bike light, and, if you've got a bit of time, offer to help that guy with the flat tire (even if you're completely hopeless at it and it's only to share the pain).

Listen
The world goes so fast, we're all busy, everything has to happen now. But sometimes, someone just needs to be heard. To get some attention. It seems so simple, but turns out to be quite difficult. Take the time, ask questions and don't jump in with your own opinion or something similar you've experienced. It can make a huge difference if someone has the opportunity to tell their story.

Be kind
Say thank you (or sorry) now and again. Be kind to everyone – why not? Give more than is expected, and be just a little bit nicer than you actually have to be. Treat others the way you'd like to be treated yourself. I may sound like your mum, but this stuff works! Shortcut to a better world.

Be thoughtful
Give compliments as much as you can. About a good deed, an impressive grade (and a C+ is one too!), a pretty top, a tasty meal, if someone smells nice. And try to really accept them too – oddly enough, quite difficult sometimes. A 'Thank you' along with a beaming smile is fab. Remember names; demonstrates you really see someone. Send a card for a birthday, bring a gift now and again, express what you feel (love, gratitude, pride).

Pay it forward
In the queue to pay for your coffee having just had a lucky break, or feeling like doing something fun? Pay for the person behind you. It'll be a massive surprise and gift for him or her, while it costs so little.

GREEN KIDS by Laura de Jong

Capturing Memories
I love investing in this. Every year we have a photo of our family taken. Choose a photographer that also captures your daily routines. These accounts will gain value as time goes by.

Choosing a School or Creche
How much time a week does your child spend there? Wouldn't it then be great if they also learn about nature and sustainability, and regularly play and exercise outdoors? Why not ask about this when visiting prospective places.

Gender-Neutral Parenting
To achieve more equality between boys and girls, men and women, it's important not to raise children with stereotypes. By saying things to your son like: 'Be a man, don't cry' and 'Pink is for girls, isn't it?', you force him into a traditional, unequal role. The same goes for girls who always have to be sweet and pretty. Pink dressing-up clothes for girls and blue cars for boys? Let your child choose! Give your son a toy kitchen to play with and your daughter a garage. Also pay attention to the kinds of toys you offer them. Rather a realistic doll than a super-skinny Barbie.

GUIDE

WEBSITES AND BLOGS

There are lots and lots of interesting sites and blogs about sustainable living, and the number's growing. Here a selection.

Avaaz / Change
Websites that through petitions and uniting communities try to change the world.
avaaz.org / change.org

Becoming Minimalist
Minimalism-expert Joshua Becker gives tips about decluttering your life and consuming less – on this blog and in books like *The More of Less* and *Simplify*.
becomingminimalist.com / simplifymagazine.com

Bloomers
Cosmopolitan blog with fair fashion (also for men), ethical lifestyle, zero waste, travel and brand tips – in English and French.
bloomers.eco – see also p. 252

EcoCult
Extensive and inspiring blog by journalist Alden Wicker, with detailed tips for sustainable fashion, beauty, travel and living (in New York and beyond), and practical information about brands, events and destinations.
ecocult.com

Eco Warrior Princess
Thought-provoking blog, YouTube channel and directory for sustainable living, by activist Jennifer Nini. After having lived the city life in Melbourne, she became co-owner of an off-grid eco farm. Shares solid and useful intelligence about conscious fashion, business, beauty, feminism, politics and technology – and because an ethical media company must be transparent, shows what she earns and from what.
ecowarriorprincess.net

EcoWatch
Environmental news-site (American, but mostly international/universal information), about climate, energy, science etc., including a special Trump Watch section.
ecowatch.com

Ethical Consumer
British, independent not-for-profit, that aims to make it easier for everyone to make ethical choices. Information about topics such as household, clothing, food, travel, energy etc.: product guides, company profiles, shopping tips and a magazine. Some information is free to access, some member-only.
ethicalconsumer.org

EWG
Website (and app) with information about more than 100,000 brands, their ingredients and impact. Also have their own certification, and lots of consumer guides (water, sunscreen etc.).
ewg.org

Gittemary
Danish zero-waste blog and YouTube channel with tips and tricks on reducing waste in food, beauty, living and more (even weddings).
gittemary.com

Good Guide
Rates and reviews (on the website and app) for over 75,000 household, personal care, food and kids' products and brands.
goodguide.com

Inhabitat
International blog about technological and material innovations, to make architecture and design smarter and more sustainable.
inhabitat.com

mindbodygreen
Extensive wellness blog for a better life, with information, videos and courses about mindfulness, food, exercise, relationships and the planet.
mindbodygreen.com

New Internationalist
International, independent and cooperatively-owned media organisation for 'socially conscious' journalism and publishing. Blog, magazine, books, and webshop for ethical living.
newint.org / ethicalshop.org

Rank a Brand
Compares brands (from magazines to supermarkets, from clothing to electronics) on transparency and policy, through for instance questionnaires and what they disclose on their website.
rankabrand.org

The Good Trade
Well designed and curated American blog about conscious fashion, beauty, food, wellness and travel, to stimulate social change through daily purchase and lifestyle choices.
thegoodtrade.com

The Green Hub
Australian blog, full of news about fashion, beauty, recipes, the ocean, home, travel and destinations, eco influencers, a brand directory and much more.
thegreenhubonline.com

The Minimalists
Blog, podcast, books (including the bestseller *Everything That Remains*) and films (e.g. the documentary *Minimalism*) with tips about living with less, by friends Joshua Fields Millburn and Ryan Nicodemus.
theminimalists.com

Trash is for Tossers
Blog and YouTube channel about a zero-waste lifestyle, by New Yorker Lauren Singer. Categories include home, food, travel, shopping and office. She's also the founder of organic, vegan laundry detergent The Simply Co. and Package Free Shop in Brooklyn.
trashisfortossers.com / packagefreeshop.com

TreeHugger
International website, one-stop-shop for news, solutions and product information.
treehugger.com

Viertel\Vor
German sustainable blogger couple, who live both in the countryside and Berlin. They discuss issues, small steps, products, interview people and much more.
viertel-vor.com

Zero Waste Home
Blog from bestselling author (*Zero*

Waste Home) and zero-waste expert Bea Johnson, full of tips (travel, capsule wardrobe, food, etc.), a webshop and bulk-store finder.
zerowastehome.com

Country directories
Overview of brands, companies and organisations in all fields, in Aus/Can/Ger/NZ/UK/US.
ecofind.co.nz / ethical.org.au / greenamerica.org / greenfinder.ca / greenguide.co.uk / greenmeberlin.com / greenmelocally.com / organicexplorer.co.nz / utopia.de

AND ALSO
1millionwomen.com.au / betterworldshopper.org / climateoptimist.org / consciousconsumers.nz / eco-boost.co / globalcitizen.org / goodnet.org / greatist.com / kinfolk.com / lifestylejustice.com / nobrandnew.com / nollahukka.wordpress.com / plastikfreileben.de / readcereal.com / smallfootprintfamily.com / thechalkboardmag.com / thecorrespondent.com / wearedonation.com

Some of my Instagram Inspiration
@beautifuldestinations
@cabinporn
@davinamccall
@diversity_rules
@dosomethingfornothing
@iconaccidental
@nasa
@shethinx
@wayofgrey
@womensmarch

APPS

Buycott
You can scan barcodes for information about products, participate in campaigns and/or make your voice heard. Millions of people from 192 countries participate (app comes from America).
buycott.com

Oroeco
Shows you what impact your actions have, calculates your CO_2 emission and what choices really make a difference for a better climate.
oroeco.com

AND ALSO
consciousconsumers.nz / ethical.org.au / ewg.org/apps / goodguide.com

---

INFORMATION

Innovators
ananas-anam.com/pinatex / blondandbieber.com / franklinonfashion.com / helenstoreyfoundation.org / paulinevandongen.nl / studioroosegaarde.net / twitter.com/elonmusk

BRAVE GENTLEMAN

Heroes
eco-age.com / facebook.com/emmawatson / katharinehamnett.com / leonardodicaprio.com / oprah.com / stellamccartney.com / twitter.com/markruffalo / viviennewestwood.com

Equal rights
caitlinmoran.co.uk / everydayfeminism.com / everydaysexism.com / facebook.com/naomi.wolf.author / gurlstalk.com / hollykearl.com / ihollaback.org / leanin.org / menengage.org / stopstreetharassment.org / stoptellingwomentosmile.com / timesupnow.com / whiteribbon.ca / We should all be feminists, Chimamanda Ngozi Adichie, TEDxEuston (and the HeForShe-speech by Emma Watson)

Diversity
blackheritagetours.com / blacklivesmatter.com / diversityrules.nl / facebook.com/coloroncovers / facebook.com/GetOutMovie / janeelliott.com (and doll tests) / Peggy McIntosh / theglobeandmail.com (Colour Code podcast) / thestreetstore.org / Gloria Wekker

Money, impact and compensating
actionaid.org/tax-power / clientearth.org / colinbeavan.com / ex-tax.com / globalcarbonproject.org / goldstandard.org – see p. 244 for offset websites / taxjustice.net

Burials
greenburialcouncil.org / naturalburial.org / naturaldeath.org.uk

Digital and self-help
digital-selfdefense.com / eff.org / gretchenrubin.com / theselfhelphipster.com / tim.blog

---

MAGAZINES

Conscious
International magazine about innovative ideas and creative solutions for positive impact. Initiatives, entrepreneurs and conscious style, travel, food, art etc.
consciousmagazine.co

Eluxe Magazine
Sustainable luxury-magazine (and website), about fashion, celebrities, bloggers, eco beauty, travel, living etc., with own webshop.
eluxemagazine.com

IMPRINT
Magazine featuring high-end sustainable fashion and design. With interviews, editorials, reports, photography and short films.
imprint-mag.com

Peppermint
'Print magazine about style, sustainability and substance.' Australian quarterly magazine, covering ethical fashion, social entrepreneurs, natural living, slow food, diversity etc.
peppermintmag.com

BOOKS

Kate Black – *Magnifeco. Your head-to-toe guide to ethical fashion and non-toxic beauty*
Christina Dean, Hannah Lane, Sofia Tärneberg – *Dress with Sense*
Cameron Diaz & Sandra Bark – *The Body Book*
Adina Grigore – *Skin Cleanse*
Chris Hadfield – *An Austronaut's Guide to Life on Earth*
Naomi Klein – *No Logo*
Safia Minney – *Naked Fashion / Slow Fashion / Slave to Fashion – see also p. 048*
Caitlin Moran – *How to Be a Woman*
Gavin Pretor-Pinney – *The Cloudspotter's Guide*
Jonathan Safran Foer – *Eating Animals*
Lucy Siegle – *To Die For: Is Fashion Wearing Out the World?*
Naomi Wolf – *The Beauty Myth*

FILMS AND VIDEO

Before the Flood
Leonardo DiCaprio travels the world to show the impact of climate change, and discusses problems and solutions with leaders such as Barack Obama and Elon Musk.
channel.nationalgeographic.com/before-the-flood (also see *The 11th Hour*, an earlier film by DiCaprio about the climate)

Bitter Seeds / China Blue
Bitter Seeds follows Indian cotton-farmers to the edge of the abyss: many of them commit suicide. China Blue tells the story of two Chinese girls trying to survive whilst working in a jeans factory.
teddybearfilms.com

Blood Diamond
Film by Leonardo DiCaprio and Ed Zwick about 'blood diamonds' in conflict areas in Sierra Leone.
warnerbros.co.uk/blood-diamond

Blood, Sweat and T-Shirts / Blood, Sweat and Luxuries
Series in which young people visit the places (and work in the factories) producing our clothes and luxury items.
bbc.co.uk

Blue Planet II
BBC series about marine life (successor to *The Blue Planet*), narrated by David Attenborough. The beautiful images and his urgent call to seriously start protecting the environment (especially from plastic) have big impact.
bbcearth.com/blueplanet2

Cowspiracy
Revolutionary film about the enormous impact of large-scale livestock farming on the environment and the world.
cowspiracy.com

Demain
Feelgood story about positive pioneers' solutions for the ecological and social problems.
demain-lefilm.com

Earthlings
Documentary about how we use animals as pets, but also to turn into clothes and food and for experimentation.
nationearth.com/earthlings-1

I AM
Film by the director of *Ace Ventura* and *The Nutty Professor*, that aims to answer two questions: what is wrong with the world and what can we do to make it better?
iamthedoc.com

An Inconvenient Truth
Groundbreaking film by Al Gore about global warming – one of the first to put this subject on the map. There's now also a sequel.
takepart.com/ait10 / inconvenientsequel.tumblr.com

The Light Bulb Conspiracy
Documentary about 'planned obsolescence' – products made to break quickly.
facebook.com/TheLightBulbConspiracy

Minimalism: a documentary about the important things
Documentary about how good and important it is to live with less, and how we can reclaim our own will.
minimalismfilm.com

Planet Earth
Innovative BBC documentary about nature and the animal kingdom as you've never seen it before.
bbc.co.uk/planetearth

Racing Extinction
Exposes how many species are threatened and how rapidly we are on the way to mass extinction.
racingextinction.com

Straight/Curve
Documentary about society's unrealistic and dangerous beauty standards. It examines the industries (fashion, media) responsible for this, and showcases the leaders fighting for more diversity – to bolster a movement for change.
straightcurvefilm.com

The True Cost
Documentary about the impact of the garment industry on people and the environment, in response to the collapse of the Rana Plaza factory.
truecostmovie.com – see also p. 250

Volta
Platform with inspiring videos about sustainability, lifestyle, nature and technology.
voltatv.com

QNOOP / TOMEK DERSU AARON

Over-fishing, whales, dolphins and oceans
A Plastic Ocean / Blackfish / Sea the Truth / The Cove / The End of the Line

(Un)healthy eating and the food industry
Eating you Alive / Fat, Sick and Nearly Dead / Fed Up / Food Chains / Food Inc / Forks over Knives / GMO OMG / In Defense of Food / SEED - the untold story / That Sugar Film /

The Truth about Food / TONY / What the Health

Gender / LGBTQ
Boys Don't Cry / Breakfast on Pluto / Brokeback Mountain / Milk / She's a Boy I Knew / Thelma & Louise / XXY

Women's rights
Erin Brockovich / He Named Me Malala / Norma Rae / North Country / Ride to Freedom: The Rosa Parks Story

Diversity
Boyz n the Hood / Dear White People / Do the Right Thing / Get Out / Our Colonial Hangover / Pride / The Butler / The Color Purple

---

ORGANISATIONS

There are many, many organisations doing good – here's a few.

Circle Economy
Puts the circular economy on the map, with projects, events and workshops around fashion, money, cities etc.
circle-economy.com

Greenpeace
International environmental organisation that puts pressure on companies and governments. Thanks to their 'Detox-Challenge' several large fashion brands have for example promised to eliminate the release of toxic chemicals into the environment.
greenpeace.org

Help Refugees
UK humanitarian aid NGO, helps those displaced by war in Europe, the Middle East and beyond. You can donate money, but also helpful items, become a volunteer, buy a Katharine Hamnett shirt or actual coats, tents or cooking utensils (for refugees).
helprefugees.org

Holstee
Tools and inspiration for a mindful and meaningful life: from weekly reflection mails to a membership in which you explore monthly themes such as kinship, integrity or adventure.
holstee.com

Refugees Welcome
Connects people who have a spare room to refugees seeking shelter. Already in 14 countries, including Australia, Canada, Germany and Sweden.
refugees-welcome.net

SOMO
Research and network organisation, which examines multinational companies and the consequences of their activities for people and the environment. On the website you'll find reports and information.
somo.nl

White Helmets
Volunteer rescue workers who go to places in Syria where public services no longer function and risk their lives to help anyone in need. They've now saved over 99,000 lives (and nearly 250 of them have died…). You can donate to buy material (white helmet: 122 euros).
whitehelmets.org

AND ALSO
campaigntoendloneliness.org / doctorswithoutborders.org / endloneliness.com.au / equalitynow.org / foei.org / icrc.org / refugee-action.org.uk / rescue.org / sundayassembly.com / theschooloflife.com / unhcr.org / womenonwaves.org / worldanimalprotection.org

---

GREEN KIDS

WWF
In many countries, The World Wildlife Fund has special youth branches, to learn about nature worldwide.
gowild.wwf.org.uk

Magazines
You'll find more information in these online magazines (or take a subscription): thegreenparent.co.uk (UK), thenaturalparentmagazine.com (Aus/NZ), ecoparent.ca (Can), greenchildmagazine.com / naturalchildworld.com (US)

A is for Activist - Innosanto Nagara
An alphabet book for toddlers about civil rights. Sounds heavy going, but learning to stand up for everyone in the community is important at every age.
aisforactivist.com

Last child in the woods - Richard Louv
Whizzing through the woods on your bike, looking for autumn leaves... Nature is the basis of many memories from your childhood. Children today spend much more time indoors, with all the consequences – including obesity and depression. This book shows why nature is so important and how to get back out into it.
richardlouv.com

AFTERWORD

You made it! I hope you've enjoyed reading this guide, and feel excited and equipped to go ahead. Because that's the major challenge: moving from knowing to doing, from words to deeds, putting your money where your mouth is – those kinds of things. So, let's rock 'n roll. And remember: it doesn't have to be perfect. What it does have to be, is more fun and better. Hopefully that'll now be easier to base your choices on. It'll probably not always be top of mind, and one subject might be more up your alley than another. No worries. As long as you make a start, and keep going. With every small step, you're contributing to a more beautiful world. And if small steps could even get us to the moon, imagine where else they could lead us...

Although we've spent quite some together these 280 pages, there's still heaps I wasn't able to show you. I've focused on what I'd like to share with you if you were my friend (and that is how it feels by now). There's so much out there, I hope you're curious about it. And that this is a good guide for you on the way to a more sustainable, smart and sunny life.

– Marieke

THANK YOU
Many thanks to everyone who's asked me questions over the years, and inquired about an international edition. If it wasn't for you, this book would never have come about. I hope I was able to give you (a few of) the answers you were looking for.

I'm incredibly honoured to have had the opportunity to interview all the fantastic experts, pioneers and innovators, and grateful they wanted to share their incredible stories and tips. I truly stand on the shoulders of giants.
This also goes for all the amazing brands and organisations I've been able to work with over the last fifteen years, that have given me so much inspiration and motivation. There's nothing I'd rather do than showcasing and putting all the important and positive things you do on the map. There are so many heroes who in their own way make the world a better place, and reach so much higher than I can. I wish I could personally thank (and hug) each and every one of you.

I also want to hug Natasha Barton. You were my favourite from the translation tests on – I'm so pleased with how you've captured my tone and language, and how we did this as a team. Thank you for being involved, diligent and big-hearted, and for helping me make my dream come true.

All the great people around the world who've provided input contributed to that too. This book wouldn't have been the same without the wonderful suggestions and useful tips from Anna Lehtola, Kelly Dent, Caroline Sommer, Anoek van der Leest, Mirjam Groten and Olivia Ellice-Flint, and the interviewed experts. Muchas gracias!

Any inaccuracies are of course down to me: I've tried to simplify complex material, which can be tricky. Luckily, then there are facts and figures to clarify in one swoop what this is all about. That, *kapow*, slap you in the face. They come from Edmé Koorstra, who was also the first to read all text, make improvements and come up with smart suggestions. Worth his weight in gold. No, priceless.

Just like the place where I was welcome to write. A large part of this book came to life in Zoku, my 'home away from home'. I owe a huge amount to all my friends there. I'd never have succeeded without you and look forward to what the future has in store for us.

The same goes for these two aces. I know nothing about children, but Laura de Jong does. Your willingness to share your knowledge and tips is much appreciated. You're a star, thanks for your support. Naomi Rachèl Timan zealously compiled the image bank. I think you'll all agree the photos in this book are awesome (thank you!).

Indeed, it looks stunning – exactly like I envisioned. A book not only good on the inside, but good-looking and modern on the outside too. Many thanks to Brechtje Baars en Leonoor Verplanken of The Green House for this timeless and cool design, and to Esther Scheide for her dedicated and detailed DTP work on this edition.

I'm so grateful to BIS Publishers for this opportunity. Bionda Dias believed in an international edition from day one and has ventured off the beaten track to make it happen. Thank you for your trust. Also, a special mention for Sara van de Ven, Marit Bohnenn and everyone from the (international) sales, PR and marketing departments who worked so hard to get this book into the shops and under the spotlight. You rock!

The original, Dutch version of this book was partly made possible by Meulenhoff Boekerij, which I'm very thankful for. They published it in collaboration with Guido A. Keff. One of the biggest gifts of this entire adventure is getting to know Guido. There's no-one quite like him, and I learn from him every day: to be positive, grateful and light. Life may be gone before you know it, but then we at least managed to realise this international edition, and made a new friend.

And there aren't many things more important than that. Without friends there's nothing. So, thank all of you for being you and being there.

That certainly also applies to Louise van Deth. Coach, friend and mentor: the smartest woman I know. You often know exactly what I need (a kick up the backside or a listening ear) and your opinions are always on the ball. Thanks for all your insights and confidence – it means a lot that you want to share your time and knowledge with me.

My parents are always there for me, willing to lend a helping hand. Whether I'm chasing a deadline, presenting somewhere or making new plans: they're doing it with me. I'd never have been able to write this book without their backing. I've got my few brain cells, education, view of the world and of course my very existence thanks to you both, and I cannot be more grateful.

I've written a good guide, but I already had one myself. Edmé is my everything: my journey, my direction, my harmony, my tune. We sing our way through life together, wandering the valleys and scaling the peaks – always enjoying the view. I know no-one more supportive, kind and loving (okay, and the six-pack helps too), and who suits me better. You've not only worked tirelessly on this book, you've also caught me, taken care of me and tossed me back up into the sky. For me, you're the very definition of good.

>> *Finished with this book? Pass it on!*

Act as if what you do makes a difference. It does.